RENEWALS 458-4574

The Ship of State

The Ship of State

Statecraft and Politics from Ancient
Greece to Democratic America

Norma Thompson

Yale University Press   New Haven & London

Designed by Mary Valencia
Set in Caslon 224 type by Keystone Typesetting, Inc.
Printed in the United States of America by Sheridan Books, Chelsea, Michigan.

Library of Congress Cataloging-in-Publication Data
Thompson, Norma, 1959–
The ship of state : statecraft and politics from ancient Greece
to democratic America / Norma Thompson.
p.   cm.
Includes bibliographical references and index.
ISBN 0-300-08817-5 (hardcover : alk. paper)
1. Political science—History. 2. Sex role—History. I. Title.
JA81 .T53 2001
320—dc21
00-012133

A catalogue record for this book is available from the British Library.

The paper in this book meets the guidelines for permanence and durability
of the Committee on Production Guidelines for Book Longevity of the
Council on Library Resources.

10 9 8 7 6 5 4 3 2 1

To Charlie

If we know in what way society is unbalanced, we must do what we can to add weight to the lighter scale . . . we must have formed a conception of equilibrium and be ever ready to change sides like justice, 'that fugitive from the camp of the conquerors.'

Simone Weil, *Gravity and Grace*

Contents

Introduction

The stimulus for this book initially came from Tocqueville's study of America. In *Democracy in America,* Tocqueville traces several oppositions—between aristocracy and democracy, between the spirit of freedom and the spirit of religion, and between masculine and feminine spheres of influence—but as he proceeds, his quest to sustain both elements of each binary appears increasingly wistful. His pessimism at the close of the work suggests that he held out little hope for the long-term reforming power of his own remedies. Scanning the democratic scene in a last summary glance, Tocqueville congratulates Americans for the justice of their egalitarian system, but admits to being saddened and chilled by the "universal uniformity" that stretches before him.[1] This parting comment is worth further note, for it would seem that the more accurate Tocqueville's judgment, the less his despair would register in future democratic ages. And I take it to be a worrisome fact that his despair hardly registers at all in our age. To be sure, Tocqueville is recognized for his prescience and influence, having almost singlehandedly spawned a "civil society" industry, with legacies both on the left (for articulating the need to reinforce communal attachments) and on

1

the right (for identifying the increasing centralization of government and its new paternalistic form). His specific policy recommendations are still relevant, whether the topic is the intermediary associations for teaching self-rule to democrats, or the proactive policies on the part of leaders for encouraging self-interest rightly understood. Yet these are subsets of the larger problem that he identifies, which is the intellectual challenge for democrats of holding alternatives in view at the same time. Tocqueville calls for a binary thinking that mirrors his own dichotomies in *Democracy in America,* but put that way, contemporary readers recoil.

Since the late twentieth century the received wisdom concerning binaries is not favorable: one of the two terms (among, for example, culture/nature, reason/emotion, or masculine/feminine) is thought always to be privileged at the expense of the other. Wherever a binary appears, a concealed hierarchy is suspected: culture is *over* nature; reason is *over* emotion, and the feminine is "a metaphor or identity for the denigrated terms."[2] Thus it is in good conscience that contemporary critics slight Tocqueville in his most trenchant criticism of American democracy—and thereby fulfill his prophecy about democratic thinking moving toward sameness, not difference. This is of considerable interest on the topic of masculine and feminine spheres of influence. Tocqueville's assessment of the *cause* of American success is unforgettable ["if anyone asks me what I think the chief cause of the extraordinary prosperity and growing power of this nation, I should answer that it is due to the superiority of their women" (603)], and yet that picture of the American female is utterly dated: "You will never find American women in charge of the external relations of the family, managing a business, or interfering in politics; but they are also never obliged to undertake rough laborer's work or any task requiring hard physical exertion. No family is so poor that it makes an exception to this rule" (601). Instead, Americans have followed the route marked out by Tocqueville as "European" leveling: "They would attribute the same functions to both [men and women], impose the same duties, and grant the same rights; they would have them share everything—work, pleasure, public affairs" (601). I do not suggest here that the radical change in the lives of American women is something to be *regretted,* for the situation is what it is, for better and worse. But there can be no glossing over the distance Americans have traveled toward accepting an androgynous standard since Tocqueville first chronicled their mores in the mid-nineteenth century.

Prior to Tocqueville's section on the democratic family, he expresses anxiety about the democratic perception of the historical process; the specter he fears is that, in a democracy, history itself is transformed into an all-enveloping process. Throughout, Tocqueville is preoccupied with combating the anonymity of this process with concrete detail. He examines the interrelated tendencies of American democrats to forget their ancestors, as if the world were theirs to live anew, and to rely to an extraordinary degree on the (invisible) standard of public opinion. His remedy is formulated consistently to counter the worst effects of egalitarianism: democrats must be encouraged to study the past, to retain a sense of the alternatives that the Western political tradition has offered, and to preserve some place as sacred from the leveling forces of democratic politics. Yet he knew that no such place could survive under the pressure of "the equality of conditions" that struck him so vividly in the United States (9). It is not just that democratic historians tend to "make great general causes responsible for the smallest particular events," whereas aristocratic historians "see a few leading actors in control of the whole play" (494); it is that each is *right* to do so: "General causes explain more, and particular influences less, in democratic than in aristocratic ages" (495). This insight, sobering as it is, should not lead us to conclude that human choice and agency are helpless before the historical process, Tocqueville argues; indeed, he wrote his book in defiance of any such doctrine that deems insurmountable "the perils with which equality threatens human freedom" (702). But he still shudders to contemplate a situation in which standards of morality and rationality are viewed as wholly centered in the living, and ideas are regarded as products of the times—the historical process itself being determinative.[3]

Whether the issue is "history" or "women" or whatever, Tocqueville locates the common denominator in the drive toward uniformity. If Tocqueville is correct, then we run a notable risk of succumbing to a history-writing in which works of the past are probed in egalitarian terms, and caricatured accordingly. This has been the case in conventional present-day depictions of the Western tradition in political thought as uniformly misogynistic. Instead of looking for genuine alternatives of masculine and feminine representations in the great works of earlier times, contemporary writers often present all previous societal arrangements as flawed precursors to our own prescribed arrangements. My goal is to escape this trap by keeping in view both the "historical rootedness" and the "transcendent ideas" to be found in this tradition—without asserting the predominance of one over the other.

In doing so I hope for the support of those who seek a productive middle ground between "essentialism" and "constructivism," terms long featured in feminist debates. The dearth of women in the Western tradition of political thought has led many thinkers to hope that with increasing attention to women's participation—from the point of view of both authors and readers—will come the radical restructuring of that tradition. Even the female characters depicted by male authors are sometimes considered suspect, since they bear the imprint of their male creators. The thought is that if women have been alienated from the tradition by having their voices excluded, then the inclusion of those voices may herald the looked-for remedy. Presumably, then, the sole scenario for bringing about the emergence of female subjectivity is a female author depicting a female character.[4] But such an appeal to the irreducibly female is essentialist, and as Tocqueville makes clear, resorting to an argument about a "fixed nature" is problematic in a democracy ["in a democracy each generation is a new people" (473)]. Pejorative synonyms associated with the term essentialism include "logocentrism," "objectivity," and "the search for eternal truths."[5] Today essentialism almost always denotes a *complacent* belief in the unchangeable core of an abstract entity, such as "nature." And so the constructionist answer to the essentialist challenge was precipitated, rejecting the vocabulary of essence and propounding the view that nature itself is the product of contingent societal transformations. I hope to identify terrain where an agreeable combination of "essence" and "construction" can be achieved.[6]

I focus my search on three high points in the tradition of political theory: the ancient Greek *polis,* the modern state, and democratic America. The standard literature on women in political thought identifies a grimly consistent form of misogynism throughout history, but I find significant differences in the characterizations of societal arrangements between men and women in each of these three cases. In a letter to Nathaniel Hawthorne, Herman Melville once remarked that "great geniuses are parts of the times, they themselves are the times and possess a corresponding coloring."[7] It seems to me that what "great geniuses" have revealed is that the distinctive correctives of one age can be profitably reconsidered in another. Accordingly, I employ my three-part structure mainly for the light it sheds on democracy. It is not that the polis leads to the state which leads to democratic America, even if the later entities take their bearings from earlier modes. It is rather that the Greek polis and the modern state represent distinct and instructive alternatives to democratic America, as captured in the superb political writings of their times. The primary texts representing each polity demonstrate that key political issues must be approached *through* writing styles—debate, dialogue, the narrative story—that are designed to be open-ended, to be critically and continually scrutinized. This shared feature is my justification for placing in contact authors and texts from across the centuries. Next to Tocqueville's elucidation of democratic America, then, I investigate depictions of the polis from Homer to Aristotle, and elaborations of the state from Machiavelli to Burke and Mary Shelley. My account aims to achieve a new understanding of the literary forms adopted by political thinkers of the polis, state, and modern democracy such that these forms are revealed to have substantive, not merely stylistic, significance. My claim is that if literary styles can be shown to be powerfully related to the political communities that are their subject matter, they also can be ranked as better or worse at ameliorating the perceived shortcomings of their political communities, and at achieving a crucial balance of masculine and feminine aspects.

Essential to this undertaking is a deepened sensitivity to literary character, for it is precisely the literalism prevailing among democratic readers that impedes their appreciation of the texts in my purview. Part of my initial dismay with feminist readings of political philosophy came from their credulous nature: if the priest in *Mandragola* says that "All women have few brains,"[8] then Machiavelli himself must believe that, too. Such readings cling to surfaces just as political scientists fear to venture beyond numbers. *Ideas* are the generating causes in my account, and understanding them in depth is the objective of this book. This means attending to the distances authors create between themselves and their characters, for those spaces are opened for *our* reflection as readers. Further, in the hands of the most profound writers, that space is uniquely redrawn, prohibiting us the comfort of leaning backwards on something firm. The most renowned example is Plato's Socrates; where Socrates appears, he ineluctably plays a dramatic role, no matter how philosophic the "plot" becomes.[9] This raises knotty questions about the historical core of the portrait—the Socrates who really existed—and Plato's literary shaping of him. These questions provide Platonic philosophy with a staggering openness. To supplant the Socratic figure seems impossible, but inspired writers of later times offer their own paradigmatic characters. Such is the character in Rousseau's *Emile,* who adds dimensions to this conundrum by blurring the real Rousseau, the narrator of *Emile,* and the character of "the tutor." How are readers to understand the status of that character? And the American entry is suitably brazen. Gertrude Stein, assuming the voice of Alice B. Toklas, composes a "Gertrude Stein" who is fit for the times: an original spirit lashing out at the indolent reader. In the process, she earns more than a place among the distinguished company assembled here.

With this list of authors from Homer to Gertrude Stein, I may safely claim originality for my overarching story line. However, I wish to take note from the start of my intellectual debts, for the critical literature in regard to every one of my texts contains exceptional readings.[10] Even where I dispute conventional views most heatedly— that is, concerning the programmatic dismissal of the Western tradition as misogynistic—an impressive body of literature already exists which rehabilitates individual writers from reductive assaults based on their depictions of women. With these insights in mind, my aim is to recast the entire tradition. In this endeavor Edmund Burke has served as a model: beginning with evidence and information that is readily available and shared, I aim to produce an account which is incisive for our time.

These chapters are excursions into texts that have demonstrated a capacity to endure and stimulate interest across great stretches of time and despite political and cultural changes of immense magnitude. Nonetheless, in today's intellectual environment of policy focused, empirically based social sciences, the question that cannot be avoided is whether the veins of thought, insight, and speculation that run through these texts remain workable as sources with potentially practical significance for the present and its predicaments. This book is my assertion that they do and that political theories derived from or inspired by these works not only can offer material useful to contemporary empirical investigators, but also encourage them to overcome their "idolatry of the factual."[11] The openness that is the byword of democratic America exalts the brute and transparent fact even as it obstructs the achievement of more enlightening and perdurable literary forms. From Tocqueville's observation that democrats in America wish to unify and make uniform all that lies before them ["the concept of unity becomes an obsession" (451)], it is but a small step to the democratic worship of number. And *counting* may be the ultimate flight from thinking beyond "the given."

The moral of my story is that democrats need to be wary of their imperious and unitary ways. In most surveys of Western political thought, the measure is provided by the rights-oriented politics of the day. From the fact that women were not citizens in earlier eras is extrapolated the position that all prior thinking exhibits a defect from which we alone have escaped. By focusing on the changing literary forms in different political communities, I establish distance enough to perceive that "our solution" is as makeshift as any. When we become attentive to the distinctive writing mode of our political community as well as to its historical alternatives, we may be able to offset what Tocqueville saw as democracy's strange power: the "mighty pressure of the mind of all upon the intelligence of each" (435). At any point in history, a successful political community correlates with a certain genius of formal expression that is usefully classified as "balanced." Our own political community needs redressing in this regard, by attending to the old books that have defined us, by holding on to images of strong human agency and free will, and by simply taking the time to think through the enduring issues of political philosophy. I want to thank all the people who have allowed me the time to elaborate these thoughts. This work was long in the making and dependent upon a wide range of teaching, writing, and research occasions. I am grateful for an Olin Fellowship received at a crucial early stage, and I thank Donald Kagan for his sustained encouragement throughout. My colleagues and students in the Program of Directed Studies have honed my wits and spurred my ambitions; among them I make special mention of the late Joseph Hamburger and David Bromwich, Peter Gay, Jane Levin, John McCormick, Maria Rosa Menocal, Jaroslav Pelikan, Steven Smith and Frank Turner. I am greatly indebted to my fellow teachers in the "Democratic Statecraft" course: David Apter, Ian Shapiro, and Rogers Smith. The issues we contested there in the best spirit of collegiality provided the intellectual foundation-stones for many aspects of this book. I profited from heated discussions in the Yale Political Theory workshop, including participants Bruce Ackerman, Vittorio Bufacci, David Hennigan, Boris Kapustin, Ian Loadman, and Fiona Miller. Students in the seminar "Women in Political Thought" tested my lineup of authors, and I appreciate their contributions to this project. Invaluable research assistance was provided by Colleen Shogan and Justin Zaremby. Outside of Yale, several friends and colleagues provided useful comments and timely criticisms, including Cliff Orwin, Patrick Deneen, Jonathan Marks, and Delba Winthrop. Harvey Mansfield was an encouraging and incisive reader. I thank the Director of Yale University Press, John Ryden, for his original enthusiasm for this work, and my editor, Larisa Heimert, for her professional attention. Kelli Farnham helped me through many a computer breakdown. Finally, I honor my family for their patient and good-humored support. This book is dedicated to my husband, in gratitude for the finest, greatest gift in the world: *homophrosyne*.

1

The Polis

One

Stories at the Limits

For a single political entity, the ancient Greek polis is remarkably varied in its literary incarnations. From Homer through Aristotle, poets, historians, and philosophers contribute to an evolving idea of the polis, such that a recognizable core exists despite the vast expanse of time that separates its origins from its culmination. Such a core apprehension of the nature of the polis has emerged from scholarly efforts to trace its features, projected and material, within the framework of specific genres. Most prominent for the relative transparency of their evidence are historical and archaeological studies. Single-author studies of the polis are deemed manageable as well, and Aristotle in particular is the subject of endless inquiry, with an alternating emphasis on historical or philosophical components of the polis. Political studies are undertaken which embrace more diffuse sources of evidence, from speeches to tragedies, comedies, and other performance occasions. The development of the polis and of Greek drama proceeded in parallel and with a reciprocating influence, each profoundly impacting the other.[1] Efforts to delineate the polis within distinct genres have produced a rich, sprawling, and unconnected profusion of material, and leaves unasked the question:

what core elements of the polis interest poet, philosopher, *and* historian? For me, this is the crucial element of the polis—its affinity for productive tension. To explore this dimension, I will consider Homer's *Odyssey* at the origins of the polis, Thucydides' *Peloponnesian War* at its breakdown, and Aristotle's *Politics* at its "resolution." In that unlikely series exists a single story in the service of the polis.

Homer stands alone among these writers as the storyteller,[2] but beyond this he "authorizes" the polis in the *Odyssey* as Odysseus and Penelope relinquish themselves to a public narrative of their union. Odysseus and Penelope are forcibly kept apart after the end of the Trojan War, yet they establish the reality of their attachment in thought and in the telling. Each appreciates that the story line is not under his or her full direction, but entails, rather, a surrender of self. Their patient and reverent bearing toward the world is a defiance of its brute materiality; they are able to subsist in imagination. The successful end of Odysseus' homecoming is the providential beginning of the polis, where masculine and feminine influences are commensurate. The polis, in its tenacity about its own narrative, will mirror this essential feature of its founding couple.

Thucydides has a less heartening story to tell of the polis, but it *is* a story. Without any bow to postmodernism, and without detracting from the historical value of *The Peloponnesian War,* I argue that Thucydides makes his *own* war out of the conflict between Athens and Sparta. His accomplishment is such that there is no getting behind him to the "real" war; competing accounts, archaeological evidence, and information added all now pass through a Thucydidean filter.[3] Homer and Herodotus each made the Trojan and Persian wars his own, but Thucydides' achievement is distinctly compelling because of his contemporaneous marshalling of the evidence.

Aristotle's monumental contribution emerges from his story of a polis unattached to any one city in history. One aspect of his success in reconstituting the polis is Homeric: his sense of urgency in connecting *oikos* and polis. Nothing matters so much for the polis as its "homecoming" and renewed link with Nature. A second aspect is Thucydidean, as Aristotle uses inherited historical exemplars, so that Athens and Sparta serve as anchors for his modification of the polis. But Aristotle refines these historical exemplars out of existence; a preferable "middle" term beckons above and beyond them. He restores and reconstitutes an old version of the polis, one more respectful toward the feminine corrective in theory than the polis ever was in practice.

An announced interest in the counterpoising ways of the Greeks—culture versus nature, reason versus emotion, public versus private—would once have been met with indifference; this is, after all, a people for whom the voice of wisdom declared "measure is best" (*metron ariston*). But now binaries are presumed to camouflage the disparagement of women, and there hardly appears room for debate on the subject. The claim is ubiquitous: women were excluded from politics in the Greek polis, in both theory and practice. In sharp contrast, I find that Greek profundity extends even into reflections on gender. The polis is indeed marked by polarities, but where polarities exist, they generate challenges to thought: how *do* things stand with men and women, with masculine and feminine? how *must* they? My look at the most telling productions of ancient Greece finds insights about men and women far more profound than even the most far-reaching charges of misogyny allow—such as the account of the *Peloponnesian War,* which locates a total of *two* "praiseworthy women" in the entire text.[4] The great writer is not dupe, but interrogator, of the subject matter. My claim is that the Greek discovery of the polis is premised not on *exclusion* but on *tension,* and when it falters, its best chroniclers take note. At its productive best, the polis produces tensions which accommodate masculine and feminine forces alike.

Homer and the Origins of the Polis

The *Odyssey* is a story of the reunion of husband and wife, seemingly a celebration of oikos (the household) rather than the polis. It has been noted that the word polis appears rarely and only once in conjunction with Ithaca.[5] Two individuals are called upon to endure unimaginable trials and uncertainties; how could their eventual reunion signify the grounding of political community? My answer is that the *Odyssey* depicts the coming together of oikos-polis in accordance with nature and in ways that mark them as inextricably connected. Only in the end is the natural sign of the constancy of

Penelope and Odysseus revealed—the marriage bed centered around the stump of an olive tree—but all along assertions of their need for each other is alternately a provocation or an inspiration to others. If Homer's "pre-political" political community is not an obvious point of departure for an examination of the classical polis, it surely is a defensible one; it anticipates nicely Aristotle's claim that the polis as a whole is naturally prior to the oikos (*Pol.*, 1253a19–20). The presumption here is that the logic of the political community is manifest already in the *Iliad* and is assumed in the *Odyssey*.[6]

Odysseus identifies as the greatest gift in the world like-mindedness (*homophrosyne*) between man and woman: "No finer, greater gift in the world than that . . . / when man and woman possess their home, two minds, / two hearts that work as one."[7] That like-mindedness which characterizes Odysseus and Penelope is hard-fought and may reasonably be called a *spiritual* accomplishment of each. For the challenges that confront them separately fall into narrow "male" and "female" types; the perils exist at either extreme. Monstrous creatures like Polyphemus and Scylla have to be dispatched or at least encountered, and so, too, do the more ordinary personages like the suitors; all seek to diminish the force of the mutual attachment of Odysseus and Penelope. It is as if each gender as a collective resists the claim that the two individuals belong to each other. The responses of Odysseus and Penelope to these challenges entail an opening of themselves to something larger than their single gender types. Their shared understanding challenges others to commit themselves to something more than mere physical survival. This will have its imprint on the polis, for in the end, Ithaca emerges as a balanced construct; this is their "life story" (23.227–230). Human remembrance is at the center of this story, for it can accommodate impossible complexities.

The significance of memory and the threat of forgetting is palpable in the *Odyssey*, then, where the very existence of Ithaca as polis is at stake. The challenges to Odysseus' homecoming, the obstacles in the way of the successful tale, are of both male and female countenance. The male version is evinced by Poseidon and his kin, featuring an outsized antagonist who is ferocious when roused—and distinctly ill-mannered. Odysseus seems to be just the heroic type to confront this kind of an obstacle, since even in the *Iliad* he is the one to live by his wits, redrafting the warrior code even while existing within it. In the *Odyssey* we are reminded of the radical nature of this shift when Odysseus encounters Ajax in the underworld; even in death, the more brawny warrior cannot forgive the slight of being passed over by his peers for the likes of Odysseus (11.620ff.). But the cunning and endurance of Odysseus are more pivotal in the *Odyssey* than in the *Iliad*—and more suggestive of feminine undercurrents. His repeated challenge is to bide his time, to suppress his appetite and his spirit (*thymos*) until a more propitious moment for its expression. His success frequently derives from his forbearance. So Odysseus resists the urge to do direct battle with Cyclops, foreseeing that even if he and his men could overcome the giant, they would still be trapped inside the cave. His ruse of concealing grown men under Cyclops' sheep is the work of no ordinary soldier. Only his taunting of Polyphemus after their escape reminds us of the older ethic, but clearly Odysseus is not enclosed by old denotations of manhood.

Later, Odysseus resists eating the cattle of the Sun when his shipmates succumb, despite the dire warnings all had received against that transgression. This single example from the *Odyssey* signals the critical spiritual dimension to the formation of the polis. Odysseus' men are warned repeatedly that the herds are the possession of the god Helios and thereby marked as sacred and inviolable. Alarmed for his men, Odysseus convinces them to take an oath vowing never to harm the cattle. And so long as food remains plentiful, the men respect the prohibition. With hunger comes weakness, and susceptibility to the nefarious leadership of Eurylochus: "Listen to *me*, my comrades, brothers in hardship. / All ways of dying are hateful to us poor mortals, / true, but to die of hunger, starve to death— / that's the worst of all. So up with you now, / let's drive off the pick of Helios' sleek herds" (12.366–369). In an instant the cattle become sustenance to men who must eat. What gives one man the strength to refrain? Odysseus is elsewhere on the island, deep in prayer (12.359)—mindful of the immortals as he struggles to situate himself properly, to make the distinctions that give meaning to a human life. He alone of his shipmates earns his homecoming, and he does so in self-abnegation. And Odysseus' singular reverence for the gods is a learned trait—the *Odyssey* opens with mention of his sacking of the sacred citadel of Troy (1.2)—and one that is of particular interest regarding the long-term implications for the polis, for how the polis fares ever after can be plotted in accordance with the presence or absence of this spiritual component.[8] Odysseus reveals new interior dimensions. Back in Ithaca and confronting indignities in his own home, Odysseus urges himself forward: "Bear up, old heart! You've born worse, far worse" (20.20). His response to physical assault by the suitors is an ominous shake of the head. There is no hint of a diminished hero, and the slaughter of the suitors and the hanging of the servant women testifies to a barely contained brutality. But it might also be said that he confronts the ordeals sent by Poseidon with a distinctly feminine appreciation for the indirect defense.

Other challenges to Odysseus' homecoming are put in terms of forgetting, and there the embodiment is often female. Threats of female sexuality abound, with the stories of the "bad sisters" Clytemnestra and Helen (first cousins to Penelope[9]) never far from mind. In Odysseus' travels, goddesses and prospective wives alike seek to envelop him in a protective atmosphere, to shield him from danger by means of a gentle oblivion. Alternatively, Scylla-like, they seek to devour him alive. But, as Odysseus observes, there is no fighting *that* nightmare (12.242), whereas he can resist the forgetfulness induced by contentment. And at the same time that the poet shows Odysseus resisting these external threats, the "inside" view on this topic is also projected. Beginning with the enchantresses like Circe or Calypso, continuing through Helen of Argos, and culminating with Penelope, a line is traceable in the *Odyssey* which signifies an eventual triumphant association of "female" and "constructive remembrance." "Happy Odysseus!" the ghost of Agamemnon will proclaim: "how well Icarius' daughter remembered you" (24.210–213).

In one way or another, the goddesses in the *Odyssey* who transfix human beings make mere animals of them;[10] these goddesses may choose also to rouse men *out* of this state. But for that sea traveler who comes too close to the Sirens, there will be "no sailing home for him, no wife rising to meet him, / no happy children beaming up at their father's face"; his fate will be to loll about in the meadows

(12.48–51). The unmindful man goes to that fate willingly. The Lotus-eaters similarly induce loss of memory such that anyone who tastes the lotus fruit wishes to graze there forever (9.106–110). As Odysseus struggles to sustain his clarity of purpose—his homecoming and renewed rule in Ithaca—he neutralizes such potent magic as practiced by the Sirens, who captivate with their enthralling tunes of the old world, or by Circe, who literally transforms his shipmates into swine. But even he has to be stirred by his men to think of his own home after Circe indulges him in pleasures for a year: "there we sat at ease, / day in, day out" (10.514–515). Circe is implicated alternately as the source of the forgetting ["but into the brew she stirred her wicked drugs / to wipe from their memories any thought of home"(10.259–260)] and credited as the helpmate in its overcoming ["But I will set you a course and chart each seamark, / so neither on sea nor land will some new trap / ensnare you in trouble, make you suffer more" (12.28–30)]. Here and elsewhere, the female is recognized both as "the problem and also the solution; [women] are the signs of our mortality, and also make it possible for life to go on," in Redfield's fitting assessment.[11] But an elevated human life "cannot go on" without an act of self-possession, and this the goddesses would disclaim of Odysseus. Even Calypso wishes to possess Odysseus forever, on her terms. Only on the order of Zeus does she release him, and this without ever apprehending the drive he feels to return home. If you only knew, she cautions him, "down deep, what pains / are fated to fill your cup before you reach that shore, / you'd stay right here, preside in our house with me / and be immortal" (5.228–231). Odysseus' decision to refuse her offer of immortality is a move—inspired by the right woman—to possess his self.

Helen, daughter of Zeus, hearkens to another world while living on in this one, and so assumes an intermediate position on this topic of remembrance and self-possession. Her role in the old Iliadic world was as a subject of song ("Zeus planted a killing doom within us both, / so even for generations still unborn / we will live in song"[12]); as a result, she is largely immune from responsibility for her role in the events. Helen in the *Iliad* is like nature itself, a given.[13] The elders of Troy look on at Helen, in wonder, but not in judgment: "Who on earth could blame them? Ah, no wonder / the men of Troy and Argives under arms have suffered / years of agony all for her, for such a woman. / Beauty, terrible beauty!" (III.187–190). But the Helen of the *Odyssey* is quite another matter. Back in Sparta and reunited with her lawful husband, Helen is not the temptress of former days; now she is subject to some more ordinary estimations of character. Her failings illuminate Penelope's triumphs, just as Helen served as contrast to Andromache in the earlier epic.[14] Notably, Helen reverts to the behavior of the goddesses by slipping in a potion to anesthetize from all human cares the company that is assembled before her. Her drug "[dissolves] anger, / magic to make us all forget our pains . . . / No one who drank it deeply, mulled in wine, / could let a tear roll down his cheeks that day, / not even if his mother should die, his father die, / not even if right before his eyes some enemy brought down / a brother or darling son with a sharp bronze blade" (4.245–251). That is formidable medicine indeed for preventing tears. And why should one *wish* to prevent tears? On one occasion Odysseus as disguised beggar asks Penelope to release him from the need to answer questions about his past: "I am a man who's had his share of sorrows. / It's wrong for me, in someone else's house, / to sit here moaning and groaning, sobbing so— / it makes things worse, this grieving on and on" (19.130–133). It makes things worse, because old sorrows relived may cut so deeply that they paralyze the individual in question; such appears to be the perpetual state of Penelope. But Helen's miracle drug should cause us to reassess whether Penelope's incessant weeping for Odysseus is a sign of weakness. To weep in remembrance may be eminently appropriate and humane, in contrast to the inhumanity of the dry-eyed witness to brutality of the poet's description. It is a stamp of our humanity that some memories *do* incapacitate us. "What other tribute can we pay to wretched men / than to cut a lock, let tears roll down our cheeks?" (4.220–221). And Penelope has her reasons for retaining her tears.

For her part, Helen is neither incapacitated by the past, nor particularly honest about her part in it. True, she acknowledges the battles fought on her behalf ["shameless whore that I was" (4.162)], but her accounts to Telemachus of her behavior while within the walls of Troy are nothing if not self-serving. In her version, she had come to regret her elopement with Paris and wished to redress her sins by conniving with Odysseus on behalf of the Greeks. But this rendition is immediately made suspect by Menelaus. His story deflects attention away from Helen's perceptiveness in recognizing the disguised Odysseus and her alleged collusion with him, and toward her heartless—and traitorous—bantering of the Greeks as they hid inside the Trojan horse. There is no like-mindedness in *this* marriage; the stories of Helen and Menelaus are well characterized as "subtle acts of self-justification, self-explanation, and mutual recrimination."[15] Consider the original scene that Telemachus and Pisistratus happened upon in Sparta. A wedding celebration was in progress for the son of Menelaus—the son who is not, however, the son of Helen. Megapenthes ("Great-Grief"[16]) was fathered by Menelaus and a slave woman. The air feels uncomfortably heavy around this domestic hearth, and Telemachus wisely requests an early retirement: "But come, send us off to bed. It's time to rest, / time to enjoy the sweet relief of sleep" (4.330–331).

Helen of Argos is the example that Penelope holds before herself as a means of governing her behavior: "In my heart of hearts I always cringed with fear / some fraud might come, beguile me with his talk" (23.242–243). For her own self-protection, she develops the strategy of freezing Odysseus' image in her mind, and hence of freezing time. This is captured most unforgettably in her weaving and unweaving of Laertes' shroud; for three years, this works to distance the suitors. But all that occurs before the events of the *Odyssey*. Now events herald the coming of age of Telemachus and therefore the end of Penelope's solitary designs. And Penelope's relations with Telemachus are noticeably strained as she is forced to factor in his involvement. His adventure in Pylos and Sparta might appear to be a much-diluted version of the travels of Odysseus, but Telemachus *has*, at least, been induced to make his move. Penelope overreacts, as she tries to insulate Telemachus from the world's hardships in a way that would protract *his* homecoming: "Oh, if only I had learned he was planning such a journey, / he would have stayed, by god, keen as he was to sail— / or left me dead right here within our palace" (4.825–827). But the recognition slowly dawns on her in the course of events that she cannot keep her son under her sway indefinitely; her past is permitted to unthaw. Penelope opens up her story to an unknown ending. This acceptance of risk is the key to *her* act of self-possession, akin to Odysseus' act of refusing Calypso's offer of immortality. Odysseus might have spurned mortal life then, but instead he maintained a higher standard for the story that would be told about him. Unlike Helen, when he speaks of being put on this earth for the sake of being the subject of song for those to come, he assumes an active role for himself as "poet" in shaping the outcome. After all, if one is careless on this matter, one could end up like the hapless Elpenor, whose story, now and forever, is of "a man whose luck ran out" (11.84)—all because he slept on the roof of Circe's house and forgot to use the ladder to descend. Or, more grimly, one might be condemned to repeat the refrain of Agamemnon: "the song men sing of [Clytemnestra] will ring with loathing. / She brands with a foul name the breed of womankind, / even the honest ones to come!" (24.221–222). For Odysseus and Penelope alike, the element of choice and self-authorship is crucial. Penelope uses the passage of time as her ally, in order to resist the claims of the moment. This makes her the "second hero of the poem," as Schein claims.[17] Each spurns the default position, using time as only humans understand it, to forestall what is immediately pressing. By committing themselves uniquely to their union in this way, Odysseus and Penelope are the cause of the oikos and polis intertwining to become something memorable.

There is no question of Penelope letting go of her memory of Odysseus, but she does allow it to recede in the determining effects it has over her behavior. So it is that just at the moment that Penelope is receiving signs that Odysseus' return is imminent, she solicits bridal gifts from her suitors, and proclaims the decisive contest for her hand in marriage. Penelope's deed is all her own, but it summons the desired response from the partner in her midst. Notably, whereas we observers may be fixated on the extent of Penelope's knowledge and the import of her timing, Odysseus never is; their movements are in step. Homer makes us feel the status of outsiders looking in at this enigmatic couple, Penelope and "the man marked out by fate to be her husband" (21.185). But if their ending is perpetually longed-for, it is not assured. Penelope and Odysseus both make themselves vulnerable to the threat that their past will leave no trace on their future. But when they take a hand in the story that will be written, they make themselves worthy of each other. Human nature may improve in the telling.

Prior to the reunion of Odysseus and Penelope, their abilities to take on the conventional features of the opposite sex are in full sight. Odysseus battles and subdues his willfulness as he teaches himself to endure the vicissitudes of fate with an accepting spirit. Penelope overcomes her quiescence, releases the hold of the past, and exposes herself to imposing risks. "Reverse similes" abound in the *Odyssey* that demonstrate the poet's expert ways of arguing for a "particular pattern" of male-female relations, as Helene Foley has traced to brilliant effect. The fame of Penelope is likened to that of a flawless king "who dreads the gods, / who governs a kingdom vast, proud and strong" (19.119–120), whereas Odysseus is imagined to be like a weeping woman, "her arms flung round her darling husband" (8.588). For as long as Odysseus and Penelope circle warily around each other, the images serve to guide them away from the extremes they seek to avoid, unconstrained aggression and irresponsible guardianship: "The characteristics associated with both the male sphere—with its special relation to war as well as agriculture—and with the female sphere—weaving and maintaining the domestic environment—are each shown to be potentially unstable in one dimension."[18] When the reconciliation finally occurs, the male and female roles are distinguished to perfection. In Penelope's great moment, when she tricks Odysseus into detailing the secret of their bed, Odysseus goes into paroxysms of recrimination. As injured lover, Odysseus is earnest and voluble—and potentially all too comical. Penelope resists the smile and proffers the apologies; her success is completed in her self-abnegation. The elemental oikos comes together, "two minds, two hearts that work as one." Their attachment is sanctioned by nature itself with that emblem of the olive tree, for the remembered image is powerful enough to form the basis of a political community. Nature, household, and city are in harmony.

The story culminates but does not close in that happy moment,

for Odysseus communicates to his newfound wife the prophecy by
Tiresias that "one more labor lies in store— / boundless, laden with
danger, great and long" (23.283–284). Just as there is no gainsaying
the past that Penelope and Odysseus have lost together, so there will
be no illusions about a secured future. Penelope receives this news
with the same strength with which Odysseus conveys it; the two are
at ease in the repose allotted to them. Their spirituality consists in an
acceptance of the terms which transcend human comprehension.
Neither presumes to inquire further. Perhaps Odysseus attained his
wisdom in the House of the Dead, when he absorbs the sobering
lesson from Achilles that men risk their souls when they seek to
become as gods.[19] Or perhaps it is the story-infused environment
itself, in which men and women keep before themselves corrective
images not just of kingly women or of weeping men, but also of gib-
bering bats, human shades, and vengeful gods of the sea. The first
great story of the polis ends when the goddess wheels on Odysseus
and demands an end to the war: "Don't court the rage of Zeus." *This*
hero obeys her, "glad at heart" (24.597–598) for the divine sanction
of his, and Ithaca's, homecoming.

Thucydides' Athens

In one of the darkest moments in *The Peloponnesian War,* the
Athenian general Nicias, "appalled by the state of affairs" before the
battle with Syracuse in the Great Harbor, calls out to each of his
captains in a last-ditch effort to raise their spirits. Thucydides reports that Nicias resorted to those all-purpose appeals "—to wives,
children, and national gods—without caring whether they [were]
thought commonplace, but loudly invoking them in the belief that
they [would] be of use in the consternation of the moment."[20] But the
appeals were hollow. As the Athenians go down to catastrophic defeat, Thucydides notes that they were so overwhelmed by their misfortune that they "never even thought of asking leave to take up their
dead or wrecks, but wished to retreat that very night"; more, they
refused to board the ships ever after (7.72.2–4). In one snapshot is
revealed the utter breakdown of the Athenian identity and all the
crucial elements that are out of balance in the polis: wives, children
and national gods; ancestors, customs, and national identity. Sensing

imminent peril, the Athenians take on the features of trapped animals; without a polis, they resemble beasts. Their end is in a pit. With the final defeat comes Thucydides' pronouncement: "this was by far the greatest reverse that ever befell an Hellenic army" (7.75.7).

Throughout his account of the events in Sicily, Thucydides elicits a retrospective impulse, for readers may well be bordering on disbelief. When earlier high points are recalled, the juxtapositions are extremely uncomfortable; the increasingly futile speeches of Nicias in Book 7, for instance, make even first-time readers of Thucydides squirm in remembrance of Book 2 and the Funeral Oration.[21] Under the leadership of Pericles, the Athenian self-presentation was at its most buoyant and the Athenian military position looked to be formidable, if not infallible. Pressing back further, readers are struck by other indicators of a foreordained Athenian victory. Indeed, the closer one gets to returning to the beginning of the work, the more principled appears the cause for pinning all hopes on the Athenians. The measures set out and explicated by Thucydides in his Archaeology (1.2–1.23), his opening segment on early Greek history and the rise to power of Athens, conduce to the sense that Athenian aggressiveness on the seas and adaptability on land equip her better than Sparta to carry out a prolonged engagement. Connor rightly remarks that "if the Archaeology were our only evidence, we might conclude that Athens should win the war."[22] Strangely, this bent toward Athens persists for many readers through subsequent encounters with the text, as if perhaps in the next time through, Athens might finally prevail.

The literary achievement of note here regarding *The Peloponnesian War* is this: the historian insinuates that Athens is on the side of history, only for "history" ever to demur. Athens is identified in the first place as the dynamo, the emphatic activating force and preeminent subject of Thucydides; almost invisibly, and in the second place, she is faulted for her activity and her *kinesis,* or movement. As Athens' defeat is assured in fact, the studied nature of this literary effect must be acknowledged; Thucydides is no transparent narrator. To follow his irony is to take up the cautionary story of the polis. This role of Athens can be emphasized without overlooking the supreme contrast that emerges in the *Peloponnesian War* between Athens and

Sparta. As in the other great works examined here, things are what they are, yet they possess a transcendent significance as well. Athens and Sparta are not only warring states but also distinctly different relations to the universe, dichotomous yet in an ultimate sense mutually indispensable.[23] Nevertheless, Thucydides marks Athens with special emphasis as the single historical entity that defines the concept of the polis, for she embodies the energy and innovative spirit that is associated both with its triumphs and its self-destruction. Her insistent self-institution portends that she, not Sparta, is the authoritative polis in Thucydides' world, that the Athenian people, "born into the world to take no rest themselves and to give none to others" (1.70.9), are *more* vital as a political experiment than the famously denatured Spartans, whose watchword is always "containment."

From the point of view of the Athenians, "Sparta was different, 'other,' almost un-Greek," as Cartledge remarks.[24] Sparta, Thucydides reminds us, "is neither built in a compact form nor adorned with magnificent temples and public edifices, but composed of villages after the old fashion of Hellas" (1.10.2). It lacks the openness that is so critical to Athens, and the secrecy of its government frustrates Thucydides' own researches (5.68.2). The personalities of Athens and Sparta are revealed early in *The Peloponnesian War* and remain noteworthy throughout. At the first assembly at Sparta, the Corinthians set out the unforgettable types: "You, Spartans, of all the Hellenes, are alone inactive, and defend yourselves not by doing anything but by looking as if you would do something" (1.69.4); the Athenians, in contrast, "are addicted to innovation, and their designs are characterized by swiftness alike in conception and execution" (1.70.2). Admittedly, this assessment is made by a neighbor intricately involved in the action, but the characterization is supported more generally in the speeches and events to follow. Regarding events in the twenty-first year of the war, Thucydides remarks that the Spartans, as usual, were "the most convenient" possible adversaries for the Athenians: "The wide difference between the two characters, the slowness and want of energy of the Spartans as contrasted with the dash and enterprise of their opponents, proved of the greatest service" (8.96.5). Thus there are compelling reasons to conclude that Thucydides identifies Athens as the creative intelligence: "[Athens'] power, created by intelligence, inevitably becomes war . . . and eventually this war destroys the civilization that brought it about. The Spartans are merely the external agents of this destruction."[25] Sparta remains intact in victory—and to the side in the *History*.

The means by which Thucydides acknowledges the superior creative intelligence of the Athenians is more intricate than is often allowed, and in surprising accord with those of his predecessor, Herodotus. It should be noted that both historians open their accounts by allowing the aggressors to speak, and both end their histories with that voice defeated and inarticulate. This one observation should be enough to discredit the old view that Herodotus is the "subjective" historian, Thucydides the "objective" one, for *both* present complex perspectives on national characters. This is not to imply in either case that they fully *identify* with the characters, as in the assumption that Thucydides, for example, allows his favored characters to speak for him, with Pericles serving as consensus figure, or that he duly expresses the ideas of his time.[26] It is rather to claim that Thucydides assumes a role and criticizes the performance at the same time. He speaks "in character," and what that character *is* he reveals in his opening two words: "Thucydides the Athenian." Taking on the ways of the Athenians, Thucydides presents them in motion, as it were, and from the inside; it is *his* war. The result is an internal view of the demise of the polis, even as he also attends fastidiously to the shifting conditions of the Greek world at large; it remains *the* war, as well.

This reading clears *Thucydides* of the ideologically driven motives of which he is so often accused in his selection of evidence, and leaves *Athens* exposed as the polis which cuts off its own moorings. There have always been critics who take Thucydides to task for the constricted nature of his subject matter and who remain insistently with the surface impression of the text. From this literal point of view, his motives may appear deeply suspect. Thucydides is said to neglect women ("no living Athenian woman, respectable or otherwise, ever surfaces in his *History*"), the household ("Thucydides has marginalized the oikos"), and the gods ("Thucydides seriously understated the religious aspect of the war he set himself to describe").[27]

Notably, these positions exclude the possibility that Thucydides omits from his presentation what his *characters* omit from their thinking, and this is the possibility that I pursue here.

The reputation that Thucydides has for objectivity and impartiality tends to conceal the magnitude of his artistic accomplishment and the connections he establishes with his predecessors.[28] When he mimics the Athenian voice (thus aspiring to capture "how they really were," the formula now associated with Rankean objectivity), his act of imitation is a creative interpretation which must pass the scrutiny of friend and foe in his audience. Imitations call for judgment; a poor rendering of the Athenians (or the adversaries they brought on) would not likely succeed in the long run. Thucydides may put words in the mouths of his speakers, but the portrait is open to scrutiny; every instance is a renewed invitation for the audience to evaluate his rendering. No one has faced this challenge more squarely than Thucydides in his famous commitment "to make the speakers say what was in [his] opinion demanded of them (*ta deonta*) by the various occasions, of course adhering as closely as possible to the general sense of what they really said" (1.22.1). Contemporary readers find it notoriously difficult to accept this combination of the literary shaping of the historical bedrock of events, but it must be at least considered that the deficiency is in the readers who expect clarity in how all of this "works." Thucydides' vaunted objectivity is real enough; perhaps, though, his exactitude is of a more inventive sort than a scientifically based age easily can assimilate.[29]

Contrary to initial appearances, Thucydides already anticipates the decline of Athens in those early "positive" moments of *The Peloponnesian War,* such as in the Archaeology and the Funeral Oration. Each offers a glimpse of the fatal turn of the polis. We must conclude that Thucydides intends criticism of the Athenian perspective from the start. When Nicias called out to his Athenian captains in Book 6, then, he spoke in a void, for the polis had long ago dissociated itself from the influence of women and the oikos, become careless of traditional practices, and embraced untrammeled change and innovation. Even an exceptional religious person like Nicias could not bring his practices into common use; his was a private attachment to the gods. This did not happen suddenly in Sicily, or arise in the commonly noted points of decline—in the Plague, Mytilene, or Melos. Thucydides informs us much earlier that the Athenians were headed for catastrophe, having separated the interests of the polis from women and the household, and severed their attachment to customary practices and remembrances. The Archaeology portends the doom of the polis, picking up the same note with which *The History* of Herodotus ends.

The initial contact that Thucydides makes with Herodotus in the Archaeology signals an important correspondence in method. If imitation is the sincerest form of flattery, then Thucydides flatters Herodotus in his opening by assuming the literary posture of the materialist and rationalist Athenians. Herodotus, it will be recalled, opens *his* work in a mocking rendition of how the Persian chroniclers account for the enmity between East and West.[30] In the relatively short time period between the Battle of Salamis in the Persian War (480 B.C.) and the outbreak of the Peloponnesian War (431 B.C.), Athens transforms itself from patriot city fighting on behalf of all of Greece against despotic Persia, to naval power convinced of its own manifest greatness, and hegemon over Greek city-states. It should come as no surprise that it is in the Pentecontaetia, Thucydides' filling-in of some of the events between the Persian and Peloponnesian wars (1.89– 117), that his contact with Herodotus is most unmistakable. Critics have long noted that Thucydides there conjures up the Herodotean world in his anecdotal treatments of character and his unique usages of archaic language. This is true without being pejorative, for it is a necessary bridge in Thucydides' account.[31] For example, a character that Herodotus and Thucydides share—Themistocles—looks back to a time when the oikos and polis were still in contact (1.136.3), and looks ahead to a point when sacred distinctions are lost from sight, in the course of elevating the concerns of the polis (1.90.3). Soon enough, the Athenians rule an empire of their own, and impose *their* distinctive political imprint. When Thucydides reproduces the Herodotean strategy of presenting in the first place the perspective of the aggressor, this cannot bode well for the Athenians.[32] It suggests that Thucydides' Archaeology should be approached with the same skepticism that we direct toward the Persian chroniclers of Herodotus.

In the opening to Herodotus' work, the Persian chroniclers spin out their rationalist fantasies about the outbreak of the Persian war. This rationalism of the Persians is associated significantly with their slighting of women, as they put forth a simplistic explanation of the war that levels all females (including immortals) according to their troublesome proclivities for being carried off by males. Mythical Greek figures—Io, Europa, Medea—are resurrected in that account either as unfortunate or willing victims of kidnap and rape; mythological women thus are treated as linked historical figures. The Greeks allegedly bring on the enmity between East and West when they overreact to the final theft, that of Helen, wife of Menelaus. The Persians place themselves in the right: "they, for their part, made no account of the women carried off from Asia."[33] Herodotus leaves clues throughout of his ironical distance toward these views: "this is the Persian story" and "not how the Greeks tell it" (1.2). These asides suggest that something is amiss among the rationalist and self-justifying Persians. And without doubt, the treatment of women is at the very center of their skewed outlook: "to take seriously the avenging of [women] is the part of fools . . . clearly, the women would not have been carried off had they no mind to be" (1.4).

Thucydides does not mention Herodotus' *History* explicitly, but his Archaeology similarly demystifies the Greek past; it also proves jarring in its treatment of women—who conspicuously disappear. In Herodotus' *History,* the Persian outlook culminates in Xerxes' impulse to "show to all a Persian empire that has the same limit as Zeus's sky" (7.8). Barely a generation later, the war is internecine, Athens has assumed the aggressive posture, and Thucydides "interprets" the role anew. When he investigates the source of the Greek conflict, he measures only quantities of power: his war reveals the greatest movement known in history, on the greatest scale (1.1.1–3), lasting "a very long time" (1.23.1), accompanied by unparalleled disasters, including earthquakes, eclipses, droughts, famines, and "the most calamitous and awfully fatal visitation, the plague" (1.23.3)— and all this evinced "from the very beginning." Past wars (mere skirmishes, really, Thucydides assures us) pale in contrast: the number of Greeks who sailed to Troy appears "inconsiderable" (1.10.5); as for the Persian War, it must be said that the vessels in the fleet at Salamis "had not complete decks," and, after all, that war "found a speedy decision in two actions by sea and two by land" (1.14.3; 1.23). For a prolonged time, over a very wide area of Hellas, states "were incapable of combination for great and national ends, or of any vigorous action of their own" (1.17). Minos is identified "as the first person known to us by tradition as having established a navy" (1.4.1), and he and Agamemnon are noteworthy for appreciating the importance of controlling the seas. The Trojan War itself came about as a consequence of Agamemnon's naval power, rather than on account of "the oaths of Tyndareus" (1.9.1). Familiar Greek heroes go unmentioned, and the cycle of history moves in accordance with the concentration of material power alone. The "real" reason for the outbreak of the Peloponnesian War, the motivating force behind this unprecedented series of events, is, Thucydides concludes, "the growth of the power of Athens" (1.23), a conclusion which he has built up to through this "unsentimental, unheroic view of the past [with] an emphasis on the drives for power, self-protection, and self-interest."[34]

The preoccupation with war and its origins in Thucydides' Archaeology remains consistent with Herodotus' proem, then. But if the impulse to demythologize is still in constant view, the centrality of women is not. Since one of the wars Thucydides contends with is the Trojan War, it is no small matter for him to eliminate all mention of Helen—but he manages to do just that. The historian is sure that "fear was quite as strong an element as love" (1.9.3) in precipitating that conflict, and he suspects that Agamemnon's superiority in naval strength bound "the Suitors" over "the oaths of Tyndareus" (1.9.1). The name of Helen is never uttered. On another occasion in the Archaeology, Thucydides again evokes a subject that calls women to mind, only to surprise our expectations with wholly male-oriented examples. The topic is "fashion." Is this the province of men? Thucydides confides that in regard to the old fashions of Hellas, "it is only lately that [the Athenian] rich old men left off the luxury of wearing undergarments of linen, and fastening a knot of their hair with a tie of golden grasshoppers" (1.6.3).[35] This is absence made palpable. Women are drawn to mind at the same time that they are excised from this version of Greek history.

The phenomenon of the disappearing Greek women occurs first in Herodotus, though well into the narrative of the Persian War. From his early story of Gyges to his closing chapters in *The History,* Herodotus traces the association between absolute (Eastern) rule and its distortive impact on public and private relations. The final drama is not the overthrow of Xerxes' forces on land and sea, but the disastrous results of the Great King's affair with Artaÿnte, daughter of his brother, whose wife he had initially sought to seduce. That convoluted story encapsulates the consequences of entangling private *eros* and public power. The Persian system of rule is susceptible to the most distressing abuses in this regard, and one of the questions that hangs heavily at the end of Herodotus' work is whether the Athenians will have the resources to combat that failing as they come into rule. The question hangs so heavily in *The History* because over the course of the work, the place of Greek women fades from sight, falling away from the balanced picture Solon had offered in Book 1 as the happiest lot: one of public, and one of private orientation (1.31–32). When it comes to depicting women in the Greek polis, Herodotus eventually has as little material as Thucydides.[36]

When Thucydides removes women altogether in his reconstruction of early Greek history, then, he is only corroborating the negative trend set out earlier by Herodotus. By Book 6 in *The Peloponnesian War,* the contrasting excesses of Nicias and Alcibiades are articulated in terms reminiscent of the Persians' confusion of public and private eros. But again, the markers are laid down much earlier, in the Archaeology. As Thucydides completes his revision of early Greek history, he pauses to reflect: "Having now given the result of my inquiries into earlier times, I grant that there will be a difficulty in believing every particular detail. The way that most men deal with traditions, even traditions of their own country, is to receive them all alike as they are delivered, without applying any critical test whatever" (1.20.1). Thucydides then introduces an example that commentators have long read as an aspersion against Herodotus. This concerns the tradition about the tyrannicides Harmodius and Aristogiton, a tradition which is critical to the topic of the exclusion of women from Greek history as well as to a proper assessment of Thucydidean historiography. Thucydides claims that the Athenian public continues to misidentify the status of Hipparchus when Harmodius and Aristogiton killed him; he was not tyrant of Athens, but *brother* of the tyrant, Hippias. "There are many other unfounded ideas current among the rest of the Hellenes, even on matters of contemporary history which have not been obscured by time" (1.20.3). The barb is commonly taken to be directed at Herodotus despite the fact that Herodotus' rendering is in full agreement with Thucydides': "This Hipparchus was the brother of the reigning prince, Hippias" (*History*, 5.55).

The key to this passage in the Archaeology is not Herodotus' rendering of the tradition, but Thucydides' own fuller account in Book 6. There he reinserts an all-important female figure excised from the original account, and explains more fully the love affair and "the sad fate" of Hipparchus that made him famous and "got him also the credit with posterity for having been tyrant" (6.55.4). That fate came about after Hipparchus solicited Harmodius, was unsuccessful, and sought to insult him in revenge. The unnamed sister of Harmodius was the vehicle. She, just a young girl, was invited by Hipparchus to join in a procession; appearing as summoned, she then was rejected by Hipparchus, who denied that he had ever invited such an unworthy participant. Thucydides goes on to fill in the details of the assassination in a way that seems to bear out his announced intention: "to show that the Athenians are no more accurate than the rest of the world in their accounts of their own tyrants and of the facts of their own history" (6.54.1). The "Athenian perspective" is the target in Book 6 as in Book 1, with the early account consistent with the Archaeology in its all-male cast of characters.

Thucydides concludes his examples of distorted history with the gibe: "So little pains do the vulgar take in the investigation of truth, accepting readily the first story that comes to hand" (1.20.3). Is not the Archaeology the first story that has come to hand in this work? Thucydides leaves unsettled the difficulty he anticipated for his readers "in believing every particular detail." This leads me to surmise that the gap between Thucydides' apparent and intended meaning extends even into "the Methodology," Thucydides' explicit historiographical defense (1.20–22). There is no mistaking the consistency of the voice that comes across in the Archaeology and Methodology— no-nonsense, rationalist, impressed only by demonstrable proofs— and yet only the former is treated by commentators as a puzzle.[37]

Where Thucydides comes across as most transparent ["In fine, I have written my work not as an essay which is to win the applause of the moment, but as a possession for all time" (1.22.4)], he may be most abstruse, for that is the voice of those same doomed Athenians who follow Pericles in imagining the memory of themselves descending "to the latest posterity" (2.64.3)—all without a Homer, or another of his craft (2.41.4).[38] And what may be most questionable of all in the Methodology is Thucydides' apparent dismissal of his immediate predecessor, Herodotus. Herodotus is not named when Thucydides refers to the "absence of romance" in *his* work (1.22.4), but the target has never been in doubt. The finality of that judgment should be reassessed, for the references to Herodotus actually serve further to open the ironical stance of Thucydides.

Thucydides exposes literarily what is happening politically. He continues to express the Athenian proclivities as he proceeds through his discussion of methodology. He promises us "the clearest data" and conclusions "as exact as can be expected" (1.21.1), for he subjects his work to "the most severe and detailed tests possible" (1.22.2). He claims that an examination of the facts will verify that his war "was much greater than the wars which preceded it" (1.21.2). In the same chapter, he signals the inapplicability of poets and chroniclers, "attractive at truth's expense." They are immaterial. Other remarks by the historian "in the Athenian mode" bear scrutiny. Thucydides holds out to us the paradigmatically Athenian posture of the intellect capable of ordering the world, at the same time that he has put it in a framework that must undermine those prospects: the Athenian way is *not* destined to succeed. Hunter notes that while "the Archaelogy points to the *arche* [empire, hegemony] of Athens, the Athens of the Funeral Oration, the very culmination of civilization, it also anticipates the problems and difficulties that will lead to the disintegration of her *periousia* [surplus], her *dynamis* [power] and her *arche.*"[39]

Thucydides presently signals the connection between his perspective and that of Pericles, by having him recount the same strategy of removing Athens and its image from the domain of the poets, and specifying the same exacting audience. Pericles echoes Thucydides' voice in his insistence that power reveals its own glory. Early in the Archaeology, Thucydides had paused to imagine the eventual demise of Athens and Sparta, and to consider how the two city-states would come to be regarded (1.10.1). He claimed that *power* (*dynamis*) is the correct signpost of their fame, rather than physical structures, and that power must be assessed soberly. That thought leads to a derogation of the poets, who muddle the appearances; Homer is specifically identified (1.10.3). If accounts of war are removed from the poets and taken up by someone desiring "an exact knowledge of the past as an aid to the understanding of the future" (1.22.4), then the memory of Athens would seem to be assured. Pericles proceeds through the same argument. He associates the fame of Athens ["the greatest name in the world" (2.64.3)] with the "imperishable monuments" she left behind, not artistic or cultural artifacts, but other "mighty proofs" of power. Once again, the poets are dismissed as irrelevant, and Homer is derided (2.41.4). Pericles speaks in the foreknowledge that "in obedience to the general law of decay," the Athenian empire, too, will fall (2.64.3). Pericles and the Thucydides of the Archaeology are fully in line.

The protest against Homer and other rival accounts begins to sound too strongly. A reassessment may be in order, and in this spirit we propose that Athens' great hero, Pericles, is a kind of "failed Odysseus" in this polis story. Pericles is untroubled by any such qualms as Odysseus had about how his story would be told. Pericles treats as burdensome the immediate past of the Athenians in the Persian War, thus freeing himself and his listeners from the cautionary lesson evinced by Herodotus. Instead, Pericles celebrates the freedom of Athenians to live as they please, an anti-Odyssean sentiment if ever there were one. For the stories the Athenians tell themselves about who they are now become presentist and thus utterly dependent on the personalities of their leaders. This situation evokes the memory of Herodotus' early Persians. Herodotus writes that a Persian subject "may not pray for good things for himself alone . . . but only that all shall be well with all the Persians and the king; for among all the Persians is himself also" (1.132). Similarly, the Athenians of Thucydides look to be well on the way to losing their individual selves. Pericles resists reciting the lessons learned in the Persian War as a theme "too familiar to my hearers for me to dwell upon" (2.36.4). As he detaches the present generation from its recent inheritances, it makes it possible for him to argue for the self-made status of the Athenians. A closer look at recent history would qualify that reading considerably, and so Pericles' move appears to be an evasion tactic, and one his successors would learn well. Unhinged from lessons of the past, Athenians can celebrate their originality: "Our constitution does not copy the laws of neighboring states; we are rather a pattern to others than imitators ourselves" (2.37.1). By the time of the Melian dialogue, the Athenians are a pattern to others only in the negative sense of having succumbed to the predictable cycle of hubris as set out by Herodotus.

In *The History,* the moment in which the Athenians take to the sea against the Persian aggressors was a great transforming one, but it was not intended to be *permanent*. Pericles, though, alludes to the freedom the Athenians experience almost as an established feature of their personality, in contrast to the Spartans, who "cannot afford the absence from their homes" (1.141.4). He instructs his countrymen to bear up, and not to think of their homes: "Dismissing all thought of our land and houses, we must vigilantly guard the sea and the city" (1.143.5). The Athenians, Thucydides relates, "found it hard" (2.14.1). In Pericles' last words on the subject, he urges them to consider their land and houses "in the light of the gardens and accessories that embellish a great fortune, and as, in comparison, of little moment" (2.62.3). Pericles sees the Athenians waver, and he promises them an unlimited world: "your naval resources are such that your vessels may go where they please, without the King or any other nation on earth being able to stop them" (2.62.2). He is inviting them to be something besides human, regarding their homes as "accessories" or mere gardens. The sight of Athenian power fills him with visions of grandeur. This prospect of always being at sea did not find such favor with Odysseus. Could the Athenians be so forgetful? The best men Pericles can imagine are those who can *take* the buffeting of the sea: "those whose minds are least sensitive to calamity, and whose hands are most quick to meet it, are the greatest men and the greatest communities" (2.64.6). They are to take it as Odysseus did, but without an apparent destination in view. To accept *this* vision of greatness really does require a vast amount of forgetting on the part of the Athenians.

Pericles heralds in an entirely new and misplaced configuration of oikos and polis. He shows a famous inability to speak to the women of Athens, again, in another foil to Odysseus on his way towards the founding of the polis. Though Pericles claims that "our public men have, besides politics, their private affairs to attend to" (2.40.2), he also calls upon his audience to "realize the power of Athens, and feed your eyes upon her from day to day, till love of her fills your hearts" (2.43.1). This "love" is at a strange remove from ordinary human pairings: how would Athens "reciprocate" the love of its citizens? Most crucially, after witnessing the prolonged "negotiations" and trials that take place between Penelope and Odysseus before their reconciliation, this "love" of Athens comes across in contrast as a somewhat unseemly desire to brook no opposition. And "brooking opposition" is at the core of the polis. All proportion seems to be lost here, and all sense of one's own. Despite his flair in speaking, Pericles anticipates a theme to come, when words will lose their meanings.

The Athenian of *The Peloponnesian War* surrenders the oikos as his destination and centering point, accepts a certain offer of "immortality," and forgets his identity. The household surrendered, the influence of women is not to be seen. Pericles' suggestion—that if the Athenians "were ever absolutely driven to it" (2.13.5), they might take the gold ornaments of Athena—bears all the marks of behavior suggested by the absence of women. It recalls Odysseus' crew, having sworn the oath never to harm the herds of Helios, cheering Eurylochus and his suggestion to slaughter the cattle, and to make amends later (when women *are* recalled), "if we ever make it home to Ithaca, native ground" (12.372). All of these issues interrelate, as the Athenians well know: "Deep was their trouble and discontent at abandoning their houses and the hereditary temples of the ancient state, and at having to change their habits of life and to bid farewell to what each regarded as his native city" (2.16.2). Pericles' attempts to assert a perfect balance between the public and private life of the Athenian must come across as strained. In a series of statements, Pericles argues that the Athenian is able to balance freedom and discipline, refinement and moderation, daring and deliberation. There seems to be some attempt to bring together masculine and feminine properties, in other words, but all this gets a different aspect altogether when he urges them to focus on Athens' power and to fall in love with it.

In the Funeral Oration and other speeches, the restricted vision of the Archaeology is protracted by Pericles. He finally gets his due in that strange and awful epitaph offered by Thucydides: "So excessively abundant were the resources from which the genius of Pericles foresaw an easy triumph in the war over the unaided forces of the Peloponnesians" (2.65.13). The polis was in need of more statecraft. After presenting the gradual reconstitution and definition of Ithaca by the founding couple Odysseus and Penelope, we confront in Thucydides the slow degeneration of Athens, the most accomplished polis of all. The failed definition of the polis instructs as well as the positive one. Athens is destroyed for its lapse of imagination, as it suppresses the oppositional mode of its origins in favor of the materialist and later, self-serving, advice of its leaders and the presentist wishes of its populace. Ultimately, Thucydides suggests, it is impossible to continue a narrative line, and his account breaks off, in midsentence, with the last line a disconcerting one: the Persian satrap Tissaphernes goes to Ephesus, where he offers sacrifice to the Greek goddess, Artemis (8.109.5).[40] Without proper care of the polis, the Athenians have lost the stewardship of their own gods and goddesses. An undifferentiated worship of a Greek goddess, by a foreigner, is the parting image. Is this the final recantation of Athenian ways? At the least, their story was imbalanced, not livable, not true.

Aristotle's New Founding

Aristotle reestablishes the vocabulary of opposites in the polis and articulates the route to an intermediate but higher third position. He accomplishes this through his distinctive process of refining conventional opinion. The story of the polis that Aristotle transmits is one of *real* attributes (no more obstacles in the form of Poseidon), yet is also *detached* from the immediate setting (the quarries of Sicily will not be the last word). Athens is no longer the sole exemplar in Aristotle's world; Sparta is every bit as pivotal to his idea of the polis, and perhaps more so. Yet even as Aristotle brings in Sparta to illustrate more fully the nature of the polis, he does not take Athens and Sparta as the irreducible alternatives. They are accidents of history, whereas the polis abides as an ideal construct, and a historical city does not stand in for the concept. Aristotle returns to Homer in foregrounding the male-female elements in the story that will be told and in the respect he shows toward the opening of that story. But Aristotle's polis is the epitome of a *political* community, and in this it leaves Ithaca far behind. At the same time, Aristotle's version has points of resemblance with the disenchanted polis of Thucydides' description; it will never be sufficient in itself for the highest human possibility. But Aristotle refuses to give history the final word. The philosopher's prerogative is to govern the facts, "since it is our intention to study the sort of political partnership that is superior to all for those capable of living as far as possible in the manner one would pray for" (*Pol.* 1260b27–29).

Aristotle's philosophical shaping of historical material is decisive for the legacy of the polis. Historical developments that must have been alarming to him, such as its loss of sovereignty, seem to inspire his most creative resistance; he responds by inventing the polis anew. Aristotle's *Politics,* more than any other work, has shaped the modern understanding of the Greek polis. Although its descriptive and normative components are blended almost seamlessly, commentators have captured its twofold properties in countless ways. On the one hand, it designates a community, on the other, a geographical place; it is the entity that develops out of the village or it refers to the citizens participating in politics; it is necessary or it is natural.[41] These dichotomous formulations give some indication of the elasticity of Aristotle's story: his approach to the polis has captivated so many for so long because it so smoothly contains these dimensions. Criticism of Aristotle's polis often is as revealing of the suppleness of the construct as is acclaim, for then commentators appear to be highlighting only one of its elements. Runciman, for example, trumpets the "doom" of the physical polis while ignoring Aristotle's normative claims; contrariwise, when Keyt accuses Aristotle of faulty logic, he does not go on to wonder why Aristotle's argument nevertheless holds sway. Similarly inconclusive is the charge that Aristotle is not objective.[42] It is not that Aristotle should be immune from the standards of evidence of history or philosophy. But every effort should be made to respond to his multidimensional construction and not to partial views of it. For better or worse, the Aristotelian polis continues to reign.

Aristotle inclines his readers toward the "natural" polis precisely at the moment when the actual polis is beginning to lose its viability; he also moves the concept away from one of the foremost dichotomies of all time: Athens and Sparta. According to Aristotle, the polis is "among the things that exist by nature" (*Pol.* 1253a2) toward which everyone has an impulse—and yet it has a founder who is "responsible for the greatest of goods" (1253a29–31). The normative argument that human beings are completed in the polis receives its direction from the historical founder. And who is that founder? He is best conceived neither as Solon nor Lycurgus but as Aristotle himself, who constitutes the polis through "the compressed ambiguity"[43] of his language. If Thucydides takes on the Athenian perspective in order to depict the weaknesses of the polis from within, Aristotle delves further back to expose its roots and to administer natural correctives. It is with literary intentions, then, that Aristotle acknowledges only marginally the two great lawgivers of the two great poleis, for their project is to be recast. Solon of Athens and Lycurgus of Sparta are put in their place by Aristotle at the same time that he grounds his reflections in common and unexamined assumptions about his "competitors" in statecraft; Athens and Sparta recede from view. The polis becomes an object of study and the political philosopher its cultivator.

Of all Athenian leaders, Solon might seem to possess the best qualities of an Aristotelian statesman. As archon, Solon was enlisted by the rich and poor classes alike to put an end to the disabling insurrections that threatened the state ("for the rich were ready to accept him as a man of wealth and the poor as a man of principle"[44]); so equitable were his land and tax reforms that he pleased neither class. He tried to steer a middle course in his political reforms as well, and by Aristotle's own admission, opened political offices to the lower classes. Solon's "no-neutrality" measure served to unify the polis by treating rich and poor as equally subject to law. He emphasized the written nature of his legislation as a guarantee of its impartiality: "the laws, the same for the wicked and the good, fitting upright justice to each one, I wrote them down."[45] These laws were allegedly "obscure

and contradictory," forcing constant resort to the juries for interpretation and judgment. In the pages of Herodotus, Solon is said to
have presented his law code to the Athenians with the understanding
that they would consult him before abrogating any of them, whereupon he left for ten years of travel (1.29). Thus were the laws advanced without the simultaneous advancing of the lawgiver. Solon's
practical wisdom is evoked in a story related later by Plutarch; when
Solon was asked whether he had provided the best laws for the Athenians, he responded: "The best they would accept."[46] Here, and
across the evidentiary record, Solon stands as the first spokesman for
the polis.[47]

It is striking, therefore, that Solon receives perfunctory treatment
by Aristotle. He mentions Athens not at all and Solon only once in
Book 1, the book most given to enumerating the parts of the polis.
There he reconstructs a line of Solon's poetry: "For self-sufficiency in
possessions of this sort with a view to a good life is not limitless, as
Solon asserts it to be in his poem: 'of wealth no boundary lies revealed to man'" (1256b30–33). Aristotle, a careful reader of Herodotus, would know Solon's famed understanding of the boundaries of
wealth. As an unheeded wise adviser in *The History,* Solon warns
Croesus, the rich and prosperous King of Lydia, that "no single person is self-sufficient; he has one thing and lacks another. . . . One
must look always at the end of everything—how it will come out
finally. For to many the god has shown a glimpse of blessedness only
to extirpate them in the end" (1.32). Croesus comes to hold Solon's
judgment in extremely high regard. But Aristotle takes the occasion
to interject warnings in his own name against the temptations of
materialism, and Solon serves merely as the prompt.

Solon's appearance in Book 2 is equally instructive, for whereas
Aristotle there credits Solon with understanding that "the leveling of
property does indeed have a certain power to affect the political
partnership" (1266b14–15), he goes on to make the all-important
distinction between "leveling" and "aiming at a mean." This latter
constructive element is decisive for statecraft as set out by Aristotle,
and he warns us not to overvalue the good that can be accomplished
through a mere redistribution of wealth. ["For one ought to level
desires sooner than property . . . further, factional conflict occurs not

only because of inequality of possessions, but also because of inequality of honors" (1266b30–40)]. Before Aristotle finally details
Solon's reforms, he introduces otherwise unknown critics: "there are
also some who blame him for dissolving the other [elements of the
existing regime] by giving authority to the court, which was to be
chosen from all by lot" (1274a2). This is unusual enough to merit a
translator's comment: "Solon was traditionally regarded as the founder of the democratic regime in Athens in the early sixth century.
The identity of the proponents of the views described here is not
certain."[48]

Aristotle eventually affirms the reforms of Solon, but not before
giving the reader the sense that they produced a general sense of
dissatisfaction and stimulated an appetite for change. Since an addic-
tion to change appeared to be the undoing of the Athenians, Aristotle
encourages us to be more critical of the Athenian lawgiver than is
usually the case. Once the passion for change is instigated, remembrance becomes an obstacle in the way of every planned action.
Thucydides showed us the Athenians losing their sense of themselves as a people by succumbing to extreme innovation. Aristotle
puts us in mind of the necessary statesman to remedy that passion,
and according to that standard, Solon comes up short.

Lycurgus is of an altogether different order than Solon. When Plutarch wrote about Lycurgus in the second century, he prefaced his
account with the following: "Generally speaking it is impossible to
make any undisputed statement about Lycurgus the lawgiver, since
conflicting accounts have been given of his ancestry, his travels, his
death, and above all his activity with respect to his laws and government; but there is least agreement about the period in which the man
lived."[49] It cannot be said that the situation was significantly different
for Aristotle writing in the fourth century B.C. Aristotle had to con-
tend with a mythical Lycurgus, and this myth would be elicited
whenever he insisted upon a strict definition of the polis: "virtue
must be a care for every polis, or at least every one to which the term
applies truly and not merely in a manner of speaking" (*Pol.* 1280b7–
8). No city-state has a higher repute in the Greek world than Sparta
for dedicating itself to military virtue ["Sparta appears to be the only
or almost the only polis in which the lawgiver has paid attention to

the nurture and exercises of the citizens"[50]], and it was the legendary Lycurgus who was credited with first forging this Spartan identity. The mythical Lycurgus is critical to Aristotle because he is alleged to have forged a unity out of the myriad elements in the polis. Herodotus reports that before Lycurgus, "the Spartans had been, in respect of the laws, the very worst of all the Greeks, one might say, and in their dealings with others, and also among themselves, the least free in communication . . . But then they changed over toward good laws [under Lycurgus]" (1.65). The Spartan lawgiver "reissued" the Spartans as the legend we know today. Such formative influence appears more than human. Herodotus reports that when Lycurgus went to the oracle at Delphi, the Pythia first asked herself whether to hail him as god or man, then said: "Nay, but 'tis rather a god that I see in you, Lycurgus" (1.65). The historian adds "that there are some, too, who declare that, in addition, the Pythia dictated to him the present constitution of Sparta." Wherever the original laws came from, they were not intended to be reformed in any of their particulars; it was a point of pride that they were not put in writing and therefore not subject to interpretation.[51] The Spartans heard and obeyed.

Aristotle's rewriting and undercutting of this Lycurgus is considerable. Of the Spartan system he is directly critical: "their legislator was not a good one" (*Pol.* 1333b23). In the entire chapter devoted to the Spartan regime, Aristotle mentions Lycurgus by name only once, and then only to remark on his lack of success in imposing the regime on Spartan women. Otherwise Lycurgus is alluded to as "the Legislator," for Aristotle will not dignify his work with a proper name. This is of the same order as his rejection of the Homeric world of myth, for the mythical Lycurgus is unaccountable, his supposed powers of speech and voice putting him beyond criticism. Aristotle therefore detaches the lawmaking role from the image. He can show in plain fact the weakness of the Spartan legislator, since "he legislated everything with a view to domination and war" (1333b13–14), such that the Spartans even "turn out children resembling beasts" (1338b13). Aristotle deems it ridiculous that the Spartans of his day "should have lost [the chance for] living nobly even while abiding by [the legislator's] laws, and in the absence of any impediment to putting the laws into practice" (1333b23–25). Disrespect for the law was never a Spartan problem, but their disinclination to reflect on the law is quite another matter. As always, Sparta's weakness is the obverse of Athen's: Sparta could not accommodate change; it could not so much recall its past for future use as memorize it for all time.

Between his extreme examples of Solon and Lycurgus, Aristotle plots his own territory in a way that makes it *more* than an intermediate position. If Aristotle's historical renderings are straightforward, his philosophical refining process is not, even though it is in some sense his paradigmatic approach. Time and again, when Aristotle appears to be on his way to advocating a simple arithmetical middle between two endpoints, he spurs us toward a more principled resolve. Hence it is necessary to attend to even slight shifts of his language and perspective to capture him in the act of specifying new meanings. So in Book 4, Aristotle suddenly appears to offer a far more positive reading of both Solon and Lycurgus, when he claims that "the best legislators are from the middling citizens. Solon was one of these, as is clear from his poems, and Lycurgus (for he was not king)" (1296a18–20). In another apparent shift in evaluation in the same book, Aristotle praises the mixed constitution of the Lacedaemonians: "Many attempt to speak of it as if it were a democracy . . . On the other hand, others call it oligarchy" (1294b20, 31–32). Commentators get caught up in disputes about whether this positive commentary is at odds with depictions elsewhere in the *Politics*. But Schütrumpf has rightly observed that the only difference between Books 2 and 4 on this topic is the description of the mixed constitution; in Book 2, Aristotle refers variously to three Spartan institutions or three Spartan groups (the kings, the elders, the people) with their associated traditional qualifications, whereas in Book 4 he is highlighting two distinct classes of the population, which reduce eventually to the rich and the poor. The variation is notable, for in regard to these latter two classes, there is an opening for statecraft: "A lessening in the tensions of the relations between the groups can be achieved either by giving the more conservative portion of the rich or poor the political power, or by permitting both to participate in holding power through a mixed constitution. The individual quality of the office holder does not play any role at all in this."[52] With this nudge toward the possibilities of statecraft, Aristotle is prepared to accede that "the middling sort of life is best" (1259a37).

This strategy is reminiscent of the teaching in the *Nicomachean Ethics* that moral virtue is a mean (*meson*), a condition of "middleness" (*mesotes*). It is significant that the virtuous mean turns out not to be the straightforward matter of an arithmetical moderation—the view commonly associated with Aristotle—but rather requires attaining the "mean relative to us" (*NE*, 1106b1), based on principle as determined by the prudent man (*phronimos*). So Aristotle's virtuous mean is considerably more vexing a matter than compiling averages. Likewise, the superiority of the "middle" status of the statesman is not determinative; the statesman's excellence is tied to an expression of principle, too. Aristotle only intimates that he is in agreement with the conventional view that the best life is a middling sort. In Athens, the philosopher cannot ingratiate himself too far with established views. Yet none of this invalidates his prior criticism of the so-called "best legislators."

A similar inventiveness regarding the condition of "middleness" is Aristotle's appropriation of the term *"politeia,"* or regime. According to Aristotle's classification, one of the six *specific* types of regime shares the *generic* name of *"politeia."* Translators often replace Aristotle's single term with two different words ("polity" and "regime," for example[53]) to keep the meanings straight. But the ambiguity in the single term serves Aristotle well. "Simply speaking," he tells us, "polity is a mixture of oligarchy and democracy," and a good mixture is one in which "the same polity [might] be spoken of as either a democracy or an oligarchy" (*Pol.* 1293b33–34, 1294b14–16). Democracy and oligarchy are emended in polity. At the same time, there is an important sense in which *politeia* (polity) represents the *best politeia* (regime), "as if it encapsulated the essence of all political experience."[54] The best possible regime in Aristotle's typology is one in which the ruling element is not explicitly identified, and therefore may be perceived differently by the citizenry. "Democracy and oligarchy exist mainly as objects of thought," Davis observes. "The problem most obvious in a democracy is that its principle of unity is only negative and needs a positive articulation."[55] The *Politics* is replete with variations on this theme in which Aristotle extends the carrying power of his terms of art and thereby encourages his readers to leave behind simple dichotomies like oligarchy and democracy, in pursuit of a superior fusion. For Aristotle works to diffuse the impact of the endpoints—here, the strong identification of the citizen as either democrat or oligarch—by incorporating both into a larger story. In his rendering, neither are good judges of things that concern themselves; they apprehend only their own interests and put forth their valid (particularist) claims to rule in an invalid (absolutist) way. The majority has a just claim to rule, according to Aristotle, "for they are superior and wealthier and better when the majority is taken together in relation to the minority" (1283a40–42). So, too, do the wealthy have a claim, "because they have the greater part of the territory, and the territory is something common" (1283a31–32). But the tendency is for each claimant to extrapolate from its starting point to push its defining principle without limit. This is undesirable for the political community as a whole; consequently, it is the states-man's challenge to attenuate the principle of the ruling element.

Aristotle earns the candidacy of the one responsible for the great-est of goods—the beneficent statesman—when he embodies a found-ing impulse apart from the extremes of Solon and Lycurgus. His state-craft aims higher than "mixing" or redistributing income; Aristotle interjects a more principled basis for effecting change. And this activ-ity of statecraft is called for at all times, "since to reform a regime is no less a task than to institute one from the beginning" (1289a4–5). The Athenian regime, unreformed, fell prey to the desire for perpet-ual innovation. The health of a political community is better main-tained with a statesman to instruct it in containing change. But this challenge must be met without making the disposition of the people unyielding; significantly, the Spartan regime proved unable to handle leisure, for only in a war-time situation did their rigid ways justify themselves. Aristotelian statecraft is more all-encompassing; human lives should be ordered in the most principled fashion: "For what is most choiceworthy for each individual is the highest it is possible for him to achieve" (1333a28–30). If life is divided "into occupation and leisure and war and peace," then, Aristotle advises, "war must be for the sake of peace, occupation for the sake of leisure" (1333a35).

In Aristotle's city to pray for, the motto "the worse is always for the sake of the better" (1333a21) is uncontroversial. This city is not expansionist, but arms itself far enough for its security. It takes on the likeness of a private individual, in the analogy made familiar from the *Republic*. And just as *The Odyssey* ends with Odysseus laying down his weapons in the midst of combat with the elders of Ithaca, the city to pray for accepts limits on its activity and aspires, finally, to a philosophical equanimity (1324a5–13). This might be identified as a distinctly *feminine* turn, as the status of the private sphere rises to correct the predictable overvaluation of the public sphere. "[Aristotle's] appreciation of the human desirability of a degree of tension between private and public affections is thus profoundly anti-Periclean," Salkever concludes, and this "in its appreciation of the dignity of the family and the private sphere, in its refusal to equate virility and virtue, and its appreciation of the dangers endemic to political life."[56]

The suggestion that the Aristotelian polis is receptive to feminine influence causes outrage among those heavily invested in the idea of pre-modern misogyny. Similarly, Aristotle's expressed wish for slaves in the city to pray for alienates a democratic audience and impedes a sympathetic reading of the *Politics*. Issues set out by Aristotle in Book 1 inescapably recur; there is no avoiding the particularly flammable mixture of issues touching upon oppression and "natural" gender distinctions. Aristotle's wish for a class of slaves is just a late reminder of the two developments of nature he posited at the start of the *Politics*. In our most basic condition he identifies a necessary conjunction of persons who cannot exist without one another: "on the one hand, male and female, for the sake of reproduction (which occurs not from intentional choice but—as is also the case with the other animals and plants—from a natural striving to leave behind another that is like oneself); on the other, the naturally ruling and ruled, on account of preservation" (1252a26–31). Male and female embody difference, and ruling and ruled affirm hierarchy; these are Aristotle's irreducibles. Democratic sentiments are offended.

Nonetheless, the *Politics* gives us grounds for recognizing something beyond and more profound than the matters that trouble egalitarians: the Aristotelian middle which is more than an intermediate.

Aristotle expresses these two forces of nature not in order to fix them for all time, but to negotiate between them on the way to enlarging our grasp of possibilities. To register "the extremes" is a tried and true Greek method for activating thought, and we underestimate its potential when we assign static qualities to this model. Aristotle's rightly constituted polis combines the two elements of diversity and unity; the concept he proposes to accommodate both is "political rule." Already in his opening move, Aristotle asserts the primacy of this rule ("ruling and being ruled in turn") as a non-oppressive mode of governance. It is a distinct and distinctly admirable human accomplishment which he contrasts with lesser forms (1253b17–19, 1255b15–20). For him, the defining element is qualitative, not quantitative, so that political rule signifies rule over the free, whereas mastery is over slaves, however many. In contrast to political rule, the science of mastery "has nothing great or dignified about it" (1255b33; 1333b27–29). Aristotle introduces his distinctive terminology of "the natural slave" in the context of a wide range of evaluative shifts and discrepancies, suggesting that he is engaged in his familiar move toward statecraft.[57]

A key point is Aristotle's claim that "the same thing is advantageous for the master and slave" (1252a34–35). Clearly such a premise is not intended to summon hideous images of racial or ethnic slavery. Instead, we are asked to imagine "those who are as different [from other men] as the soul from the body or man from beast—and they are in this state if their work is the use of the body, and if this is the best that can come from them" (1254b16–19). Aristotle provides an analogue to our white-collared versus blue-collared workforce late in Book 1 when he speaks of wage labor being performed by "those who lack any art but are useful only for their bodies" (1258b24–26). By the end of the *Politics*, Aristotle prays for farmer-slaves in his city to pray for, for *someone* has to produce the food, and best of all would be if there existed a readymade class of people who were drawn to physical and not intellectual labor. If we were to reword Aristotle's wish as one for a stable and contented service economy, perhaps it would coincide after all with the wish lists of democrats.

It is also critical to recall that Aristotle's targeted audience is the class that fancies itself the "natural masters," so that his vocabulary of "natural slaves" may well have been intended to be the less incendiary, more effective means for correcting their perspectives than by direct criticism. If numerous obstacles arise in the course of establishing the entity of the natural slave, might not a "natural master" come to light as problematic as well? More crucially, Aristotle undermines conventional assumptions about what a master–slave relation implies by his series of negative claims. His negative definitions serve as a check against overdetermining the content of "the natural." He brings to the forefront what is *not* the slave by nature. First of all, the *female* is not a natural slave; it is the mark of barbarism to equate them (1252b4–5). Second, slaves "according to law and by force" are not the same as "natural slaves." As has been noted, natural slavery offers its advantages (1255b12–15). The master should be responsible for instilling virtue in the slave (1260b3–5), for the natural slave "wholly [lacks] the deliberative element" (1.13); he perceives, without having, reason (1254b18–24). His physical appearance is no reliable guide to this state of his soul. "Nature indeed wishes to make the bodies of free persons and slaves different as well [as their souls]— . . . yet the opposite often results" (1254b27–32). Time and again, nature's intentions are foiled, whether in identifying slave or master: "But while nature wishes to do this [from the good should come someone good], it is often unable to" (1255b3–4).

Aristotle converts the ugly reality of slavery into an intellectual conundrum: Nature is flawed in terms of human striving for the good. He combines the series of mostly negative formulations of the "natural slave" with affirmative claims that the most flourishing human condition is one in which the soul rules the body—"and the better rule is always that over ruled [things] that are better" (1254a24–25). Hierarchy is critical to the project of the polis because of its diverse elements, and diversity is productive not in the clashing of different elements but in their ordered arrangement. According to Aristotle's understanding, a proper hierarchy does not insult, but respects, the dignity of different contributors. This may all come down to Aristotle's basic dispute with democrats: whether diversity is best managed as a project of statecraft ["For whatever is constituted out of a number of things—whether continuous or discrete—and becomes a

single common thing always displays a ruling and a ruled element"
(1254a28–30)], or left alone, in deference to the free expression
of self.

Aside from the naturally ruling and ruled, the different contributors to the polis receive their paradigmatic expression in "male" and
"female." And under the rubric of political rule, Aristotle places the
unique subset of "marital rule." This might appear to suggest an equitable arrangement, since in the notion of "ruling and being ruled in
turn," sympathy extends both ways, as the ruler and the ruled typically imagine themselves in the position of the other. But spouses do
not actually "change places" in that arrangement, and Aristotle's contemporary readers frequently disparage his description as unacceptably male-dominated. The implications of his musical image are
considered objectionable: "[T]he one ruled is like a flute maker,
while the ruler is like a flute player, the user [of what the other
makes]" (1277b27–28). Add to this Aristotle's assertion that man
and woman have different "virtues" and different "works," and it
becomes clear how far he strains egalitarian beliefs: "moderation and
courage differ in a man and a woman. For a man would be held a
coward if he were as courageous as a woman, and a woman talkative
if she were as modest as the good man; and household management
differs for a man and woman as well, for it is the work of the man to
acquire and of the woman to guard" (*Pol.* 1277b20–25). Aristotle is
far from sharing our hesitation about identifying *natural* gender distinctions: "For the male, unless constituted in some respect contrary
to nature, is by nature more expert at leading than the female, and
the elder and complete than the younger and incomplete" (*Pol.*
1259b39ff.). This has provoked persistent claims that Aristotle is
trapped in the conventional thinking of his time, that, for instance,
"it is because women and the household have a specific role to play in
the natural order of things that their functions should not be tam-
pered with.[58] Since democratic writers believe in no such "natural
order," it must be that Aristotle is revealing the prejudices of his time
in invoking Nature.

The alternative is worth posing: that *democrats* are being conventional when they find victims in every form of rule other than their
own, and deny the distinctions between the sexes that in other ages

might have pointed toward complementarity. Perhaps there is no infallible way to adjudicate between Aristotelian and democratic claims, but at the least Aristotle might be cleared of what critics commonly *claim* of him: that he appeals to the natural order as a means of perpetuating conventional oppressive practices.[59] Certainly Aristotle uses male-female as one of the foundational oppositions of the cosmos, with ramifications everywhere; it is an opposition that he wishes to carry into politics in specific ways. But it is community forged through difference that is at issue, difference which human beings exacerbate in the progress of civilization ["the works are divided, and they are different for a man and woman; now they provide for one another, placing the private things into the common (*koinon*)" (*NE*, 8.12)]. It is in their distinct contributions to the oikos that Aristotle identifies the move of male and female toward community, a community that in the best case is a noble prototype of the polis. Natural difference, or complementarity, is at the very center of this arrangement based on commonality. To all appearances, the rule belongs to the husband; in practice, husband and wife govern each other: "The relation of husband to wife seems to be in the nature of an aristocracy; the husband rules in virtue of fitness, and in matters that belong to a man's sphere; matters suited to a woman he hands over to his wife" (*NE*, 1160b23ff.).

To speak of "spheres" is to acknowledge natural distinctions. Thus, although marital rule is political in Aristotle's sense, husband and wife do not alternate rule because of the male's *thymos,* which is indomitable (*Pol.* 1328a6–7). Aristotle tells us in the *History of Animals* that in all cases except the bear and the leopard, the female is less spirited than the male: "With all other animals the female is softer in disposition, is more mischievous, less simple, more impulsive, and more attentive to the nurture of the young; the male, on the other hand, is more spirited, more savage, more simple and less cunning" (608b1ff.). Of course, women have *thymos,* too, but in a "rightly-constituted" marriage, the woman defers to her more spirited mate, while manifesting her own superior nurturing qualities.[60] Democrats predictably read such passages defensively, on the assumption that more spiritedness is better than less. But this is hardly borne out by the movement of Aristotle's argument. There are the intriguing literary allusions, for one thing, which subvert and suggest the *need* for a woman's "greater cunning," as a means of coping with untenable situations of male display. Aristotle's seemingly inappropriate allusion to Sophocles (in the *Ajax*) to support the view that "to a woman silence is an ornament" is just one famous instance in which he calls into question the surface meaning of the text in admiration of the female role.[61]

The common charge that Aristotle associates male with soul and "form," female with body and "material" cannot be upheld; humans are composite beings, but composite beings who identify ourselves primarily in terms of soul, not body. Aristotle moves toward intellect, or *nous,* which leaves behind all contact with the status quo. More specifically for Aristotle, we regard ourselves most of all as *nous,* or the capacity to be grasped by intelligibles. It is the activity of *nous* that for Aristotle constitutes the fullest human happiness ["in power and dignity it very much exceeds all. It may even seem that this *is* each one" (*NE,* 10.7)]. Crucially, *nous* "enters from outside," as Aristotle remarks in the *Generation of Animals,* and therefore it transcends "the generative contributions of both male and female. As a consequence, male and female may *both* be likened to matter . . . in relation to that mysterious 'outside' source."[62] The highest human possibilities for Aristotle concern one's openness to thought—a thoroughly ungendered thesis.

In retrospect, it appears that Aristotle only begins his ruminations within the limits of conventional thinking. His story of the polis ensues in a rejuvenated series of dichotomies: a reassertion that the polis depends on the oikos, that politics should heed philosophy, that public and private spheres call for balance. At the start of Book 7 in the *Politics,* Aristotle introduces the dispute "whether the political and active way of life is choiceworthy, or rather that which is divorced from all external things—that involving some sort of study, for example—which some assert is the only philosophic way of life" (1324a25–29). The highest life that comes to light is a spiritual one, with all that suggests for conflict with the demands of the polis. The polis "to pray for" emulates the contemplative life of an individual. Aristotle brings us full circle; in common with the *Odyssey* and the *Peloponnesian War,* his work ends "in prayer." We recall that the male and female elements of Odysseus' world are intensified in his attempt at homecoming; there is nothing androgynous about either Odysseus or Penelope even when their similes are "unbalanced." The complementarity that they illustrate on a basic male-female level is augmented in the "like-mindedness"—*homophrosyne,* their two hearts working as one—that connects them. The virtues of Aristotle's male and female similarly cohere; a shared intellectual life and a shared community is their best destiny. Athens and Sparta do not have the last word.

Two

Plato's Socrates

T wo of the knottiest themes in Platonic scholarship have barely concealed masculine and feminine dimensions which pertain to our investigation of literary form. The first controversy in the scholarship is about the status of kallipolis in the *Republic:* is it a blueprint for reform of a real city, or is it an intellectual exercise intended to exert a cautionary impact on would-be political idealists? The second controversy concerns the figure of Socrates in the whole range of dialogues: can we extract an identifiably "historical" figure (at least in the "early" dialogues), or must Socrates be regarded primarily as the literary character of Plato? The controversies are related, for the teaching that one discerns in the *Republic* will hinge on the prior relation that one posits between author and character. The controversies are operative, for the two English translations of the *Republic* most favored on college campuses today are in silent warfare on how to resolve them. Since there seems to be no way to avoid taking sides and no hope of persuading readers across the lines, I note without further defense my alignment with those who attend seriously to the literary and dramatic characteristics of the dialogues, who reject a literalist interpretation of kallipolis, and who regard the stipulated "historical Socrates" within Platonic texts as a phantom.[1] I will go so far as to speak of both "kallipolis" and "Socrates" as constructs, though they are assuredly constructs of a different order. Kallipolis, the "city-in-speech," never existed except in human imagination; perhaps—who knows?—it was conjured up in the imagination of Socrates in just this company. What we have, in any case, is the text. On the other hand, Socrates really existed, but our access to him is similarly restricted to Plato's (and other writers') reconstruction of him. But there is no reason to regret these circumstances; in the Platonic text lie riches still untapped—particularly regarding his ingenuity in the use of gender. For it is *Plato* who has provided us with the rival constructs of "Socrates" and "kallipolis."

In a locution that is highly significant, Socrates claims in the *Republic* that he and his companions in their founding activity are "like painters" who consult the divine pattern to draw the outlines of their city (500e). Then again in the *Phaedrus,* he draws the famous analogy between the painted image and the written word: "The productions of painting look like living beings, but if you ask them a question they maintain a solemn silence. The same holds true of written words; you might suppose that they understand what they are saying, but if you ask them what they mean by anything they simply return the same answer."[2] It is the act of *painting* that will be associated here with an inveterate masculinity, and the main image in question is kallipolis. Like Frankenstein's Creature, kallipolis is created wholly by men, marked by male desires, a male perspective, and male assertiveness. When it finally collapses, it is a boy's delight: its destruction is total and almost instantaneous, with the blame leveled squarely on an insidious female presence. Meanwhile across the dialogues, Socrates suggests a partiality toward the feminine; in the *Republic,* he turns his companions away from their first impulses toward wholesale reconstruction of their political order toward a distinctive interiority. It has been well-noted that philosophy itself is gendered female in the *Republic,* following a decisive shift in Book 6 as a serious defense of the contemplative life begins.[3] Outside of the *Republic,* Socrates is pictured in remarkable deference to female characters—like Diotima, Aspasia, or "the beautiful woman" who appears to him in a dream in the *Phaedo*. Towards these women, Socrates is not ironic, not challenging, not rude; as Blair notes, "women seem to be . . . the only teachers from whom Socrates ever learned."[4] The feminine associations are especially intriguing when they can be shown to affect the movement of the argument, as is surely the case on the topic of kallipolis.

If "Socrates talking" is a gendered counterpart to "the interlocutors painting" in the *Republic,* that is admittedly only a single appearance of a complex and changeable character. For this reason especially, the *Phaedrus* serves as an important preface to our *Republic* argument. In the *Phaedrus,* painting, writing (signified in the single Greek word, γράφω), and talking are lined up as explicit themes, and Socrates reveals himself there as utterly dependent upon his Platonic inscription. For Plato offers us in the *Phaedrus* a spectrum of possibilities from purely oral communication to the most settled written expression. Or, rather, he gives us the extremes on that spectrum from which to deduce the mean at which he seems to aim. At one end, there is a view of foundationalism as epitomized by "Egyptian" writing from the Theuth and Thamus story. At the other end is Socrates, the most famous illiterate of the Western world, and the anti-foundationalism that he represents. Plato's suggestion may well be that we discover a preferred model of writing in perceiving the flaws at the limits. Our final object here, then, is to discern behind the masculine painted image of kallipolis (with all of its excesses) and the feminine-oriented talk of the character Socrates (with all of his vulnerabilities and his concealed powers of persuasion), the balancing presence of Plato. The Socratic way is feminine and has to be mended by being put into print.

Talking in the *Phaedrus*

In the Egyptian myth that Socrates recounts in the *Phaedrus,* Theuth, the scribe of the gods, approaches King Thamus in order to promote the art of writing among the Egyptians. According to Theuth, writing is bound to help them improve their wisdom and memory. King Thamus (Ammon, to the Greek world) abruptly disagrees: far from being a recipe for memory and wisdom, he claims, writing will aid the Egyptians only in recollection and in garnering the reputation for wisdom: "what you have discovered is a recipe not for memory, but for reminder. And it is no true wisdom that you offer your disciples, but only its semblance" (275b). Socrates proceeds to affirm that position: "Then anyone who leaves behind him a written manual . . . on the supposition that such writing will provide something reliable and permanent, must be exceedingly simple-minded" (275c). The opposition is clear: on one side, there are the real-life Egyptians who disregard the advice of Thamus (and fulfill his prophecy by becoming preservers of the dead letter); on the other, there is Socrates, who, following Thamus, opts for self-sufficiency and a thinking which renews itself in the moment.

Since Socrates left behind no written manuals, readers of the *Phaedrus* have often assumed that this is *the* defining passage on the subject of writing for Plato. When King Thamus rejects the offer of writing, he explains his reasons in terms to which Plato is thought to subscribe. In Derrida's famous restatement, writing is the secondary and inferior mark of an original knowledge: "It inscribes in the space of silence and in the silence of space the living time of voice. It displaces its model, provides no image of it, violently wrests out of its element the animate interiority of speech. In so doing, writing estranges itself immensely from the truth of the thing itself."[5] But this view makes of Plato a mere amanuensis. The deconstructionist reading of the *Phaedrus* treats Socrates as the unproblematic authority figure, as if Plato obviously subscribed to a single position articulated there by his teacher—the critique of writing—and did the best he could under the circumstances, namely, to write down the conversation. This view, strange on the face of it, requires the reader to disregard the self-reflexive elements of the narrative and therefore to overlook key dramatic tensions: "Socrates [is] master in a scene of instruction to which Plato, who obediently *writes it down,* is both admiring witness and guilty party."[6] The admonition against writing takes on a different aspect if one acknowledges Plato apart from Socrates—and there is no more reason to equate Plato with Socrates' position here than to suppose Plato is advocating a hieroglyphic system; his own example is equally distant from each.

"Egypt" and "Socrates" are better viewed as dueling characters in

the *Phaedrus*. Egypt is offered as an outer limit to the Greek world in
a way that is familiar to us from Herodotus: "Just as the climate that
the Egyptians have is entirely their own . . . and their river has a
nature quite different from other rivers, so, in fact, . . . most of their
customs are the exact opposite of other folks" (2.35). This would
include, of course, male and female arrangements ["Among them the
women run the market and shops, while the men, indoors, weave"
(2.35)]. Phaedrus observes after listening to the Theuth-Thamus
story that "it is easy for you, Socrates, to make up tales from Egypt or
anywhere else you fancy" (275b). Egyptian tales are particularly easy
for Socrates to make up, since so much comes to the Greek world
already imprinted. There are the priestly scribes familiar to us from
The History who have been recording events since time immemorial;
there are the customs that show reverence for the ancestral and the
unchanging; there is the inventiveness in numbers, calculation and
geometry; and finally, there is the hieroglyphic writing that is frozen
in meaning and decipherable only by initiates. These Egyptian associations span the Platonic dialogues, from Plato's turn toward Egypt
for a tale of pre-history in the *Phaedrus,* to his use of an Egyptian
priest in a later dialogue for his story of Atlantis."[7] There (in the
Timaeus), Critias relates to Socrates a story of Solon's visit to Egypt,
where Solon is told that "the greatest action which the Athenians
ever did, and which ought to have been the most famous" was utterly
lost to their memory.[8] As the Egyptian priest goes on to enlighten a
famous wise man of Greece, the almost imperceptible equation is
made between the ancient records of Egypt and the Egyptians as a
source of wisdom: "in mind you [Greeks] are all young; there is no old
opinion handed down among you by ancient tradition, nor any science which is hoary with age." In the *Laws,* Plato has the Athenian
stranger praise the "astounding" legislation in Egypt which forbade
innovation in painting, represented postures, and other such things:
"And they are still not allowed to—not in these things or in music
altogether. If you look into this you will find [it so] for ten thousand
years—not 'so to speak' but really ten thousand years."[9] In matters of
body and soul alike, Plato's Egyptians seek a fixed state. Socrates
refers engagingly in the *Phaedo* to the "virtual" immortality that the
Egyptians gain in their custom of embalming; the corpse "will remain

almost entire for ages and ages; and some parts of the body, such as bones, sinews, and so forth, even when decomposition has occurred, are virtually immortal."[10]

Thus does Plato underscore the foundationalist propensity of the Egyptians to put down their mark for all time. When Socrates draws his famous analogy between the silences of writing and painting, his words have particular resonance for the Egyptians and their practices of inscription. The pivotal contrast is between the Egyptian hieroglyphic writing which directly imitates the object it represents, and Greek alphabetic writing that represents oral speech: "Egyptian hieroglyphics, handed down without innovation, guarded and controlled by the sacred priests of Ammon, dependent upon memorization and repetition . . . exemplifies the nature of nondialectic writing . . . which Socrates condemns."[11] Plato is not evoking an Egyptian myth (through Socrates), then, in order to classify or capture the historical Egyptians, but rather he discloses one variation of foundationalist writing. Without pushing the connection too far, there is a masculine coloring to this foundationalism. After all, no one in the *Phaedrus* fits the Egyptian mold more exactly than Phaedrus himself, who seeks the attention of another man through his act of memorizing speech.[12]

A focus on the factual accuracy of the portrait of Egypt is misplaced, then, since a quite specific reputation of Egypt is legendary, and it is to that reputation that the characters appeal.[13] A caricaturing of "the other" persists in contemporary times despite the preoccupation with overcoming this practice. For his part, Plato (like Herodotus before him) shows no such inclination to depict the Egyptians apart from their traditional associations, using these indicators for his own purposes and with good conscience. Egyptologists and other scholars may well protest against the misleading historical representations that result. "None of these references shows a profound or first-hand knowledge of Egypt," Lefkowitz comments in an overview of Plato. "Moreover, his chronology is shaky."[14] Moreover still, Plato's depictions of Solon and the Egyptian priest in the *Timaeus* show a suspicious resemblance to Herodotus' depiction of the Egyptians in *The History*. But Plato's overlap with Herodotus appears less than incriminating if we ascribe intention to both of their characterizations of Egypt and Egyptian writing, and allow what is transmitted—by Greeks about Egyptians, and by Egyptians about themselves—into the category of the historically significant. Some element of stereotyping will find its place in these remembrances, as here, in which the impulse to record, codify and calculate one's way to (virtual) immortality comes across as a faintly *masculine* conceit.

Plato's other outer limit in the *Phaedrus* suggests the stereotypical female analogue, in none other than the figure Socrates. With particular force in this dialogue of "Talk itself, Absolute Talk,"[15] Plato takes Socrates to task for disesteeming the art of writing; his (feminine) risk is one of leaving no mark whatsoever. In the *Phaedrus*, Plato discloses to us that Socrates is not, after all, a self-made man, for his destiny is always to be a character. To be a character (in part historical, in part literary) is the appropriate fate for a philosopher like Socrates who does not know what he is about—and delights in entertaining the most monstrous possibility: "[I direct my inquiries] to myself, to discover whether I really am a more complex creature and more puffed up with pride than Typhon, or a simpler, gentler being whom heaven has blessed with a quiet, un-Typhonic nature" (230a). Socrates' quest for self-knowledge attracts the attention of the young, who see human possibilities as unbounded and who may be drawn to the prospect of his pushing the limits of convention. His life activity could be considered exemplary, if only its contours could be identified. But Typhon has a hundred heads and a tremendous voice. In Socrates' quest for self-knowledge, might he have gotten carried away with *his* tremendous power of speaking?

Socrates refers in the *Phaedrus* to the "unquestioned legitimacy" of living speech: "The sort that goes together with knowledge, and is written in the soul of the learner: that can defend itself, and knows to whom it should speak and to whom it should say nothing" (276a). But how often does Socrates say nothing? Here in the *Phaedrus,* we have cause to marvel more than once about the company Socrates keeps to indulge his passion for speeches. "The action of this dialogue presents Socrates as the lover of Phaedrus. One wonders why."[16] The practice of engaging in speech whomever he happens upon may keep him honest and identify him as a democrat at heart, but, absent Plato, it also delegates Socrates to the ephemeral. When his fellow democrats one day demand that he justify his way of life, he stands before them vulnerable, without apparent roots. If this is an admirable human achievement, it is not *obviously* a beneficent one for the polis. In the event, the man of speech was famously unable or unwilling to defend himself successfully. Plato does him one better: he gives us the man *and* the defense.

The character Socrates is of no small relevance to democrats, who are prone to overenthusiastic celebrations of the immediacy and vitality of spoken exchanges over written ones. Plato's suggestion seems to be that the cost of choosing this route is to lose control over one's story. In the case of Socrates of the *Phaedrus,* Plato shows us an historical appropriation in process. When Socrates is pictured in Nature, out of his element ["a stranger being shown the country by a guide" (230cd)], he seems not to be himself. Socrates conceals himself, takes on the voices of others, and is forgetful (237a-243e, 257a, 263d). He admits to being no more than a vessel (235cd). And most unnervingly, he attributes his performance to divine inspiration (238c). These are positions that Socrates does not suffer easily in other people at other times.[17] Socrates even defends the proposition that "the greatest blessings come by way of madness, indeed of madness that is heavenly-sent" (244ab). This has proved rather trying for scholars looking to establish the identity of Socrates: "[All] the splendours of Socrates' discourse cannot conceal its provocative paradoxicality. Nowhere else . . . does Socrates describe the philosopher and himself as being divinely possessed."[18] Perhaps we are being reminded that the story is not Socrates' to tell. For all his talk, Socrates has been appropriated—and this by an author who does not say a word.

Socrates in the *Phaedrus* not only contradicts his teachings from other dialogues, but he also seems unable to stop recanting his teachings in this one. To be sure, the frequent recantations allow one to explain away what might appear troubling at any single moment: "It is the inspired Socrates who praises inspiration. When the inspiration is over, he is once more the servant of the Logos."[19] If in the palinode, Socrates again assumes the voice of another (Stesichorus), eventually he renounces that posture, too, when he and Phaedrus move on to the discussion of the art of rhetoric. That stance is recanted in its place when Socrates spins out the Theuth-Thamus myth. But all of these disclaimers cannot help but erode the characters' discursive ground, as is brought home to us by Phaedrus when he cannot recall from one moment to the next which questions have been "cleared up" (277b, 277d). This vulnerability is evident even before we take into account the last and most disruptive recantation of all, when the Egyptian myth of Socrates is recanted by Plato's written text. The integrity of every previous argument is uncertain.[20]

Plato, for his part, never becomes a character in this dialogue; he is Writing itself, the Absolute Writer. Insofar as Plato can be said "to appear" in the *Phaedrus,* he has a brief stand-in as a tree: Socrates reclines under the plane tree (*platonos*) and is made to declare that trees cannot teach him anything (230d). And there is a suggestion about how things stood for the student Plato, for Socrates evidently preferred Isocrates (279a).[21] Even with these intrusions, however, it must be acknowledged that Plato remains paradigmatically anonymous.[22] It is in recognition of his anonymity that the trend in Platonic scholarship today is to cease looking for his theories, as if he wrote treatises, and instead to be increasingly dialogic in approach. In the *Phaedrus* Plato writes of Socrates who is unmindful of writing. The Platonic dialogue draws the reader into interpretive action capable of transcending the static character of the text.[23] In truth, this dialogue is not simply about the debasement of writing, or about the status of writing as "a dangerous gift."[24] It would be more accurate to claim that the *Phaedrus* is about the difficulty of establishing a workable foundation that avoids the twin dangers of the loss of memory associated with a vaguely feminine orality and the rigidity of memory associated with a vaguely masculine literacy.

The character depictions of the *Phaedrus* thus have a concrete import for democrats. They are to be warned that at the one extreme, texts are deadening and dehumanizing when reified: Phaedrus becomes the nonchalant accomplice to "As wolf to lamb, so lover to his lad" (241d). At the other, oral conditions are associated with loss of memory—a special failing of democrats, who tend to forget their ancestors and to neglect their descendants. Socrates himself fails to detect Phaedrus' "trick" of slightly editing Lysias' text in his recapitulation (263e-264a).[25] Plato is there to map out the dangers in the "real life" characters of Socrates and the Egyptians. The heightened focus is on a form of writing that serves as a corrective to political ills. The model of writing that Platonic dialogues embody is illustrative of the craft most called for in democracy, as Plato maneuvers between the spontaneity of self-expression and the discipline of self-rule. He shows us a careful balancing of opposites, over against democracy's predilection to settle on one element of dichotomies: *talk,* not writing, and unequivocal talk at that. The democratic impulse is to reduce everything to the lowest common denominator, to treat different individuals as indifferently distinct bodies. The example of Platonic dialogue suggests that democratic statecraft may be essential if democracy is not to degenerate into the disruption and chaos that led the ancient thinkers to fear it as a path toward eventual tyranny.

Painting Kallipolis in the *Republic*

A promising opening for an inquiry into the "painted" nature of kallipolis is Aristotle's famous commentary on the *Republic* in his *Politics,* where he draws together "Plato's Socrates" and "Socrates' kallipolis." Aristotle seems to be at one with Plato in his feminine leanings. Yet in large part readers have been too mystified by Aristotle's understated commentary to appreciate his accomplishment. The puzzlement concerns the same two issues of Platonic scholarship with which we began: whether kallipolis is meant to be taken literally as a blueprint or as cautionary exercise; and whether Socrates is historical figure or Platonic character. By contemporary assessment, Aristotle's combination of answers appears muddled, for he takes kallipolis "straight" at the same time that he differentiates between Plato and his character Socrates. However, when these two issues are sorted out with further attention to our themes of the gendered nature of kallipolis and of the character of Socrates in Book 5 of the *Republic,* it can be shown how Aristotle commends—and invites us to revisit—the reconciling qualities of Platonic writing.

In Book 2 of his *Politics,* Aristotle repeatedly singles out Socrates as the specific target of his criticism (1260a22–23; 1261a11; 1261b32; 1262b3–7; 1263b29–30; 1264b6); it is only in distanced summary that the name "Plato" comes up, as Aristotle acknowledges his originality (1274b9–11). Then again, Aristotle refers to "the Socrates of the *Republic*" (1342a33) as if it were the individual character, in a single variation, with whom he were disagreeing. This version is in line with the Socrates presented here, a subject who defies all attempts to be broken down into historical fact over against literary shaping. *Socrates* is an original, according to Aristotle, and so is *Plato,* and it is only because Plato gave lasting form to Socrates that the Socratic activity of philosophy remains vital at all. But Plato's protagonist does not hold still for our leisured inspection. The juxtaposition between the static form of kallipolis and the talking of Socrates is at its extreme in Book 5; not surprisingly, this is also the unnamed range of Aristotle's attention.[26] When Aristotle isolates the discourses of Socrates for special attention ["All the discourses of Socrates are extraordinary: they are sophisticated, original, and searching. But it is perhaps difficult to do everything finely" (1265a10–13)], he bypasses the view that there are significant and divergent stages of *Plato's* development to be addressed. Recognizing that he is contending with *two* men of genius, Aristotle pays tribute to the younger writer. Along the way, he alerts us to the premise of his own strategy in the *Politics* of detaching and interrogating a single frame of Socratic discourse.

Kallipolis is introduced in Book 2 of the *Politics* as one of the regimes spoken about in Aristotle's time which is "held to be in a fine condition" (1260b35). Ever since, Aristotle's critics have been stymied over how much he leaves unsaid about the *Republic* in his criticism. It is this "unsaid" that is the clue to the feminine dimension. Aristotle focuses attention on the single-dimensionality of the city-in-speech, and in this relentless emphasis he combats the facile appeal to number on the part of the founders. Or rather, in Aristotle's rendition of kallipolis, Socrates stands alone as mastermind as he poses qualitative issues of the best life, and (in our view) then mirrors the opinions of his interlocutors by attempting *quantitative* responses. Socrates errs in "the presupposition that he adopts," that is, "that it is best for the city to be as far as possible entirely one" (1261a14–16). And he errs again when he supposes the city to be one when "all say 'mine' and 'not mine' at the same time" (1261b17–20). That argument, according to Aristotle, blends what should remain distinct: the collective and individual senses of the term "all." Likewise Socrates covers over distinctions that are certain to reveal themselves, for close kin will know each other by appearance (1262a14–17). In making property common, Socrates' legislation "has an attractive face" (1263b13), but this is to remain on the surface and neglect the *real* paths toward commonality, education through "habits, philosophy, and laws"(1263b40). In sum, Aristotle criticizes the unifying urge that comes about through an imposition of (masculine) will on material conditions. The need is glaring for the addition of some moderating influence. And it hardly seems likely that that need will be met by eradicating distinctions between the sexes: "it is odd that in order to show that women should have the same pursuits as men [Socrates] makes a comparison with the animals" (1264b1–5).

Thus Aristotle settles his readers in Book 5 of the *Republic,* before the "female drama" (451c) is fully underway, and certainly before the ascent to philosophy. In other words, Aristotle reproduces in his account the same experience of the want of a feminine aspect that prompts Socrates to introduce his three great waves: the requirement for equal training of male and female guardians, the communism of women and children, and the call for the philosopher king. Those waves are presented as a challenge to the equilibrium of Socrates ["But to present arguments at a time when one is in doubt and seeking—which is just what I am doing—is a thing both frightening and slippery." (450e/451a)], as if the intervention of Glaucon and Adeimantus were required for Socrates' peace of mind. But it is the interlocutors who are undone by the experience, as they are shown what their muscularity amounts to; they will be considerably less giddy about kallipolis than they were at its genesis. Socrates contributes the saving feminine addition, deftly changing the direction of the account such that by the end, Glaucon is open to hearing of the "two in one" and the forms: "each is itself one . . . . each is an apparitional many" (475e-476a). Socrates' talk is galvanizing, and his listeners approach the state in which they begin to comprehend the limitations of their earlier construct. This is the state that Aristotle recreates for *his* readers as well. But could not Aristotle have *said* this, in a more straightforward manner? Not and remain true to the Platonic

construct at hand, since confident assertion on the part of the founders is the structural defect of kallipolis; its correction is not to be
found in the direction of full explanation. Aristotle's pithy commentary on the *Republic* is a great tribute to Plato's literary form, for it
leaves readers, like the interlocutors at the end of Book 5, bored with
the childish painting of kallipolis—and hanging on every word of
Socrates.

This interpretation is predicated on the view that Socrates gives
voice to the prejudices and conventional opinions of his interlocutors
without simultaneously partaking of them. No doubt this is a difficult
point to establish, since the successive waves are presented by Socrates alternatively from a self-centered, male perspective or through
the detached speculations of the animal breeder.[27] The first wave
may well resemble egalitarian principles from contemporary America in its call for male and female guardians to receive the same
education and training ["If, then, we use the women for the same
things as the men, they must also be taught the same things" (451d)],
but it is still marked by questionable formulations regarding the natures of men and women. Just how seriously are these natures being
probed, when the talk incessantly is of dogs? "The females of the
guardian dogs must guard the things the males guard along with them
and hunt with them" (451d).[28] When Socrates brings the discussion
back to the human species, he goes to extreme measures to keep in
view the male standard: the women guardians, he insists, must exercise naked in the gymnasium alongside the men, even if they are all
wrinkled and unpleasant to the eye; no one who is serious about
virtue should find this at all comical (452b-e; 457a). Socrates finds
the occasion to formulate a conventionally male chauvinist position:
"Do you know of anything that is practiced by human beings in which
the class of men doesn't excel that of women in all these respects? Or
shall we draw it out at length by speaking of weaving and [cook-
ing] . . . those activities on which the reputation of the female sex is
based and where its defeat is most ridiculous of all?" (455c-d). Glaucon submits that this is virtually always the case. The epitome of this
approach is reached with Socrates' conclusion that men and women
seem to differ as do the bald and the long-haired (454c); it is hard to
imagine a clearer assertion of the male paradigm. When childbearing

absolutely must be conceded, the language shifts back to that of animal breeding: "the female bears and the male mounts" (454d).

In the second wave the male perspective is sustained, for even as it is introduced with the stress on commonality, the unquestioned assumption is that the women and children are the *objects* of this arrangement: "All these women are to belong to all these men in common, and no woman is to live privately with any man. And the children, in their turn, will be in common, and neither will a parent know his own offspring, nor a child his parent" (457c-d). And the *equal* treatment soon is left behind as Socrates and Glaucon entertain ideas about how to manage "erotic necessities" to best advantage (458d). The touchstone is to be "the marriages and the procreation" of Glaucon's hunting dogs and noble cocks (459a). Socrates asks: "Do you breed from all alike, or are you eager to breed from the best as much as possible?" Glaucon's answer: "from the best" (459a). Before long, Socrates and Glaucon have entered into alarming agreements about the extensive subterfuges that will be necessary to assure the best mating procedures among the guardians: "It's likely that our rulers will have to use a throng of lies and deceptions for the benefit of the ruled" (459c). And the mandates happen to coincide with the inclination of the speaker, as when Glaucon agrees to the proviso that the man who performs best in a military campaign may kiss whomever he wishes (468c).

Finally there is the third wave, "the biggest and most difficult," which is described by Socrates in the context of a crisis moment regarding the project's viability, and is said by him to be the "very paradoxical" source of his hesitant speech (472a-473e). Here the bias is glaring. After all the concern with equal training and equal opportunity for male and female guardians, the culminating pronouncement addresses men in particular: there will be no rest from ills unless "the philosophers rule as kings or those now called kings and chiefs genuinely and adequately philosophize" (473c-d). Readers may try as they will to resolve the contradiction by replacing Socratic terminology with the neutral "Philosophical-Ruler" or by summoning the "Philosopher-Queen" to battle. Notwithstanding these emendations, the contradiction remains—and at the very peak of kallipolis.

Kallipolis, most beautiful of cities, is an indifferent composition at best; Socrates' brush stroke is blunt. It is only when readers expect perfection that its flaws are taken so hard and so personally. The best evidence that kallipolis is no object for emulation is that even within Book 5, Socrates begins its subversion.[29] The decisive move occurs when the assembled company join in recognizing that it is high time to distinguish who they mean when they say philosophers must rule (474b-c). Here is the opening for the feminine aspect, for when the need to distinguish is felt, aspirations toward balance are soon to take hold. Saxonhouse documents the significant turn that now occurs in Book 6, as both "the object of philosophy and the process of philosophy itself are described in feminine terms."[30] And Socrates emphasizes the gendered references by suddenly shifting them. He attempts, for example, to explain to his disbelieving interlocutors that philosophers are more worthy to rule their city than anyone; this entails combating their views about the "useless" and "vicious" nature of philosophers. Following his image of the ship in which is distinguished the true philosopher from the sophists and charlatans who impersonate him (and where the philosopher is male), Socrates turns to discuss the ways in which sophists corrupt even the finest natures, the potential philosophers: "So these men, for whom philosophy is most suitable, go thus into exile and leave her abandoned and unconsummated" (495c). Throughout, the sexual imagery is pronounced: "other unworthy men come to her—like an orphan bereft of relatives—and disgrace her." The crudeness of the image only emphasizes the point the more that *philosophia* is gendered female, quite apart from whether individual philosophers are male or female. It is destined to leave its imprint in the minds of the audience.

The elaboration of who the philosopher really *is* culminates, finally, in the divided line, where the basic division is between things seen and things intellected (509d). Socrates' image formalizes the terms of an ascent through the material, visible world towards conceptual clarity and unity. Now Glaucon readily understands how the perplexities caused by the impression of things are liable to incite the movement of thinking. "Some things are apt to summon thought," Socrates explains, "the things that strike the sense at the same time as their opposites" (524d). The suggestion is that the material obstacles that kept arising in the interlocutors' attempts to institute a society of absolute equality and justice might be overcome as they ascend to a perspective in the intelligible world, where contradictions and opposing forces might issue in some more agreeable outcome. Of his many elaborations on this point, perhaps none is more famous than that in the *Phaedo*. After his leg chains have been loosened on the day he is to die, Socrates reflects upon the strange nature of pleasure: "how astonishing the relation it has with what is thought to be its opposite, namely pain! A man cannot have both at the same time. Yet if he pursues and catches the one, he is almost always bound to catch the other also, like two creatures with one head."[31] Physical sensations offer up confusing data in this way and may stimulate the search for conceptual unity. As Cropsey writes, the "routine position" of Socrates is that "the intelligible is a unity to which the multiplicity must be referred."[32] Socrates' interlocutors follow this move, and even can conceive that under the proper direction, an entire city, especially one which has as its greatest good "the community of pain and pleasure" (464b), might be led to reflect on what, more precisely, it *is*.

The divided line appears to be vertical with its sections representing a movement from low to high, from less toward more clarity. Any serious consideration of its significance, however, soon is transformed into a series of dualities. The line begins to emerge as a single-pole ladder, with rungs protruding from each side; one side being physical, material, quantitative; the other mental, psychological, qualitative. The former is Being; the latter is Knowing. The ways of characterizing the two are familiar, ubiquitous, and endless; reason and revelation; Truth and Light; Light and Truth, *Urim* and *Thummim*. From low to high, Socrates explains the two ways. First there are images and imagination, then objects and belief (or fact and fiction, event and opinion). Third up from the bottom we find counting and thinking (or reason and revelation). Near the top are Ideas (the Forms) and Understanding (the Recognitions).

As though the divided line itself is not enough, is one side only, Socrates follows it with a visual, allegorical version of it, the Cave. Perhaps this is to demonstrate that knowing requires being; that proportions require demonstration. In any case this image of counteracting forces surely contrasts with the still profile of kallipolis. In this immediate application of the divided line, the reasoning with this "geometric" tool already exemplifies the interlocutors' own ascent beyond artifacts to a stage of rational account-giving. But then Socrates and Glaucon use the geometrical model to transcend geometry: "the intelligible geometrical features of the line serve Socrates as bases, as 'suppositions' in the strict sense, for leading Glaucon—and us—to an understanding of the difference between the intelligible and the visible and of the different levels within each of them."[33] The image of the cave provokes their higher imaginative powers, causing them to project it upon their civic lives—and come to a novel insight about the "real" cave. At first, Glaucon speaks of the "strange prisoners" that are being described, but after Socrates replies "They're like us" (515a), he has to agree. Their political world is just such a closed construct, where image-makers constitute, freeze, and distort their world. Not only are the prisoners bound, but they so relish their bonds that they would kill the man who tried to release them (517a). It is a stunning insight: an imagined picture thereafter actively transforms the world they see. Politics, bound up with conventional prejudices and rigidities, appears masculine in orientation. But that singular figure who makes the ascent, "a man who is released and suddenly compelled to stand up . . . to walk and look up toward the light," and finally compelled to look at the light itself (515d-e)—that figure is moved by philosophy, with its insistently female associations. The symmetrical image provokes a thinking beyond gender.

Kallipolis reveals some unnerving consequences of taking human beings for a blank slate, including two that go in opposite directions: unrealistic abstractions from human nature, and all-too-realistic concessions to conventional opinions. Both of these tendencies are revealed in Book 5 of the *Republic*. There is the much-noted fact that the equality of training of male and female guardians entails the eradication of specifically female qualities; women are to take on the attributes of men. And there is concurrent tendency for conventional prejudices against women to be aired as obvious fact (455c-d; 469d). These factors show the basic "historiographical" weakness of kallipolis: it is both too removed from human possibility, and too unaware of its grounding in fallible conventions.

By the end it appears that the interlocutors have put together a construct from a decidedly male perspective, complete with conventional prejudices against women, and that that construct lands them "in an underground cave-like dwelling . . . with their legs and necks in bonds so that they are fixed, seeing only in front of them" (514a). More provoking still, it is a "female touch" that is responsible ("by nature") for the liberation of the single prisoner. The female drama does not enumerate the wondrous institutions of communal sex, as perhaps was the hope of the assembled young men, but rather introduces the saving female influence, the "heroine" Philosophy. The growing awareness in the ascent of the interlocutors is of the unbalanced qualities of their own political commitments, and of the need for a new sense of proportion as a goal that might draw them forward. Within the context of the *Republic,* the aim is the impossible goal of the perfect polity, a conjoined, harmonious polity perfected for the ages. Socrates shows it in all its impossibility as a warning to us not to abandon the present for some far-off utopian future; that way lies totalitarian horror. At the same time, however, an awareness of the need for balance provides a goal for humanity. The philosopher-king will never come to power. But philosophy, with its feminine associations, and monarchy, with its male attributes, may, if partially and imperfectly achieved in balance, offer the prospect of the best possible political system. The "authentically Socratic debate," writes Loraux, "pits feminine against masculine, playing it out as far as possible."[34]

But Plato as writer never takes *Socrates* as a blank slate. Socrates stands as a challenge to the political reality of his times, but this challenging aspect is firmly grounded in *his* idiosyncratic origins. Plato integrates the shared stories that were told about his remarkable teacher and his own rendering of his philosophical import. Critics speak of the "warts and all" portraits of Socrates—he is not whitewashed, not idealized—but neither is he drawn in facile imitation. As Ausland remarks, "We tend inappropriately to expect either historical or fictional characters, whereas Plato employs historical figures for theoretical purposes."[35] Unlike in the case of Socrates' painting kallipolis, when Plato profiles Socrates, he succeeds in depicting a changeable entity. As an intelligible whole, the *character* Socrates successfully accommodates seemingly impossible masculine and feminine tensions, whereas Socrates' creation, kallipolis, does not. Plato's accomplishment, first in the *Phaedrus* and then in the *Republic,* is to bring historical markers and philosophic meaning into accord, grounding his subject in the visible world—as one essential but not exhaustive component of the "real" Socrates.

Beyond the "rational accounts" of the understanding and the "forms" of pure intellection, Socrates places "the Idea of Good." That zenith is described as the locus of all meaning—"what every soul pursues and for the sake of which it does everything"—and so as simultaneously inescapable and fugitive: the soul is "at a loss about it and unable to get a sufficient grasp of just what it is" (505d-e). And so the Idea of Good looks to much of the world like Socrates himself. "Only Socrates himself has knowledge of the Forms," Sedley claims, and adds "it is typical of Plato to indicate Socrates' possession of knowledge without putting any such claim into Socrates' own mouth."[36] The analogy has the virtue of highlighting the supervening intelligence behind the literary construct: Socrates does not claim the Idea of Good as his own, anymore than Plato assumes the credit for Socrates.

Socrates' kallipolis and Plato's Socrates come together at one brief moment in the *Republic*. After kallipolis has been constructed, there is the dramatic suggestion of the authorial voice, with Plato appearing in the role of "Ariston's son": "Shall we hire a herald," Socrates asks, "or shall I myself announce that Ariston's son has decided that the best and most just man is happiest, and he is that man who is kingliest and is king of himself" (580b-c).[37] It is the subtlest of reminders that Socrates without Plato would have spoken in vain.

2
The State

Three

The Rhetoric of the State

T he shorthand version of the ideal evoked by the ancient polis is equilibrium. Poets, historians, and philosophers in the Greek tradition transmit a story of the polis that puts human flourishing in terms of balancing two poles of existence: nature-culture, private-public, female-male. As such, it is easy to underrate, as if the formulas "all in measure" or "the golden mean" were sufficient to ground a community. In the everyday realm, one of the poles predictably dominates the other. But if the historically existent polis is beyond anyone's reach, in certain written documents we find a standard insisted upon according to which the polis is judged. Inscribed ways of avoiding two extremes and attending to the middle way are found throughout the Greek tradition, and in different strategies of writing are scattered a full accounting of the rise and decline of the polis. We see, for instance, that the delicate symmetry as envisaged in the *Odyssey* fails over time, and that in the sequence of the Persian and Peloponnesian wars, the Greeks of our inherited texts begin to lose sight of their productive tension. The equilibrium of the polis surely has been lost when Alcibiades in all seriousness advocates constant motion for Athens and predicts that the Athenians will wear themselves out if they sink into inaction (*Pel. War,* 6.18.6). When the *oikos,* the private, and the female all recede, the polis is on the road to self-destruction. And because the modifications offered by the best of Greek writers is to the overdevelopment of the public and male elements, their perspective comes to sight as a feminine one.[1]

In contrast, the shorthand version of Machiavelli's *"stato"* is antithesis. Most prominently, he teaches that there are republics or principalities, new modes or old, *fortuna* or *virtù.* The first chapter in the *Prince* humorously reveals one division after another (a "typically Machiavellian rattle of antitheses," in Pocock's rendition[2]) in anticipation of the ubiquitous binaries to follow. Principalities, Machiavelli claims, "are either hereditary, . . . or they are new. The new ones are either altogether new, . . . or [not] . . . they are acquired either with the arms of others or with one's own, either by fortune or by virtue."[3] Some occasions call for one extreme, some for the other, but to attempt a compromise is madness, and potentially fatal. Machiavelli abjures "all in measure" for the scheme of either/or: "men should either be caressed or eliminated" (*P,* 10).

Here even more than in the case of the ancient Greeks, contemporary readers may discern in the binaries of the text an implicit hostility towards women. There is the notorious passage in *The Prince* in which Fortune is compared to a woman who must be beaten down ["it is necessary, if one wants to hold her down, to beat her and strike her down" (101)]; the suspicion is that the female is being likened to the passive material that is to be reshaped and fashioned by the male actor. Hanna Pitken encourages this reading in her book-length study of Machiavelli: "As a political theorist, Machiavelli is difficult, contradictory, and in many respects unattractive: a misogynist, frequently militaristic and authoritarian, uncomplimentary about human nature."[4] It is not hard to see why Machiavelli provokes this reaction, and yet one cannot journey far into *The Prince* before the symmetries become unsettled and the neat divisions subverted. It is noteworthy that in *The Prince,* the beating of Fortune is advised at the same time that her victory is assured, and this has to affect the meaning of the image. Kahn suggests that readers view these so-called permanent distinctions with caution: "Throughout *The Prince* Machiavelli sets concepts in polar opposition to each other and then shows how the opposition is contained within each term so that the whole notion of opposition must be redefined."[5] On closer look, the Machiavellian antithesis appears neither simple nor misogynistic.

One undeniable effect of Machiavelli's oppositional game is to release the hold of the ancient standard—in the service of a new form of political community, *lo stato*. Machiavelli inaugurates this move with his opening declaration in *The Prince:* "All states, all dominations that have held and do hold empire over men have been and are either republics or principalities" (5). Here the state suggests a more shifting center of power than the polis, with the emphasis on the "effectual extent" of a single person's domination: "the true ordering of the state is not what appears to the public, but what goes on behind the scenes."[6] Machiavelli's creation of the state takes its leave of the ancients, among whom "many have imagined republics and principalities that have never been seen or known to exist in truth." In contrast, he vows to leave out "what is imagined about a prince and [discuss] what is true" (61).

In this posture Machiavelli creates the distinct literary form identified here as "modern rhetoric." The allure of Homeric storytelling is replaced by the clipped cadence—and irresolution—of a rolling tape. "There are two kinds of combat: one with laws, the other with force. The first is proper to man, the second to beasts; but because the first is often not enough, one must have recourse to the second" (*P*, 69). Thucydides' procedure of establishing Athens as object lesson for all time is repudiated by Machiavelli as he weaves together past and present, fact and fiction, secular and sacred. His historical exemplars, for instance, range from the Bible to city square: "Moses, Cyrus, Theseus and Romulus would not have been able to make their people observe their constitutions for long if they had been unarmed, as happened in our times to Brother Girolamo Savonarola" (*P*, 24). And Aristotle's careful evocation of the philosophic corrective is dismissed as a futile gesture: "he who lets go of what is done for what should be done learns his ruin rather than his preservation" (*P*, 61). Accordingly, Hariman rightly describes "modernity" as less a matter of new ideas than as resourceful strategies of writing: "Modernity then is less a process of empirical discovery and more a process of invention, in the rhetorical sense of the term—the generation of the means for persuasion."[7]

The most characteristic resource of modern rhetoric is facility in the art of antitheses, an art for which contemporary readers largely have lost sympathy. Machiavelli is just the first specialist in this dramatization of extremes, where the world is made up of two kinds of people and one challenge is just to keep up with the march of candidates: foxes and lions, men and women, readers of *The Prince* and readers of *The Discourses*. What prevents these dichotomies from ensuing in hierarchies? Only subtlety in presentation, for surely dichotomies might equally well lend themselves to overly rigid, overly deterministic accounts. For this reason contemporary readers are quick to find dubious hierarchies in modern texts—and in principle, their suspicions may be warranted. But from Machiavelli onward, there *are* occasions of success which establish that the antithetical strategy of modern rhetoric is a perfectly good alternative to the equilibrium of the Greeks.

Edmund Burke, Mary Wollstonecraft, and Mary Shelley constitute one cohort of writers on the modern state who are practiced in the artful extreme and in the school of Machiavelli. From Machiavelli they inherit a sensitivity to the shifting center of the state, and show inklings of their own about how it might be inscribed otherwise. The strategies they adopt are comparable in that they each take up the antithesis of "masculine" and "feminine" aspects as a means for thinking about reform. That no essentialist conclusions need follow from this rhetorical posture is suggested by the fact that Burke stands in as the paradigmatic "feminine" writer, and Wollstonecraft as the sometime "masculine" one. The best modern writers are not seeking for the hegemony of one extreme over the other (need it be said? only the masculine posture *asserts* itself thus) but instead remonstrate with readers about the missing or diminished element. Read sympathetically, Burke, Wollstonecraft and Shelley each impel us to think through our gendered stereotypes—not only in their limitations, but in their discernment as well.

Burke's tactic is to juxtapose his deeply layered, labyrinthine style to the metaphysical clarity of the revolutionaries and to show thereby how their ways are inadequate to the depths of human nature. When he renders the life of chivalry in contradistinction to the revolutionary type in his *Reflections on the Revolution in France,* his locution is of lost illusions and of a lost world: "the age of chivalry is gone,—that of sophisters, oeconomists, and calculators has succeeded; and the glory of Europe is extinguished forever." The demand for clarity among the sophisters, oeconomists, and calculators (which Burke had already mocked in his youthful *Enquiry:* "a clear idea is therefore another name for a little idea") comes to sight as a troubling Jacobin—and specifically masculine—disposition, and contributes to the sense that the French Revolution itself was anti-female. "The Revolution labeled women secret agents of the past," Mona Ozouf notes, "always busy maintaining tradition in the present, protesting by their very existence the idea of the rupture with the past and the omnipotence of the idea of the future."[8] Burke, advocate of numerous feminine ways, accepts the role of outspoken agent of the past.

Mary Wollstonecraft penned a reply to Burke on the instant, and in her *Vindication of the Rights of Men* accuses him of being the dupe of his imagination, even as *"she"* (that is, Burke's imagination) whispered that he was "departing from strict truth." In Wollstonecraft's rendering, Burke's assumption of a stereotypically feminine posture only diminishes the status of women through his playacting of "rhetorical flourishes and infantine sensibility."[9] She points up the potentially tyrannic excess of that stance when she asks whether "there can be an opinion more subversive of morality, than that time sanctifies crimes" (*Vin.,* 85). But in the process of contradicting Burke, Wollstonecraft takes on an exaggerated role of her own: "What salutary dews might not be shed to refresh this thirsty land, if men were more *enlightened!*" (93). Hers is a neat reversal of his heuristic tools, which still, of course, leaves them employing analogous strategies. It is true that Wollstonecraft's firm voice falters on occasion in this *Vindication* ["I glow with indignation" (38)], and that she abandons the tactic altogether in her later one ["women . . . ought to endeavor to acquire human virtues (or perfections) by the *same* means as men, instead of being educated like a fanciful kind of *half* being"

(126)]. Nevertheless, even in her halting play with these oppositions, she shows her affiliations with modern rhetoric and imparts the gist of its workings.

Mary Shelley's part in the modern rhetorical tradition was assured when, in composing *Frankenstein,* she gave to the "masculine principle" a gigantic and monstrous form, and yet still elicited a troubling feminine aftermath. This effect is strange, but well-attested. On the one hand, her work marks the moment when the French Revolution and the Scientific Revolution are confounded; the impulse to dispel illusion and to reason from the ground up is henceforth the reigning one, effectively blunting the "feminine principle." So it appears, and on his death bed Victor Frankenstein counsels Walton to avoid his own example: "Seek happiness in tranquility, and avoid ambition, even if it be only the apparently innocent one of distinguishing yourself in science and discoveries" (241–242). The disconcerting outcome of Frankenstein's ambition had been death to the female character (Elizabeth, the fiancée; the innocent Justine Moritz; the Creature's companion). Even so, Frankenstein reconsiders: "Yet why do I say this? I have myself been blasted in these hopes, yet another may succeed" (242)—and the familiar hubristic cycle seems assured. On the other hand, there is something newly unnerving in the threat repeatedly evoked by the fiend: "*I will be with you on your wedding night*" (195, 213). This world is secular through and through; why, then, does the implied sexual collusion of creator and created take on such otherworldly effects? The incessantly masculine commitments of Victor Frankenstein bring on opposing volitions, and raise questions about the workings of gender. We are reminded of Aristotle's overly virile Spartans who make themselves susceptible to feminine rule, and yet the aberrance here seems more deep-seated. Not since Machiavelli has an author so gloried in the mutually determinative battle between male and female. "Though it has been disguised, buried, or miniaturized," write Gilbert and Gubar, "femaleness . . . is at the heart of this apparently masculine book." Perhaps, but then "femaleness" must stand in for something more than "being female," as maleness is more than "being male." For it is a basic division of *self* that Shelley unearths: "The civilized man or woman contains within the self monstrous, destructive, and self-destructive energy."[10]

And what is to become of the state? In the best case, accommodations might be made through statecraft to check the excess, a lesson in plain alliance with the corrections formerly explored in regard to the Greek polis. But Mary Shelley—and modern rhetoricians in general—do not exalt a stable ideal as a means of effecting that check. Their contact points with the ancient Greeks are many, and yet their writings on the state betray a self-consciousness about the lack of a beneficent natural environment that must distinguish them. It is no accident that Shelley's creature is left roaming the Arctic at the close of the novel; rather, as Veeder speculates through the geographical markers in the work, it indicates "the persistence of male forces that cannot be satisfied by southerly motions toward women."[11] Despite the closeness in the enterprises of Burke, Wollstonecraft, and Mary Shelley, contemporary readers are slow to connect them. Here, then, the alliances of modern rhetoric will be reconsidered, as a way of opening up the richness of this shared mode. When Burke sought to restore a dignity to a feminine perspective; when Wollstonecraft sought to extend the application of the masculine perspective; and when Shelley pursued their intertwined fates, each was picking up on a Machiavellian lead, to seek for change in a vocabulary of untried possibilities.

Machiavelli's Lucrezia

A single theme in the works of Machiavelli—the rape of Lucretia—provides the occasion for us to connect two objectives: the depiction of the constitution of the state through Machiavellian rhetoric, and the vindication of this rhetoric from charges that it is anti-female. If in Greece, the crux of political community comes to sight through women and war, in Rome, it is through women and founding. And ancient Roman stories of women and founding are transmogrified by modern rhetoric, since Machiavelli is interested solely in "what is true." In his *Discourses* he claims to make possible "the greater understanding" of the first ten books of Livy. Readers must be pardoned for losing sight of the original, however; the power of Machiavellian rhetoric is such that the old tales lose their singularity. As traditional elements of the story are broken down, a distanced stance by the readers becomes unviable. This is particularly striking in Machiavelli's rejoinder to the story of the rape of Lucretia as that story was inherited primarily from Livy. Lucretia appears briefly but significantly in the *Discourses,* where Machiavelli makes short work of the legend that she inspired the republican foundation of Rome with her guiltless suicide. And Machiavelli offers a more extended treatment of Lucretia in his comedy *Mandragola.* In his retelling, fraud replaces force such that there is no rape, no suicide, no revenge—and no story. With the bracketing of the story goes the centrality of the virtuous female character; his Lucrezia does not edify.

In Livy's account, the events of 510 B.C. unfold with the Roman soldiers idle, having failed to take Ardea by assault and now settled in for a prolonged siege. The young officers take the occasion to entertain themselves lavishly, and during one bout of drinking in the quarters of the king's son, Sextus Tarquinius, they converse heatedly about the virtue of their wives. The competition grows between the men, as each strives to praise his own wife more extravagantly than the last. Finally Collatinus utters the fateful challenge: "Stop! What need is there of words, when in a few hours we can prove beyond doubt the incomparable superiority of Lucretia?"[12] The men agree to ride on horseback the several hours to Rome, to visit their wives without prior notice in order to observe their behavior. The wives of the royal princes are discovered in gay company, enjoying a party late into the night "with a group of young friends" (98). With Lucretia, it is otherwise; she and her servants are found deep in labor, occupied at their spinning under the lamplight. "Which wife had won the contest in womanly virtue was no longer in doubt" (98). Lucretia fortifies that impression as she warmly welcomes her husband and his friends and sets about preparing a supper for them. At this fatal supper, Livy remarks, "Lucretia's beauty, and proven chastity, kindled in Sextus Tarquinius the flame of lust, and determined him to debauch her" (98).

Days pass at the Roman camp, until Sextus Tarquinius finds the occasion to slip back to the house of Collatinus with a companion. The unsuspecting Lucretia offers hospitality to the prince and companion of her husband. Then deep in the night, while the household sleeps, Sextus Tarquinius slips into the bedroom of Lucretia armed with a knife and intent on violating her. He cajoles, lies, and finally threatens death to make her submit to him, but nothing affects her resolve—until he preys upon her sense of reputation: "If death will not move you, dishonor shall. I will kill you first, then cut the throat of a slave and lay his naked body by your side. Who will not believe that you have been caught in adultery with a servant, and paid the price?" (98–99). Lucretia yields, and Sextus returns to the camp, convinced of his conquest.

After the outrage, Lucretia summons her husband and father to the scene, asking each to bring a trusted companion. Collatinus brings Brutus, known popularly as "the Dullard" and a half-wit. At the time, Brutus was intent on deflecting the king's attention from himself as a potential threat, and so affected madness (97). In front of these gathered men, Lucretia describes the outrage, accuses Sextus Tarquinius, and elicits their promise to avenge the crime. The men attempt to put the woman at her ease: "It was the mind, they said, that sinned, not the body: without intention there could never be guilt" (99). But as Lucretia proclaims her innocence, she reveals the knife that will found republican Rome. Stabbing herself fatally, she declares: "I will take my punishment. Never shall Lucretia provide a precedent for unchaste women to escape what they deserve" (99).[13] As the stricken husband and father look upon this death scene helplessly, Brutus steps forth, drawing the bloody knife from her body and vowing to put down the Tarquins: "never again will I let them or any other man be King in Rome" (99). This is the transforming moment for Rome, prompting the needed vigor for the Romans to expel the tyrants and to found the Republic. The Romans rush to honor Lucretia by expelling the Tarquins from their soil: "when Brutus cried out that it was time for deeds not tears, and urged them, like true Romans, to take up arms against the tyrants who had dared to treat them as a vanquished enemy, not a man amongst them could resist the call" (100).

Machiavelli refers explicitly to the story of Lucretia three times in the *Discourses,* and in each case the point of contact overlaps with that of his more extended treatment in *Mandragola.* Since *Mandragola* is the only comedy that is entirely original to Machiavelli, it is to be noted how consonant are the "literary" and "political" treatments. This is the vaunted homogeneity of Machiavelli's writings, and a consistent feature of modern rhetoric more generally. The literary works lend themselves to political allegory, the political works contain literary dimensions, and frequently in modern rhetoric (as with Rousseau), the confusion between literary character and political theorist is complete. This is essential to the workings of this rhetoric in which immediacy is achieved and the reader is implicated at every turn. Machiavelli "counsels us to theorize," as Streuver observes: "Readers are drawn in—in the process of inspecting considerations they find themselves defending their complicity or hostility."[14] These are not stories for the ages but forced tonics for readers in corrupt times. And once this Machiavellian tonic is experienced, there can be no simple reversion to old ways.

In Machiavelli's first mention of Lucretia in the *Discourses,* he dwells on the good use Junius Brutus made of her death scene: "he was the first among her father and husband and other relatives to draw the knife from the wound and to make the bystanders swear that they would never endure that in the future anyone should reign in Rome."[15] Biding his time, Brutus waits for the moment when he can control the ending of the drama. Machiavelli does something of the sort, too: he rewrites the part of Brutus such that the *bystanders* are pulled in. In Livy, Brutus takes the burden wholly upon himself.[16] The sensory impact of their respective scene-making is emphasized; the more graphic the detail, the more immediately the moment can be shaped for use.[17] Of the sudden transformation of Brutus, Livy writes that "a miracle had happened" (99), but in Machiavelli's world the change is accounted for more prosaically. Brutus, discontent, understands his own weakness and therefore simulates madness, creating a safe distance between himself and the prince. Machiavelli allows that some might counsel a more moderate policy, that of standing neither so close to the prince as to be caught in his ruin, or being too far from the scene so as not to profit from the ruin when it comes. "Such a middle way would be the truest if it could be observed," he remarks, "but because I believe that it is impossible, one must be reduced to the two modes written above—that is, either to distance oneself from or to bind oneself to them" (III.2; 213). Brutus accepts the constraints of his situation and therefore triumphs; in his modern rewriting, he need not take upon himself alone the crimes of the land. We shall see that Lucrezia's is a triumph of a comparable sort in the final scene of *Mandragola;* the modern Lucrezia shall live and prosper within the conventions of her city.[18]

In Machiavelli's next reference to Lucretia in the *Discourses,* he corrects Livy's account by claiming that the fall of Tarquin the Proud was only accidentally related to the rape, since the king had already created the disposition in the Romans to revolt. The legendary status of Lucretia is more than slightly eclipsed: "If the accident of Lucretia had not come, as soon as another had arisen it would have brought the same effect" (III.5; 217). Machiavelli thus extracts from the story the inherited dictates, such as the "precedent" left by Lucretia ("Never shall Lucretia provide a precedent for unchaste women to escape what they deserve"), and refuses readers the solace of passive admiration of such an ideal. As Streuver writes of *The Prince:* "It is as if we must read each exemplary narrative as enclosed in quotation marks: they are cited, not told. . . . It is impossible to evade the issue of use; the citations are our investigative acts, not theirs; in our domain of experience, rather than in some distanced domain of the past."[19] Machiavelli's extended treatment of the Lucretia theme in a *comedy* effectively brings home the point that historical exemplars must not console or enervate but only toughen readers. Lucretia is not to be the towering figure that stirs the virtue of republican Rome and instills the reverence of posterity; she is, rather, an upstanding woman with little room to maneuver when her husband, mother, and Confessor all press her urgently to become a whore and an instrument of death. Machiavelli's genius is in assuring that under the circumstances, we readers congratulate her agility—and partake of her thinking.

Finally, Machiavelli transforms the outrage by the king's son into an example of the disruptions that women bring into politics. Lucretia becomes an example well-suited to his chapter in the *Discourses* entitled 'How a State is Ruined Because of Women': "one sees that women have been causes of much ruin, and have done great harm to those who govern a city, and have caused many divisions in them. As has been seen in this history of ours, the excess done against Lucretia took the state away from the Tarquins" (III.26; 273). The challenge here is to remain with Machiavelli in his language of effects and in his neutrality. He has deftly assumed the perspective of the Tarquins in this instance; if certain prominent acts of violence are needed to keep the state secure, other acts of violence are gratuitous and therefore worthy of condemnation. This is the category in which he assigns the rape of Lucretia. Machiavelli's subject matter is not feminine capriciousness, as D'Amico notes, "but rather that the abuse of women can cause rulers to fall."[20] Machiavelli even gives credit to Aristotle for observing that tyrants are put down most often "on account of women, by raping them or by violating them or by breaking off marriages" (III.26; 273). It may reasonably be assumed here that Machiavelli puts aside issues of morality of the act itself and attends only to its likely effect; such is his usual procedure. When Brutus resorts to killing his own sons, for instance, Machiavelli refrains from any moral assessment and comments that there is no remedy "more powerful, nor more valid, more secure, and more necessary" (I.16; 45). In *The Prince* Cesare Borgia's butchery in having Remirro placed in the piazza "in two pieces, with a piece of wood and a bloody knife beside him," is all part of Machiavelli's example of "the great foundations for future power" that Borgia laid for himself (27, 30). In the Machiavellian world "excess" is not committed lightly.

And Machiavelli's sole reference to Aristotle in the *Discourses* in the above passage appears fitting, since Aristotle there assumes the remarkable perspective of advising tyrants on how to keep their regimes secure. That is an (exceptional) Aristotle with whom Machiavelli can converse, and definitely *not* the Aristotle of the *Nicomachean Ethics* who suggests that there are some things a good man would never do. Machiavelli wants his prince to be cognizant of ordinary propensities [in *The Prince* he notes that what makes a prince hated above all "is to be rapacious and a usurper of the property and the women of his subjects" (72)], but to be able to consider *anything*. Not only can Machiavelli himself imagine an amoral conquest of Lucretia which still works to sustain the state, but in *Mandragola* he will make his audience imagine it, too.

Turning to *Mandragola,* we note that there Machiavelli remakes "Lucrezia" into the "new case" for the modern world, with immediate applications. One of the first indicators of this occurs in the Prologue, when the speaker addresses the (female) audience directly; Lucrezia is introduced as the shrewd young woman tricked by Callimaco

Guadagni: "And I would wish that you might be tricked as she was."[21] This is a startling way to introduce an account of a rape, and quick notice that the reader must release preconceptions about Roman Lucretia in order to understand her Florentine personification. But "personification" summons the Florentine Lucrezia too hastily. The bulk of this comedy is spent unfolding "the deception," according to which Callimaco will be invited into the household with permanent conjugal rights. For a good part of the action, Lucrezia is a mere verbal image. Before she finally appears in Act 3, she is evoked only in speech and through her urine sample, demanded of her by her husband on orders from the Latin-speaking "doctor" Callimaco. The picture is of an utterly caged being: "Locked in the mind of her zealous devotee, Lucrezia as icon is less free or independent or autonomous than any matron at her loom. Fully dependent, she first appears as both property of her husband and creature of Callimaco's imagination, which would possess her as well."[22]

Lucrezia's fate is to be the beautiful, well-mannered and "extremely honest" (or "chaste") wife of Messer Nicia Calfucci. The plot begins as Callimaco Guadagni, a Florentine who has spent twenty years in Paris, hears of her beauty, and develops such a passion to possess Lucrezia that he returns to his native city to accomplish the seduction. "Who can be blind to the irony of a man leaving Paris in search of a woman?"—Sumberg asks,[23] and what is more, the man has never set eyes on her. The genesis of the deed (men-talk) thus recalls Livy's account and "the competition of insatiable masculine desire."[24] And it would be Paris where Callimaco had been residing for the previous twenty years, the first decade at the behest of his guardians, the second, because it struck him as more secure than his own land, which Charles VIII had invaded. Already in the prologue we are alerted that "in all things, the present age falls off from ancient virtù" (11), and indeed, "patriotism" seems to have fallen off quite considerably. But the image of Lucrezia rouses Callimaco, formerly given over "part to studies, part to pleasures, part to business" (13). He vows to confront her chaste nature "which makes war" against him, alien as her nature is to "the things of love" (14).

Callimaco enlists the aid of Ligurio ["a parasite, the darling of malice" (10)] to bring to pass what would seem to be an unlikely

event, for Lucrezia's virtue is legendary. But Ligurio's oft-noted resemblance to Machiavelli bodes well for the project. Callimaco and
Ligurio fix upon three items in their favor: the stupidity of her husband, Nicia Calfucci; the desperation of the couple for a child; and
the dubious morality of her mother, Sostrata [who, according to
Callimaco, "used to be good company" (14)]. The first and third
items become important as the drama unfolds, but the action is precipitated by information that the married couple is childless and
desperate for an heir. There is repeated emphasis in the play on
identifying and taking advantage of the *desires* of others. Callimaco's
desire for Lucrezia is nearly debilitating [with his new passion, he
confesses to not knowing *where* he is (13)]; Nicia's desire for a son
blinds him to every aspect of the deception, whereas Ligurio is in the
position of power, for he only desires what Callimaco desires: "I desire for you to satisfy this desire of yours almost as much as you do
yourself" (18). Under Ligurio's direction, then, Callimaco becomes a
doctor well-versed in fertility potions. As such, Callimaco convinces
Nicia that though he does possess an infallible fertility drug ("mandragola") for his wife, it has the distressing attribute of causing death
to the first person who then sleeps with her. With almost no resistance [he does not want to get caught (25)], Nicia accedes to the suggestion that they meet this challenge by carrying off a young man
("the sacrificial inseminator"[25]) from the streets of Florentine to take
upon himself the poison of the drug. This is Callimaco's entry.

Persuading Lucrezia to go along with this scheme is the real novelty of Machiavelli's revision, and this feat is accomplished on the
allied front of family and faith: Sostrata and the "ill-living *frate*" (10),
Frate Timoteo. Sostrata accedes to the plan in an instant, as she is
intensely anxious about the possibility of being disenfranchised,
should her daughter remain childless. Frate Timoteo is a more interesting challenge, for though money-making is never far from his
thoughts, he is no dupe, and he seems to share Ligurio's trait of being
able to identify the effective truth of things. Ligurio feels the need to
test him in his capacity to absorb scandal, and so invents an abortion
scenario which requires the frate's participation ["by persuading the
abbess to give the girl a potion to make her miscarry" (31)]. This
scheme is a nice prelude to the genuine plan in its incidental refer-

ence to the life that must be sacrificed: "you don't offend anything but a piece of unborn flesh, without sense, which could be dispersed in a thousand ways" (32). Timoteo shows himself adequate to the task: "So be it in the name of God" (32). But this is just a small joke. There is no piece of flesh to be disposed of, just Callimaco's desire to be accomplished. Timoteo is brought in.

At the same time that Ligurio successfully extends the conspiracy, Callimaco threatens always to cause it to self-destruct. In fact it is only the examples of Nicia's terrific pomposity that delay our recognition of how weak-minded a "prince" we have in Callimaco. Early on, Callimaco finds cause to imagine himself in a moment of colossal significance: "I've got to try something, be it great, dangerous, harmful, scandalous. Better to die than to live like this . . . I'm not afraid of anything, but will take any course—bestial, cruel, nefarious. . . ." (17). But from the start, he takes every direction from Ligurio, and he becomes increasingly dependent upon him ["Oh don't leave me alone" (27)], even swearing he will go to his death before the outcome of the plot (40). At one point Sostrata addresses her daughter as "sniveller" (36), but the only snivelling done in this comedy is from Callimaco: "Miserable me! Will it ever be possible for me to live with so many worries, disturbed by these fears and these hopes? . . . Woe is me, for I can't find rest anywhere!" (39).

All finally depends on Lucrezia. Before her appearance on the stage, she is revealed through the words of Nicia as a woman of spirit, neither acquiescing easily to his importunate demands for her urine test ["How much labor I've endured to make this stupid woman give me this specimen! And it doesn't mean she doesn't care about having children, because she thinks about it more than I do; but as soon as I want to make her do the least little thing, I get a big story!" (23–24)] nor displaying an undue regard for his presence ["she stays on her knees for four hours, stringing together Our Fathers before she comes to bed, and she's a beast for enduring cold" (24)]. She is familiar with corruption at the highest levels; Nicia recounts how "one of those *frati* began to hang around her" (28) after she had vowed to hear the first mass for forty mornings. How, without a miracle, is her transformation to be made credible for a modern audience?

Lucrezia is presented in converse with her mother about the

"most strange" series of events. She correctly identifies Nicia's desire for a son as the precipitating factor; she shares the desire, without the accompanying blindness. But all forces are locked against her: "I'm in a sweat from what I'm going through" (35), she confides to Sostrata, in an image which marks her transformation. Sostrata turns her over to Frate Timoteo, now revealed as an astute reader of history. "Truly, I have been at my books more than two hours studying this case, and after much examination, I find many things both in particular and in general, that work for us" (35). There are unexpected precedents to be found. Did not Lot's daughters sleep with their father? "Because their intention was good, they didn't sin" (36). Lucrezia might similarly sleep with the stranger in good conscience, for it was at her husband's bequest, and besides, her end "is to fill a seat in paradise" (36). Urging adultery, Timoteo succeeds with the line that did *not* work with Roman Lucretia: "the will is what sins, not the body" (36). Lucrezia accedes, adding, "I don't believe that I shall be alive at all tomorrow."

With the morning, all desires appear to have been met. Nicia is exuberant, after locking "the poor young man" in the bedroom with his wife, and spending the night at the fire with Sostrata, talking about the son he would have and about the stupidity of Lucrezia, "and how much better it would have been if, without so many goings-on, she had given in at first" (51). Ligurio relishes the details provided by the cuckolded husband, who proudly retells how he "touched and felt everything," to assure that the "captured" Florentine was a healthy specimen (51). And Callimaco relates the great pleasure he took in lying with Lucrezia, though he confesses he was of "troubled mind" (52) until he made himself known to her and declared his love: "I . . . made her understand . . . how easily, on account of her husband's simplicity, we could live happily without any scandal, promising her, whenever God did otherwise with him, to take her for my wife" (52). This is the one point on which Callimaco strays from Ligurio's instructions. Ligurio's counsel included an ugly threat: "tell her of the good you wish her; and how without scandal she can be your friend, and with great scandal, your enemy" (42). But a dramatic change has overtaken *Callimaco,* who now expresses the wish for a permanent relationship, an eventual *marriage* between himself and Lucrezia, just as soon as the temporary inconvenience of the husband is removed. Callimaco has come to desire respectability—not an inclination he picked up from Ligurio.

Indirect discourse is a specialty of Machiavelli's, and with the conclusion of *Mandragola,* it appears to be a specialty of Lucrezia's, as well. Callimaco offers her reactions to their night together in the same noncomprehending way that Nicia tells of her nightly prayer ritual. Just as Nicia's recounting of Lucrezia adds a challenging dimension to every one of his assumptions about her (including that she is the source of the infertility), so now Callimaco's summary rendition suggests dimensions of rule that he does not fathom. He seems not to be aware of his own language shift as he describes her reactions. Lucrezia, Callimaco relates, concluded that the combination of his own astuteness, Nicia's stupidity, Sostrata's simplicity, and Frate Timoteo's wickedness had forced her hand: "I'm determined to judge," she is said to have concluded, "that it comes from a heavenly disposition which has so willed; and I don't have it in me to reject what Heaven wills me to accept" (52). Lucrezia bows to the new arrangement, in the most submissive of terms: "Therefore, I take you for lord, master, and guide; you are my father, my defender, and I want you to be my every good; and what my husband wanted for one evening, I want him to have always" (52–53). As Lucrezia goes on to fill in the details of their continuing arrangement, Callimaco is so overcome with happiness that her imperatives go unnoticed: "You will, therefore, make yourself his close friend and you'll go to the church this morning, and from there you'll come have dinner with us; and your comings and goings will be up to you, and we'll be able to come together at any time and without suspicion" (53). *He* is smitten, *she* is in control; the power is behind the scenes.[26] This is the end of Ligurio's reign, as he uncharacteristically asks: "But what do we do now?" (53). The answer is that they will all go to the church, as instructed, to receive the blessings of the highest authorities.

Livy's Lucretia is modernized to perfection in Machiavelli's Lucrezia, for as D'Amico notes, "in the private world she proves to be the most astute and, perhaps, Machiavellian character in the play. She converts momentary satisfaction into a new order."[27] So far has the modern world fallen off from ancient virtù that great, self-sacrificing heroines no longer speak a comprehensible language. But Lucrezia adapts, and spurs our thinking; within the constraints of a corrupted time and place, her indirect rule is an example of immediate use. What we have, in sum, is a set piece instructing us in how to conspire successfully against a "malignity of fortune" such as Nicia represents. By the end, Lucrezia has become contemptuous of Nicia's traditional ways, for hers is the "new case." Nicia notices some slight change in his wife the next morning. "Why don't you go?" (53), Lucrezia demands of him. For all intents and purposes, Nicia does just that. Contrary to popular representation, Machiavelli brings the indirect, feminine rule to sight as more than equal to the assertions of the prince. The wise and well-mannered Lucrezia, like Penelope, is "fit to govern a kingdom" (17), but she is Penelope with an edge, without illusions about love.

At the close of Machiavelli's *Mandragola,* it would appear that all the characters have accomplished their desires, and without anyone suffering palpable harm. Nevertheless, the projected attitude is one of watchful enjoyment; there will be other desires to agitate this scene, and other occasions for deception. Yet if the equilibrium is precarious, more than that is not sought. The male and female leads arrive at a mutually satisfactory settlement, one that, to be sure, would not be mistaken for the highest friendship between husband and wife as discussed by Aristotle, for the all-important stability and community of his vision is left far behind. Lucrezia is paired with her husband and her lover without any obvious regard for either. Thus the example of Machiavelli's Lucrezia is removed in every way from her ancestor in Livy. It appears that for Machiavelli at least, historical exemplars should serve as bracing reminders of our capricious lot, and of the consequent need for agility in affairs of state as well as in affairs of the hearth.

The new alignment of writing and political community that occurs with Machiavelli can be traced in turn through Burke and Mary Shelley. This series of readings shows how markedly modern writers diverge from the ancient case; each refuses the inclination to *capture* an object-image as part of their political corrective. The ancient writers in our survey put a permanent stamp on an equipoised polis, whereas the moderns shun the appearance of resolution in their writ-

ings and refuse any posture which might suggest a stable and beneficent ordering of the world. Following Machiavelli, the modern rhetoricians aligns the fluidity of their literary boundaries with those of
the state.

Burke's Queen of France

Even a work like *Mandragola* carries an allegorical meaning, despite "its being so light" (*Mandragola*, 10). Sumberg states blankly,
for instance, that *Mandragola* "is a guide on how to carry out a
conspiracy against a corrupt regime."[28] Nicia is the unfit prince, ruling by fortune rather than virtue. Ligurio, the Machiavelli-figure,
knows just how to remedy that situation: "I'll be the captain, and get
the army in order for the battle" (47). Politics spills over its borders
into private lives. It is noteworthy that allegories, like stories more
generally, make room for distinctive masculine and feminine elements. In this respect, it is a surprisingly small step to move from
Machiavelli's *Mandragola* to Edmund Burke's *Reflections on the Revolution in France*. In the rhetoric of the state, strong male and female
predilections tend to be easy to isolate, whatever their allegorical
force may be. Interpretations vary widely, in keeping with the possibilities of that form. At best, these modern texts are both "pressing"
and "open-ended" in their formulation of the political problem.

Burke's very title reveals something of the new phenomenon of
modernity. It is not "the French Revolution" but "the Revolution in
France." Like a fire or a disease, this revolution, "the most astonishing that has hitherto happened in the world" (*Reflections,* 9), can
sweep from one national house to any other, respecting no boundaries; it could afflict the whole world if not checked. And the episto-
lary form of Burke's *Reflections on the Revolution in France and on
the Proceedings in Certain Societies in London Relative to That
Event in a Letter Intended to Have Been Sent to a Gentleman in
Paris, 1790* is itself a depiction and demonstration of the form of
human community he is attempting to defend. *Reflections* purports
to contain Burke's thoughts and feelings just as they happened to
arise, "with very little attention to formal method" (9), but few works
reveal so much preoccupation with literary method. Ideas spill out at
a high velocity in a kind of "stream of consciousness" that accords

with the workings of the mind itself. The text circles and spirals and returns again and again to its core themes which are thereby slowly and organically transformed. The letter is anything but a treatise; it does not move from one proposition to another, with the reader "immersed in a world like the real world, in which judgments of fact and reason and value are continuous."[29] The letter is at the same time utterly clear *and* stubbornly resistant to easy appropriation or summation. There are no reader-friendly demarcations; no table of contents, no chapter-headings or subheads, no index. Attempts to outline the work have not met with success. When we attempt to assess Burkean ideas, we have to do all the work of classifying and analyzing the material in our own minds. And any such effort soon convinces us that no part of the text can be cut or skipped over without damaging the whole. Past, present, and future are inextricably intertwined. Once readers are inside this text, they have entered an organic political community.

The letter seems to be the appropriate vehicle for delivering to the gentleman in Paris the news which is calculated to stun, from one who was thought to be a friend and who was assumed to be likeminded. Concerning the late proceedings in France, Burke writes to C. J. F. Depont, "it is my misfortune to entertain great doubts" (*Reflections*, 4). To his contemporaries, Burke's political record seemed at odds with his stance. He had opposed the religious persecution of Catholics in Ireland. He had defended the American colonies in their revolution and declaration of independence. For years he worked to impeach Warren Hastings for oppression of the people of India. But on the issue of the French Revolution, Burke left his party and sacrificed his friendship with the Whig leader Charles James Fox. This, despite the fact that to most observers at the time, the French Revolution appeared to be the second act of the American Revolution. Burke seemed to have needlessly invented a career crisis for himself; it was the time that Wordsworth later would recall: "Bliss was it then to be alive / But to be young was very heaven." Burke wrote during the peaceful year of the Revolution, Mosher reminds us, before the rise of the Jacobins or the French wars or the massacres or the terror: "It should always be stressed how early in the Revolution Burke came to his views about it . . . No other philosophical writing on politics succeeded in predicting so accurately and with such relevant specificity the course of subsequent events."[30] In academic circles, Burke's prescience still rankles.

From the outset of Burke's letter he calls the Revolution a "monstrous" tragicomic scene and fiction (9, 32). In a phrase, what he fathomed was *Hominem non sapient* (160), "they know not man." To Burke, each human society is a carefully balanced organism that has been nurtured, grown and tended slowly and with care over generations. The "state of Nature" to Burke was not, as it was to Rousseau and others, a primitive stage which mankind has left behind; the state of Nature is society today. To tear such a society apart by revolution is to commit a crime against nature. The threat created by the Revolution in France, as Burke saw it, endangered the vital roots of the organism that is society. Property was to be confiscated to ensure that it belonged to no one. Religion was to be abolished in favor of atheism, a belief in nothing. Political legitimacy was murdered, leaving nothing in its place. And civility, manners, respect, and all the attributes of dignity would be scorned or eradicated, leaving nothing to smooth relations between human beings. To Burke, this was nothing less than the end of history's painstakingly evolved human achievement.

It seemed that the forces of both revolution and capitalism were enthralled by an abstraction. In the grip of a metaphysical vision, the revolutionaries wished to traffic in a clear and simple entity, "man," capable of being counted, predicted, directed. "Simple modes of polity are infinitely captivating" (54), Burke suggests, because they satisfy our desire for system, order, and presumably, justice. The problem is that to the degree that "they are metaphysically true, they are morally and politically false" (54); human affections are slighted. Reason, under this approach, is not informed by the passions, but is employed to suppress and confine them. Glimmers of misogyny emerge in the clarified atmosphere. Carefully balanced human interaction is to be replaced by a single, triumphant concept: instrumental Reason.[31] "On the principles of this mechanic philosophy," Burke writes, "our institutions can never be embodied in persons, so as to create in us love, veneration, admiration, or attachment. But that sort of reason which banishes the affections is incapable of filling their place" (68).

Burke counters "this mechanic philosophy" by declaring that he wants to reassign "prejudice" to its proper role, for we English, he claims, "cherish our prejudices to a very considerable degree" (76). This language is intended to stir up an age that had defined its own enlightenment against prejudice; certainly, Burke could have chosen a less explosive word. For him, prejudice is the attachment felt for established practices and institutions; consequently, more neutral words were available—attachment, commitment, affinity—which did not suggest such a strong sense of "pre-judging." And Burke acknowledges elsewhere that not *every* prejudice is worth defending, that there are "false," "vulgar," and "antiquated" prejudices. Thus his rhetorical audacity and inventiveness still astonishes. He invests other words with his own particular meaning and significance, especially those beginning with the letter "P." To line them up and to analyze and make sense of the list as a whole would be most un-Burkean, but scattered as they are across the text of the letter, they imbue the reader with the sense of a complex interlinking, a psychological, intellectual, societal balancing of public and private, masculine and feminine, indeed of all dualities, into a comprehensive political community. Passions inform our reason, principles express natural law, prudence is the practical application of principles to particular events, presumption favors any settled practice, prescription is any ancient, unquestioned possession, precedent is the law's natural process, partnership is the spanning of past, present, and future, property is the guardian of liberty, party—in Burke's famous definition—is "a body of men united for promoting by their joint endeavors the national interest, upon some particular principle in which they are all agreed." But of all the "P-words," "prejudice" is most important. For Burke it holds together—in balance—reason, motive, passion, emotion and affection, the self and the community, one's best instincts and habits, character and conduct. Society and the self exist in a reciprocal relation, capable of perpetual reconstitution. That the reader may be shocked by this use of the word "prejudice" only compels it to be given fresh attention.

Burke similarly provokes his readers with his formulations about what is "natural" and what is "unnatural." Nature is "wisdom without reflection, and above it" (29), he claims. *You* men of theory are at war with nature (43), he charges, while in England, "*we* have not yet been completely embowelled of our natural entrails" (75). These are confident formulations about the simple matter of things, but Burke's distinctly modern usage of "nature" is to be noted: nature is neither "form" nor "end." He introduces nature claims to confront the elemental shift that Jacobinism represents, for it is not mere thuggery, but the precursor of what would later be called "totalitarianism." Burke identifies Jacobinism as the attempt to eradicate prejudice, and *therefore,* nothing less than a distortion of human nature; the Jacobins move outside of politics in an attempt to remake human beings. And once man is held up as "self-making" without limit—that is, without a role for the accompanying prejudice of religious establishment, of historical traditions, of culture—then unprecedented political excesses will follow. Burke agrees with his opponents that it *is* the prerogative of man "to be in a great degree a creature of his own making" (*Reflections,* 81), but he reminds us further that we are not, after all, self-created. Grant human beings the highest dignity in the world, Burke allows, but do not forget that they are *part* of that creation and not the authors of their own existence. Human beings do not have the option of blithely dispensing with the whole of their past, even if they do have the ability to choose among their traditions and inheritances.

In *The Origins of Totalitarianism,* Hannah Arendt offers her strong support to Burke's attack on the abstract concepts of the French Revolution. The brutal reality of the Holocaust, she says, "appears to buttress [Burke's] assertion that human rights were an 'abstraction,' that it was much wiser to rely on an 'entailed inheritance' of rights." Burke's arguments, Arendt concludes, gain added significance when we look at the condition of those who have been forced out of their political communities. "If a human being loses his political status, he should, according to the implications of the inborn and inalienable rights of man, come under exactly the situation for which the declarations of such rights provided. Actually the opposite is the case. It seems that a man who is nothing but a man has lost the very qualities which make it possible for other people to treat him as a fellow man."[32]

For all their vigor, Arendt's words in praise of Burke are atypical among twentieth-century readers. This critical reception might be passed over in silence, except for the fact that Burke's rhetorical project is so frequently dismissed as unworkable in principle. The claim is that when Burke exposes the elements of revolutionary discourse, he simultaneously undoes his own. Predictably this charge is directed against the most famous passage in the *Reflections,* on the spectacle of events surrounding the forced march of the King and Queen to Paris and culminating with Burke's apostrophe to Marie Antoinette. Nothing in Burke's letter has drawn more scorn and derision. Even his close friend and editor called it "pure foppery."[33] Ever since, Burke's charge that his opponents' rhetoric relies on the "magnificent stage effect" and "grand spectacle" (57) has been turned against his own writing. "Burke's distinction between his own historical veracity and the theatricality of revolutionary rhetoric—a distinction vital to his ideological project—thus threatens to collapse in its most critical moment."[34] The claim is that Burkean rhetoric gets the better of Burke himself, that his argument has no more objective justification than the renditions of his adversaries.

This attack on Burke appears in a range of specialized readings, from the Freudian ("Burke's life was a set of variations on oedipal themes. . . . Decrying [the Jacobins'] aggressive masculinity represented the recurring need to deny his own masculine oedipal conquest") to the feminist and post-structuralist versions.[35] Interestingly, these critics almost invariably turn to Burke's *Philosophical Enquiry* to fill out the mind-set revealed in his mature *Reflections.* Mitchell claims, for instance, that Burke's gendered language is not just a matter of aesthetic decorum but is "a figure for the natural foundations of all political and cosmic order, the universal structure of domination, mastery and slavery."[36] Since this critical move is made as early as 1790, in Mary Wollstonecraft's *Vindication* ["But these ladies may have read your *Enquiry* . . . and, convinced by your arguments, may have labored to be pretty, by counterfeiting weakness" (79)], it is worth a glance back at the work that Burke's critics find so damning.

In the *Enquiry,* Burke posits a basic division at the root of human experience, and seeks to describe the origin of the ideas of the sublime and the beautiful with more refinement and symmetry than was the norm. He complains there that those ideas were "frequently confounded," and he imagines further that if *any* remedy were to be found, "it could only be from a diligent examination of our passions in our breasts" (*Enquiry,* 1). Since Burke believed that our ideas of the sublime and beautiful are linked to the passions, they looked to be as elemental—and potentially foundational—as any matters could be.[37] He marks an "eternal distinction" between the sublime and the beautiful, and elicits their gendered dimensions: the sublime is associated with preservation of self and masculinity, and the beautiful with society and feminine attachments. "For sublime objects are vast in their dimensions, beautiful ones comparatively small; beauty should be smooth, and polished; the great, rugged and negligent. . . . beauty should be light and delicate; the great ought to be solid, and even massive" (113).

Burke's hope was to draw attention to those occasions in which the human imagination seemed to be affected similarly by external stimuli, so as to "supply the means of reasoning satisfactorily about them" (13). He provides his readers with any number of controversial claims in the process. Critics never fail to note his remark, for instance, that women are aware of how beauty almost always carries with it an idea of weakness and imperfection, "for which reason they learn to lisp, to totter in their walk, to counterfeit weakness. In all this they are guided by nature" (*Enquiry,* 100). Nevertheless it must be said that Burke qualifies the truth-revealing qualities of *all* human language in the *Enquiry,* and locates an irresolution at the very heart of "the political and cosmic order." All of his claims must be read in the context of the author's insistence on the mystifying potential of human reason: readers are cautioned time and again about the gap between argument and example. And Burke notes from the start that he has no intention of *defining* these terms with any fixity: "I have no great opinion of a definition. . . . For when we define, we seem in danger of circumscribing nature within the bounds of our own notions . . . instead of extending our ideas to take in all that nature comprehends, according to her manner of combining" (12). Throughout he combines a respect for the immediacy of our ideas of the sublime and beautiful with a humility about what human reason amounts to, even in its "satisfactory" exercise. For, as he acknowledges in his concluding section, our words do not even resemble their objects (153–154). And, most insistently, the effect of *clarity* is no part of Burke's ambition (56–57).

The tone is not at all what is commonly suggested, then, when Burke's individual statements in the *Enquiry* are extracted for purposes of explaining his rhetorical moves in the *Reflections*. While always retaining his ability to make discriminations, Burke strives for openness to the complexity of nature. His readers tend to concentrate on only one part of his enterprise, with the result that the critics of the left and his critics of the right hardly seem to be speaking of the same author. Conservative critics note that Burke permits no appeal to principle beyond politics, that he argues from circumstance in the manner of a liberal. "However much Burke eulogized tradition and fulminated against the French Revolution," Weaver concludes, "he was, when judged by what we are calling aspect of argument, very far from being a conservative." Leo Strauss notes the "premodern conception of natural right" to which Burke reverts and stresses his verdict that "what the wisest individual can think out for himself is always inferior to what has been produced 'in a great length of time, and by a great variety of accidents.'" It is liberal writers who are more likely to associate Burke with "essences": "His image of man's intricate and complex nature as the essential reality that must be preserved in society is the exact contrary of the revolutionary's view of man as an obstruction to the beneficent sunburst of human liberty."[38]

The complexity of Burke's rhetorical posture in the *Reflections*—and his Machiavellianism—is therefore often strangely underestimated. Thus his florid description of the Queen of France is frequently mistaken for mere nostalgia. But when Burke places Marie Antoinette in company with the ancient Lucrezia, he does so with the recognizably *modern* purpose of toughening his contemporary readership rather than reassuring or consoling them. As with Machiavelli's "new case," Burke evokes Lucrezia only to register the passing of her world. In the course of praising the dignity of the Queen of France throughout the unseemly events of October 6, 1789, he writes: "I hear, and I rejoice to hear, that the great lady. . . . has lofty sentiments; that she feels with the dignity of a Roman matron; that in the last extremity she will save herself from the last disgrace; and that, if she must fall, she will fall by no ignoble hand" (66). In truth, the restraint of Burke's prose shields no horrors from the reader. Pocock misses the chilling edge of Burke's depiction when he comments on this passage that "Burke seems to imagine Marie Antoinette committing suicide like Lucretia, to save herself from rape. She was in fact guillotined" (223, n. *lii*). Lucretia, in fact, did not "save herself" from rape, any more than Burke imagines here that in the end, Marie Antoinette will escape execution. He has already noted with acerbity that the "massacre of innocents" was "unhappily left unfinished" on the sixth of October: "What hardy pencil of a great master from the school of the rights of man will finish it is to be seen hereafter" (64). And he closes the account with an unambiguous epitaph to the age of chivalry: "Never, never more shall we behold that generous loyalty to rank and sex, that proud submission, that dignified obedience, that subordination of the heart which kept alive, even in servitude itself, the spirit of an exalted freedom" (66). The "accumulated wrongs" that the Queen bears (66) are noted without elaboration, in keeping with Burke's own manner of reserve. For all that, his Marie Antoinette surely will be slaughtered, presumably after further indignities.

Burke has also given the impression to many readers that he was writing in a vacuum, unaware of the pornographic material circulating in abundance about Marie Antoinette at the same time that he penned his tribute to her. But there is nothing naive about the way he transforms the Queen from target of the tabloids to noble emblem of a civilized community; his approach is deliberate. Burke does not dignify the obscene publications by direct engagement, but certainly he was *aware* of them: "We spurn from us with disgust and indignation the slanders of those who bring us their anecdotes with the attestation of the flower-de-luce on their shoulder" (73).[39] Instead of disputing the aspersions, he *shows* his readers the elevated stance of the Queen, through his writing which embodies the achievement he praises. He knows the power of good writing over bad; his strongest demonstration of the truth he tells is in the way he enters into its spirit. His rendering startled his first audience though his sources were widely available,[40] but once published, his account was exceedingly difficult to ignore or to refute. At the other extreme, the obscene pamphlets may have been distributed widely but they were without individual conviction, for there was no originator, no responsible source to stand behind the accusations. In contrast, Burke marks his ground and stands it, thus providing an example that many readers were eager to take up and reproduce in their own names.

For his boldness in historical perspective Burke is seen as presumptuous on another front. When Burke intones "History will record that on the morning of the 6th of October, 1789," his critics may move in for the kill.[41] But whoever reads to the end of the sentence finds something other than great impertinence on the part of our historian: "the king and queen of France, after a day of confusion, alarm, dismay, and slaughter, lay down, under the pledged security of public faith, to indulge nature in a few hours of troubled, melancholy repose" (62). Burke has taken a page from the father of history here, for Herodotus begins his *Persian War* with a similar parody of the historian's role. He depicts the "Persian chroniclers" offering up their far-fetched and self-serving explanation of the war at the very start of his work as a way of acknowledging his *own* vulnerabilities and temptations as a historian. The combination of grave assertions by the Persian chroniclers and ridiculous subject matter of their so-called history is fair notice that the writer of the parody recognizes the temptations at hand; so, too, with Burke. Of course, Burke intends what follows to be a serious part of the record, but was there ever a less-insolent opening move made by a historian than Burke's—to *presume* that the royal couple had fallen asleep? It is tempting to see this move as a slight joke at the expense of the omniscient observer.

Finally, the most common charge directed against Burke's authorial posture is that he simply appeals to the traditional morality around him, an appeal that is not justified by anything more than historical accident. So he is preoccupied by "pleasing illusions" and regrets that henceforth they are to be dissolved (67). But in his lament that "all the decent drapery of life is to be rudely torn off," Burke is doing something considerably more powerful than appealing to the conventions of an earlier generation that were more to his liking; his intentions are towards retrieving "the elemental" rather than the "the traditional." This can be brought out more clearly by considering this entire scene as a rewriting of a mythical Greek story, Herodotus' Gyges story. Burke's rendition is a more secular version but is otherwise quite recognizable. His hope seems to be one—Machiavelli-like—of bracing his readers for the real harshness of their surroundings.

In Herodotus' Gyges, "retribution" is a critical feature in the tale of a masculine invasion into the feminine sphere. King Candaules, reports Herodotus, "fell in love with his own wife; and because he was so in love, he thought he had in her far the most beautiful of women" (*History,* 1.8). The events begin when Candaules summons his servant to his quarters. "Gyges," Candaules says, "I do not think that you *credit* me when I tell you about the beauty of my wife . . . Contrive, then, that you see her naked." Gyges cries out, for the shame of it, but nevertheless is convinced to look upon what he should not. Feminine modesty and dignity are violated, and, to condense the story, the regime comes toppling down, and generation after generation feels the aftershock, altering the course of history. The gods were stirred: "But this much the Pythia said: that the Heraclids should yet have vengeance on a descendant of Gyges in the fifth generation" (1.13).

Burke's modern rendition leaves us more at a loss about the regaining of historical equanimity; surely no cycle exists to resituate a people, once the historical moment has passed. His famous passage begins thus: "It is now sixteen or seventeen years since I saw the queen of France, then the dauphiness, at Versailles, and surely never lighted on this orb, which she hardly seemed to touch, a more delightful vision. I saw her just above the horizon, decorating and cheering the elevated sphere she just began to move in—glittering like the morning star, full of life, and splendor, and joy. Oh! *What a revolution!*" (66). With this exclamation, Burke's letter shifts from Marie Antoinette to focus on the two opposing characters: the revolutionary, and his opposite, the man of chivalry. They exemplify the contrast between thinking and feeling, and contain the clues to why traditions and memories are to be revered. The Queen is like a sun, a source of warmth. The revolutionary extinguishes the sun with "cool calculation." In contrast to the revolutionary is—or should be—the gentleman of chivalry. But they do not rush forward. "Little did I dream," Burke says, "that I should have seen such disasters fallen upon the Queen of France in a nation of gallant men, in a nation of men of honor and of cavaliers. I thought ten thousand swords must have leaped from their scabbards to avenge *even a look* that threatened her with insult—but the age of chivalry is gone. That of sophisters, oeconomists, and calculators has succeeded; and the glory of Europe is extinguished forever" (66). Burke sums up all this in the famed sentence "All the decent drapery of life is to be torn off." In these words we hear echoes of a shocking story, so fundamental that we can trace it back through the centuries.

Herodotus' Candaules was not a Greek, but a barbarian, and so could not be expected to understand that this formation of the political community must not be destroyed by the violation of "looking." Burke, on the other hand, is appalled that the French, "a nation of men of honor and of cavaliers" would fail to protect their Queen. This was a matter of self-interest as well as honor. As in chess, a Queen is more important than a King, and she was *theirs*. In the stark revaluation of the naked humanity of governance lies the cause of national disaster. When a spectacle is made of beauty, when nobility is exposed to the searchlights, as in the march to Paris, all illusion is dispelled and cannot be resuscitated. "The unbought grace of life," Burke concludes, "is gone!" (67). And in its place? Not the looked-for liberation. As the "decent draperies" of life are torn away, the aggressor is hurled into the chaos that the state-of-nature theorists would have recognized: "a king is but a man, a queen is but a woman; a woman is but an animal, and an animal *not* of the highest order" (67). This is the horrifying perception that brought Hannah Arendt to the side of Edmund Burke.

The decent drapery symbolically represents an understanding that masculine and feminine are distinct realms, in a distinctive equilibrium and mutually dependent upon maintaining a fine balance. To disrespect the distinction is to upset the balance and to risk great damage to human society in every regard. To transgress in this way is not only to recognize that human beings are animals, but to elevate that animal nature above humanity's social conventions. Once such transgressions become conventions, politics become impossible. At the core of these accounts is feminine sexuality. Supremely powerful by nature,[42] it can only be maintained and managed through modesty. Once woman loses the ability to avoid shame, she adopts a masculine politics. Once Candaules' Queen is stripped of her privacy, she begins to issue commands that cause the murder of the King and initiate a cascade of political horrors.

Little wonder, then, that critics since Mary Wollstonecraft have directed their objections against Burke to his rendering of a kind of "feminine" principle. On the very surface of the *Reflections* is Burke's intercession on behalf of this feminine element, which recognizes contingency and displays a sense of finitude; he aligns himself with the force that attends to history and that urges us inwards, to a moral or spiritual examination. This feminine principle is attached to traditions that maintain the strength of social affection across communities, as White explains.[43] It is linked with creativity, the unconscious, interiorization, and mystery, and opposes a "masculine principle" which employs power, with reason, to meet immediate objectives. That impulse calls for exactitude, precision, and an intellect which functions in line with scientific or empirical observations. The urge to limitlessness and to mastery is revealed. To Burke—quite apart from any oedipal themes of his own—the Jacobins represent the masculine principle gone mad.

The patent nature of these masculine and feminine dimensions in Burke's work makes it puzzling when critics imply that it is a sufficient reason to discount his project to catch him, for instance, "enforcing a gendered semiotic code." According to Zerilli, Burke intends this code to make inconceivable the notion of political women: "the aggressive political woman whose threat to the sexual economy of chivalry and the aristocratic order is both *evoked* and *managed* in the author's prose."[44] But since Burke is not concealing this rhetorical strategy, correctives to his account need to go further. After all, Mary Wollstonecraft penetrated the workings of this rhetoric instantly. What she was *not* able to do was to detract from its plausibility.

Burke offers in his prose a corrective to the kind of thinking Jacobinism represents: "I cannot conceive how any man can have brought himself to that pitch of presumption to consider his country as nothing but *carte blanche,* upon which he may scribble whatever he pleases." He is suggesting in his language of "monstrous fictions" that without this corrective which respects received inheritances, the result of this presumption is not just one-sided or lacking in proportion, but somehow ghastly. "We are taught to look with horror on those children of their country who are prompt rashly to hack that aged parent in pieces and put him into the kettle of magicians, in hopes that by their poisonous weeds and wild incantations they may regenerate the paternal constitution and renovate their father's life" (84). To convey the human cost of the uninhibited male drive, Burke holds up for reverence the receding feminine principle.

By many accounts Wollstonecraft accurately gauges Burke's intentions when she attempts to disjoin his combination of judgment and the "feminine virtue of sensibility," urging instead that "we must feel the evil of wicked acts strongly, sympathetically, with the weight of a judging conscience that is neither masculine nor feminine."[45] Yet frequently she elides into a posture that in her own terms is suspiciously "masculine" in its elevation of "the *regal* stamp of reason"(62). "Intent on rejecting this feminine psychological and political model," Poovey notes, "she substitutes for Burke's feminine paradigm a description of human nature and society anchored in 'masculine' behavior, in confrontation and conquest."[46] This has resulted in the quaint predicament for readers of having to choose between Wollstonecraft's 'male' voice of Reason or Burke's 'female' voice of Sentiment—hardly a decisive rebuttal of Burke. And Wollstonecraft does not fully commit to this posture, such that after accusing Burke of "a moral antipathy to reason" according to which "reflection inflames your imagination, instead of enlightening your understanding" (37, 38), she interjects her own emotion-laden terms: "I pause to recollect myself; and smother the contempt I feel rising for your rhetorical flourishes and infantine sensibility" (96), leaving her subject to the charge that she is reproducing the same feminine stance that she reviles in Burke.[47] Though she aspires to a judging conscience that is neither masculine nor feminine, in practice she alternates between stereotypical versions of each. And turgid prose seems to destroy the atmosphere required for Wollstonecraft to sustain her intended variances, such that her *Vindications* alternate between lectures "for" and "against" the value-free commentator.[48] Burke remains more consistent, and stands largely unrefuted. But it turns out that his language of monstrous fictions is just a tease: Mary Shelley more fully and unforgettably elaborates the gender quandary that results from wholly masculine-driven conditions.

Shelley's Monster

The literary merits of *Frankenstein* may be questioned from time to time, but as allegory, it is recognized as one of the most fertile ever devised.[49] It invites speculations about its political significance without encouraging readers to settle the issue too comfortably, for at the heart of the text is a prudent vagueness about the human condition. There is a jittery, unfinished nature to *Frankenstein* which is not due just to its nightmare vision but also to its moral, as readers are pulled both to sympathize with the characters and to chafe at the self-generated plight. Burke's language of masculine and feminine principles is fitting here, to accommodate an alternation between the pull of particular human attachments and the universalizing drive of reason. The arrangement of those two forces becomes ever more disquieting in Shelley's novel; in the tradition of Machiavelli and Burke, this story does not console. To those interested in statecraft and the construct of the state, Mary Shelley conveys the desperate inadequacy of human creations ever wholly to match their aspirations.[50]

On one level of *Frankenstein,* Mary Shelley issues a feminist critique analogous to Burke's in the *Reflections.* Burke died in 1797 and so did not live to encounter the nineteen-year-old author of *Frankenstein* (the version considered here is the original, published in 1818). But he would have found a soul-sister in this author who depicts the "metaphysical" process by which the scientist Victor Frankenstein projects a dehumanized and anti-female world. "For the simple purpose of human survival," Mellor observes, "Frankenstein has eliminated the need to have females at all. . . . his creature is male; he refuses to create a female; there is no reason that the race of immortal beings he hoped to propagate should not be exclusively male."[51] Like Burke, Shelley conveys grave alarm by the imbalances she perceives taking shape, violently, at the birth of "the age of Reason." The solitary creating man, through his vast powers of consciousness, gives external form to his deepest thoughts, and creates a being which resembles him—except bigger, and a thousand times more hideous. The egotism appears fundamentally life-offending.

Readers would be tempted to dismiss the whole roster of female characters in *Frankenstein* as weak and helpless casualties if not for the obvious invitation to judge the world behind that female lot.[52] And in *Frankenstein,* the characterizations turn back upon the deficiencies of the environment of the Promethean "knowledge-seekers." In Victor Frankenstein's narration of his life, he tells the story of how his father "came like a protecting spirit" to "the poor girl" (Victor's mother) he was to marry; this patronizing language recurs throughout. Turning to his own fiancée Elizabeth, Victor admits to admiring her understanding and fancy, but more, he "loved to tend on her, as [he] should on a favorite animal" (63, 65). Worse yet, he reveals that when she came to live with him in his childhood home as his orphaned cousin—orphaned for all practical purposes, that is, since her *mother* had died—he found her "gay and playful as a summer insect" (65).[53] Then there is the sweet and amiable Justine Moritz, on whom the monster plants evidence, implicating her in his first murder. Justine's confessor so torments her that she confesses to the crime she did not commit: "He threatened excommunication and hell fire in my last moments, if I continued obdurate . . . I had none to support me; all looked on me as a wretch doomed to ignominy and perdition. What could I do?" (114). But though Justine's fate is to be executed unjustly, she is characterized in the end not by weakness but by a "radical purposiveness which releases her."[54] Here again, the shortcoming in character is hardly intended to be *hers,* as Shelley ends this last scene in Volume 1 with Justine perishing and Victor bemoaning *his* fate: "But I—I was a wretch, and none ever conceived of the misery that I then endured" (117).

For a long time Victor Frankenstein's self-pitying analyses serve to screen what is actually his repudiation of domesticity. When he is involved in his original research, he becomes feverish, driven, unconscious of the need to sleep or eat, and utterly oblivious of his human connections: he forgets his family, his fiancée, his friends. His intellectual and emotional activities are totally disconnected: "The more fully I entered into the science, the more exclusively I pursued it for its own sake" (78). Furthermore, he is utterly unthinking about the thing he is putting together. He makes it eight feet tall simply because "the minuteness of the parts formed a great hindrance to my speed" (82). Shelley describes the great moment as Frankenstein discovers the principle of creation: "After days and nights of incredible labor and fatigue," the scientist writes, "I succeeded in discovering the cause of generation and life; nay, more, I became myself capable of bestowing animation upon lifeless matter" (81). And then occurs the final indignity: when the being opens his eyes for the first time, and Frankenstein beholds its watery eyes, black lips, and gigantic stature, he rushes from the room in horror (86), and leaves his progeny to fend for himself.

The thing is a monster of a man, but after that first night in which ensue the "wildest dreams" for the creator, it is clear that it is *woman* who is menace to Victor Frankenstein. Possibly readers let pass Frankenstein's early remark about his upbringing with cousin Elizabeth: that his mother had immediately "determined" to consider her his future wife, "a design which she never found reason to repent" (65). But Victor's dream reawakens his and our discomfort with the arrangement, as Frankenstein recalls his dream that after kissing Elizabeth on the lips, her features became transformed, "and I thought that I held the corpse of my dead mother in my arms" (86). Mother, wife, and sister blur, and Victor "feels himself failed by women on every side."[55] Just then, he wakes, and spies the wretch. "Oh! no mortal could support the horror of that countenance" (87).

Thereafter, the Victor Frankenstein character takes on more and more effeminate features. His first human contact after engendering the Creature is his friend Henry Clerval: "I grasped his hand, and in a moment forgot my horror and misfortune; I felt suddenly, and for the first time during many months, calm and serene joy" (88). Victor repeatedly refers to his "beloved" Clerval (183, 210), and it is only the sight of this comrade that restores his thoughts to "all those scenes of home so dear to [his] recollection" (88). Here and again Elizabeth is "remembered" subsequent to Clerval: "Can any man be as Clerval was; or any woman another Elizabeth?" (235). Victor's behavior is unusual enough to make his father suspect that his son has become interested in another (212). In truth, Victor acknowledges at one point that "the idea of an immediate union with my cousin was one of horror and dismay" (179). This acknowledgment comes later for Victor Frankenstein than for the reader.

The domesticity from which Victor Frankenstein flees, meantime, is precisely the Creature's most heartfelt desire. Cantor and Moses note that "in a curious way [the Creature] ends up speaking for the value of domestic life in opposition to Frankenstein, who, in his heroic quest as a creator, rejects the ties that would bind him to a conventional family. The Creature longs for precisely the warmth of hearth and home that its creator fails to appreciate."[56] Critics have long noted that the ideas of "the warmth of hearth and home" have their source in Rousseau, both in his *Second Discourse* and in *Emile*.[57] And the Creature does appear to embody that strange image of Rousseau's at the beginning of *Emile:* "If man were born big and strong, his size and strength would be useless to him until he had learned to make use of them" (*Emile,* 38). The Creature is that "newborn man," and so is monstrous, and yet since he presents himself as material for the transformative education, he is potentially the natural man as well, for his acquired skills are fully in line with his genuine needs. The scenario in *Frankenstein* is as idyllic as any in *Emile,* as the Creature conceals himself in a hut and observes the natural rhythms of life of the De Lacey family. Eventually, the Creature learns to speak English alongside of "Safie," and in his own words he recounts that "every conversation of the cottagers now opened new wonders to me" (147). But with his increase of knowledge and ability to communicate comes bitterness about his own state, and in particular, about the "blind vacancy" of his origins: "No father had watched my infant days, no mother had blessed me with smiles and caresses. . . . I had never yet seen a being resembling me, or who claimed any intercourse with me. What was I?" (149).

In his mature state, the being expresses his willingness to forgive his creator for making him a monster, *if* Frankenstein will do one thing: create for him a female mate. Here again, creature and creator articulate opposing drives. Since the monster has been educated in works of the Western canon [*Paradise Lost, Plutarch's Lives, Sor-*

rows of Werther (155)], he knows the vocabulary of his wretched isolation; he is like Adam, apparently created with no link to any other being in existence, but "no Eve soothed his sorrows, or shared his thoughts" (159). The monster's charge to Frankenstein is to remedy that isolation: "This alone you can do; and I demand it of you *as a right* which you must not refuse" (171). Frankenstein begins to capitulate and gathers the appropriate female corpses to put together a new monster blend. But midway through, he refuses to continue. Frankenstein argues to himself that the male monster has already murdered once. "*She* might become ten thousand times more malignant than her mate," he speculates, and notes that: "*He* swore to quit the neighborhood of man, but *she* had not; she might refuse to comply with a compact made before her creation" (192). In a sudden urge not (fully) explicable to himself but evident enough to the reader, Frankenstein destroys the uncompleted female: "the remains of the half-finished creature lay scattered on the floor, and I almost felt as if I had mangled the living flesh of a human being" (197). Henceforth, as Veeder notes, Frankenstein is inextricably bound to the monster: "The monster's following him south indicated the tenacity of their male bond, the impossibility of any real union between Promethean and woman."[58]

In each of these pivotal junctures, then, the weakness of character of Victor Frankenstein is opposed to more appealing predilections of the Creature. But Mary Shelley has not given us a simple morality tale; she makes us account equally for the intertwining ways of creature and creator. In one of Victor Frankenstein's more unpleasant moments, for instance, he insinuates that his father is to blame for the horrid turn of events because he had failed to explain to Victor the advantages of modern science over the ancient principles of Agrippa. "It is even possible [if he *had* so explained it], that the train of my ideas would never have received the fatal impulse that led to my ruin" (68). If this tendency in Victor Frankenstein is blamable, so much the more is the Creature's murderous revenge: "I am malicious because I am miserable" (171). So Mary Shelley stresses the ruthless nature in which his first murder victim, "the sweet young William," is dispatched: "I gazed on my victim, and my heart swelled with exultation and hellish triumph: clapping my hands, I exclaimed, 'I, too, can create desolation'" (170). If the Creature—in all justice—can demand of his creator: "How dare you sport thus with life?" (127), he can be said to take on a more ferocious game.

In popular culture, the monster is commonly referred to as "Frankenstein," indicating just how interlinked the actions and characters of the two are perceived to be. Significantly, though, contemporary critics by and large do not join in this same reading; instead of blurring the two, they tend to sympathize wholly with the Creature. Lipking catalogues this collective identification with the "victim": "Late-twentieth-century critics, when they look at Frankenstein's creation, no longer see a Monster, as earlier generations did; they now see a Creature. And other aspects of that creation—for instance, Victor Frankenstein's genius—they do not see at all."[59] In my terms, democratic readers are here bringing to bear on a modern text their own dogma; this includes the aforementioned denial of genius, an unrelenting compassion for the victim, and a propensity to find a single, didactic teaching in favor of the female element. "Mary Shelley's tale of horror is no fantastical ghost story," Mellor concludes, "but rather a profound insight into the probable consequences of 'objective'—gendered—or morally insensitive scientific and technological research."[60] As Shelley's moral becomes thus simplified, it necessarily loses its distinctive modern feature of play with antitheses. When readers offer up final statements on behalf of *Frankenstein,* they are holding on to an idealism that it seems intended to puncture.

Because of Mary Shelley's particularly eventful life, readers are tempted to overdraw her commitment to a feminist agenda. So Moers discerns a distinctly female mythmaking at work as a consequence of Shelley's traumatic and almost-constant pregnancies: "[she was] not a secure mother, for she lost most of the babies soon after they were born; and not a lawful mother, for she was not married—not at least when, at the age of eighteen, Mary Godwin began to write *Frankenstein*. So are monsters born."[61] Such readings are well-intentioned, but have the effect of earmarking the novel in a way that diminishes its hold on the modern consciousness. My view is that *Frankenstein* transcends solely female mythmaking, as the commonplace and the mysterious come together in an inexplicably effective way. The entanglement of masculine and feminine forces is complex and applicable more generally to our construct of the divided self.[62]

Notably, Shelley refuses to tie up the last threads of her tale, for to do so would convey a unipolar conclusion. After the monster flees the scene where his female mate was destroyed, he proceeds to kill the kin of Frankenstein and to pursue his creator to the North Pole, to his death. But having killed off most of her characters, Mary Shelley does not finish off her monster, who remains looming over the globe. In the tradition of Machiavelli and Burke, Mary Shelley devises a myth of an endless quest for the enmeshing of masculine and feminine propensities.

Four

Rousseau/Tutor

ousseau's tutor in *Emile,* and in the sequel *Emile and Sophie, or Solitary Beings,* marks a transitional moment between political communities. In the figure of the tutor, Rousseau looks back appreciatively to the Machiavellian tradition of shifting, opportunistic rhetoric in the service of the ruler of a state, then ultimately turns forward, toward democracy's resistance to ambiguity, and presses for uniformity. The peculiar blend of "Rousseau" and "tutor" that occurs in *Emile* advances the connection drawn in earlier chapters between literary form and political community in the modern age, as well as the dramatic new turn this association has taken since the ancient world of the polis. This literary maneuver evokes the crux of Rousseau's seminal creation, the Great Legislator, that superior intelligence described in the *Social Contract* as having "no affinity with our nature, yet [who knows] it through and through" (162). The fluctuating pedagogical identities of *Emile* are more numerous and complex than is suggested by my "Rousseau/tutor," but that label may in the first instance convey the distance Rousseau travels from the ancients. As is conventional among Rousseau's critics, I use the single terms Rousseau, tutor, or narrator as if it were clear where each identity begins and ends. Unlike others, however, I regard these oscillating roles as highly significant. The Legislator exists in the overlap. The compound voice in *Emile* seems to aim at achieving those qualities of the "original language" Rousseau posits elsewhere that "would persuade without convincing, and depict without demonstrating."[1] This literary construct adds up to the most convincing depiction of the Great Legislator that Rousseau ever produced—someone both "of" and "not of" the world, full of capacities to deceive us, for our own good, and to reveal thereby whatever goodness of nature is still recoverable. The unstable contours of the Great Legislator seem to mirror those of the state. Rousseau's rhetoric, however, will not bear the strains of inconsistency on which Machiavelli thrives. In *Emile* Rousseau addresses instability, approaches balance, and then gives way to the totalitarian temptation, demanding a unipolarity that he himself—as revealed in his sequel to *Emile*—cannot sustain.

Emile was often referred to as a novel. Rousseau calls it a romance (416),[2] in accordance with its coming-of-age narrative: Emile's education is detailed from early childhood to the day he announces to his tutor that his wife is pregnant with their first child. But at every turn, the chronological development of Emile's life seeps into the world of politics. "Let mothers deign to nurse their children," the tutor counsels, "morals will reform themselves, nature's sentiments will be awakened in every heart, the state will be repeopled" (46). From the details of an ordinary boy's education, the readers' eyes are repeatedly pulled away to matters of state. "This ought to be the history of my species," the tutor announces (416). The temptation is ever-present to map the work politically: "The correspondence between Emile and the people extends beyond the immature stage of tutor and legislator, to blossom into a striking parallel between Rousseau's theory of the family and his doctrine of the state."[3] Or Rousseau's conception of history can be seen as implanted in the lives of his character; his abiding concern is how to reinstate the authority of natural desires over against social artifice.

What may appear to be a Rousseauian nostalgia for the ancients is in fact a Machiavellian use of exemplars, to clarify our own situation, particularly regarding the crucial question of male and female.

Whereas the ancient-modern contrast for Rousseau always serves to illuminate weaknesses in his own age, it is not for purposes of restoring old practices that he appeals to the ancients, but rather for the sake of understanding the different possibilities of sexual politics: "the choice between antiquity and modernity . . . is not one between the subjection and ascendancy of women. More properly it is one between two different modes of the ascendancy of women—a covert ascendancy (under which men maintain their masculinity) and an overt ascendancy (under which masculinity is attacked and ultimately obliterated)."[4] In the former case, it is clear that Rousseau *loves* Lucretia: "All the great revolutions [in Rome] came from women. Due to a woman Rome acquired liberty" (390). His undeniable preference is for sharply demarcated spheres for both men and women as in Rome, but using examples from history in the style of Machiavelli, Rousseau transposes an ancient arrangement into a version he would advocate for his own time. Contemporary readers may well take offense when they detect in this democratic-leaning thinking a less-than-full commitment to contemporary democratic requirements, as when it is declared in *Emile* that "woman is made specially to please man" (358). But the charge of misogynism lodged against Rousseau obscures his importance to the significance of male and female in the development of political thought.

The Rousseau/tutor posture may usefully be contrasted to the "classical" position of Aristotle in the *Nicomachean Ethics*, in which the moral educator stakes his teaching on the presentation of himself as a straightforward and honorable man. In his *Ethics*, Aristotle, too, allows his ethical teaching to unfold in chronological stages, as if readers were experiencing their own moral development as the book unfolds. The markers are not as specific as in the case of the imaginary pupil Emile, whose age is noted as he progresses through the four stages of his education.[5] But, like Rousseau, Aristotle incorporates only as much teaching as the student of ethics can handle at each stage, as the student first obeys ethical strictures out of habit, then begins to reason through the virtues, and finally—at best—is persuaded of their right reasoning. Looking back at the *Ethics* after going through these steps, readers must be struck by how Aristotle retains a single voice throughout, from his careful assertion early on regarding the supreme importance of habit (110323–25), to his unexpected but still acceptable distinction in Book 6 between natural and ruling virtue (1144b4), to his assessment that the happiest life is too *serious,* finally, to be composed solely of childish pursuits (1176b34–36): the childlike component is not driven out of the happiest life, but reason is added to it. Aristotle does not patronize immature views, he allows for questioning at the dawn of reason, and he elevates the contemplative life without repudiating his opening moves. The single voice is established as trustworthy on all levels.

Rousseau could not accept the single voice that Aristotle establishes because somewhere beyond the Greek "virtuous circle" exists the authoritative voice of philosophy. That route makes possible the predominance of certain kinds of human beings as educators, those who by nature are proficient in reasoning. But the supervening principle for Rousseau/tutor is that the child must never be thwarted by personal authority but only by physical necessity: "As long as children find resistance only in things and never in wills, they will become neither rebellious nor irascible and will preserve their health better" (66). The only authority that the tutor will invoke is that of brute necessity. The language throughout is of sense, and not reason. Emile, who is to be considered "abstract man" (42), is admittedly an "imaginary pupil" (50) whose solidity is assured by the fact that he is imagined to be just an ordinary boy. Emile is pointedly invoked as of "common mind" (52). When eventually Sophie is brought in to the education as the destined wife of Emile, we are told that if "Emile is no prodigy . . . Sophie is not one either" (393). With this combination of ordinary material and extraordinary teacher, then, Rousseau/tutor presumes to undergird his imaginative venture. The methodology avowed by Rousseau/tutor is "to make a test of his own practice on his pupil. He will soon sense, or the reader will sense for him, whether he follows the progress of childhood and the movement natural to the human heart" (51).

When critics find fault with Rousseau for not supplying a convincing portrait of the Great Legislator, they tend to treat the tutor as a self-contained character, directly analogous to Wolmar of *La Nouvelle Héloïse.*[6] But Rousseau/tutor is a creation of its own order, an unreal mixture of a biographical individual and an imaginative literary construction. In that strange amalgam where the literary figure—now character, now narrator—brushes up against the author of the *Discourses,* the autobiographical impulse does not yet take over. The result is a figure who is haunting, even unearthly: "In reading this work, one will see with what liberality I treat myself" (51). However accidentally Rousseau came to his device, he recognized and developed its full potential.[7] The grounding of the teaching in *Emile* takes a wholly new path, but given the boundless liberties that are taken in the constructing of Rousseau/tutor, it is no small feat on his part to keep it rooted. The tutor is to be endowed with all of the qualities needed to make a man, and with him, we "suppose this marvel found" (50). That inexplicable and creative force apparently will justify itself according to its progeny.

The unusual character development gives Rousseau a silencing mechanism in regard to his reader, as it precludes the space for any kind of combative reactions. Rousseau has a way of anticipating all criticism of the tutor's position and throwing it back upon the reader's inadequacy, as in: "I proposed to say in this book all that can be done and to leave to the reader the choice—among the good things I may have said—of those that are within his reach" (406). The narrative device adopted by Rousseau/tutor envelops the reader in what is by no means a pleasant experience ["If you are only a pedant, it is not worth the effort to read me" (118)]. This posture has been nicely described as Rousseau challenging the reader "to a moral duel" whenever there is a doubt about their complete identity of vision and feeling.[8] As he exercises oversight over the reader, the historical touches are of crucial importance. The truth claims work on several different levels. "Jean-Jacques" steps in several times as the named tutor (99, 111, 181) and anticipates that role familiar from Rousseau's final works. Several of Rousseau's major works are cross-referenced or incorporated, resulting in a rhetorical achievement that presages the destabilizing discourses of the modern and postmodern world.[9] And with this strategy of mixing up autobiographical elements with the literary persona, Rousseau appropriates the reader in a wholesale way. He may bully the recalcitrant ["Is it my fault if you, always the dupes of appearance, take it for reality?" (227)] or appeal to a higher ground ["I show from afar—for I also do not want to say everything—the roads deviating from the right one in order that one may learn to avoid them" (249)], but he never fails to position himself offensively in relation to his reader. One senses in Rousseau/tutor the "recourse to authority of a different order, which can compel without violence and persuade without convincing" (*Social Contract,* 164). His voice reaches all.

To all appearances, the most thoroughgoing rule by the tutor is no more than the everyday resistance of things. The tutor's conspiratorial mode of teaching is acceptable, even necessary, but it must be masked: "it is of the most extreme importance that the child not perceive the intention to distract him, and that he enjoy himself without believing that one is thinking of him" (69). The warnings against being caught are ubiquitous: "A single proved lie told by the master to the child would ruin forever the whole fruit of the education" (216).[10] In the process, Rousseau is redefining "deception" such that the crucial distinction is, as Gourevitch notes, not fact/fiction, but fiction/lie: "Only deceptions that distort our moral perceptions and judgments are, strictly speaking, lies."[11] Rousseau/tutor and the pupil Emile provide guidelines for comprehending the Great Legislator's role *vis-à-vis* "The People" and "the people."[12]

If the tutor's work is rightly described as a process of clearing away the corruptions of society [he preaches "a difficult art . . . that of governing without precepts and doing everything by doing nothing" (119)], it is also an aggressive reforming of "nature" which has definite repercussions regarding male and female roles. Nature is improved (not merely conformed to, or obeyed) when the spheres are differentiated to the extreme.[13] Rousseau's argument for the complementarity between the sexes is a self-consciously constructed one: he is concerned with evoking images of male and female nature to which Emile, but especially Sophie—and his female readers—will respond. As the agents of men's socialization, women are the targets of this education; as the first sentence announces: "This collection of reflections and observations . . . was begun to gratify a good mother who knows how to think" (33). Sophie's approbation must be secured, not commanded. Methodically and deliberately, the tutor in *Emile* turns his pupil away from "love of wisdom" to "love of Sophie":

"Rousseau solves by love of women the problem Plato solved by love of wisdom, philo-Sophie in the place of philosophy."[14]

Since Rousseau is relatively explicit in his prescriptions regarding male and female roles through his characters Emile and Sophie, the allegorical nature of *Emile* is a matter of some controversy. As a couple, Emile and Sophie appall many contemporary readers because their sharply differentiated roles seem whimsical and unfairly oriented toward Emile. Sophie is specifically rendered to be the right woman for Emile, and the tutor makes assorted remarks about her education that offend readers today, such as "In fact, almost all little girls learn to read and write with repugnance. But as for holding a needle, that they always learn gladly" (368). Such statements understandably have caused readers to conclude that Rousseau's sharp differentiation between the sexes relegates women to the secondary, inferior role and, accordingly, to lesser, supportive-only functions. Similarly, such an approach has been taken to justify the conclusion that Rousseau is nostalgic for the supposedly male-dominated world of the ancients.[15]

The political urgency of these interpretations is striking—and they are not the less urgent for being unsubstantiated. None accounts adequately for the position of the tutor. To pursue a truly effective allegorical reading of *Emile* means getting beyond perceived slights against Sophie and accounting for the rule of the tutor.[16] It cannot be denied, for instance, that Emile is more fully manipulated than Sophie; after all, it is he who is under surveillance from birth to adulthood. All authority lies in the tutor's hands, "this rare mortal . . . this marvel" (50). The assumption of such extraordinary powers is unnerving: "A governor! O what a sublime soul . . . in truth, to make a man, one must be either a father or more than a man oneself" (49–50). The single being who is parent to Emile often sounds desirous of living *for* him "In making this useful quest for you, I [make] it for both of us in common" (442); his belief is that "you ought to be wholly involved with the child—observing him, spying on him without letup and without appearing to do so, sensing ahead of time all his sentiments and forestalling those he ought not to have" (189). Rousseau/tutor, narrator, pupil, and, significantly, Sophie as well, become one inseparable, inalienable, indivisible entirety, a vision of perfectible mankind made whole: The People, the General Will, the Law and the Legislator undifferentiated and unassailable.[17] In the marriage of Emile and Sophie, Rousseau/tutor has created the conditions for redressing the personal, social, and political balance. But in his revolutionary ardor to pursue the perfectibility of man, Rousseau insists that all be drawn into a totality that inevitably must destroy balance.

The tutor's ability to comprehend both Emile and Sophie seems to be because he *contains* the same assemblage of countervailing forces that each gender represents. On the one side, there is the detached, but piercing sight of a truly free man, who "wants only what he can do and does what he pleases" (84); on the other, the "empire of gentleness, skill, and obligingness" (408). The tutor is both in one.[18] Throughout the work, the failings of Emile and Sophie illuminate his exceptional standing: Emile and Sophie are formed as highly gendered beings, at the same time that Rousseau/tutor—and Emile and Sophie as comprehended by and within him—appears to be *beyond* gender. At the close of the work, this is brought out with force when, Emile and Sophie married at last, the tutor describes his own ecstasy: "How many times, as I contemplate my work in them, I feel myself seized by a rapture that makes my heart palpitate! How many times I join their hands in mine while blessing providence and sighing ardently!" (480). It is, as Starobinski charges, a *strange* ecstasy,[19] and, for better or worse, it is one that Rousseau could not leave in place, in keeping with his stress on the impossibility of taking on in any sustained way the philosophic voice of authority. Rousseau is no more an optimist in the end than Machiavelli. "I show the goal that must be set; I do not say that it can be reached" (95). It is an ancient insight that human nature is inadequate to receive the full imprint of philosophic ideas, but it is a modern amendment to charge the unsuitability of philosophy for eliciting natural goodness. Rousseau's rhetoric disallows such comforting stories as *Emile* seems to be.

In Rousseau's *Emile* we confront some familiar modern features, for there the author behind the scenes depicts a capricious world in which the human condition may be ameliorated through its harsh rhetorical education. The combination of the tutor's despotic reach over Emile's life and the secret machinations brought to bear on Emile's education takes to a new level the realism of modern politics.

But what is of even more interest here is how Rousseau retracts from the ending he gives in *Emile* in his sequel. *The Solitary Ones* is of high interest not because of what happens to the lead male and female characters—the adultery of Sophie or the adventures of Emile—but because of Rousseau's treatment of the tutor, for that gets to the heart of the rhetoric being employed.

The mildly critical impulse that Plato exhibited towards Socrates is nothing next to Rousseau's subversion of *his* exceptional character, the tutor. We have seen that Socrates was portrayed so realistically by Plato as to seem to become a historically identifiable figure in the dialogues. Even if his historicity is an illusion, his endurance as a character is real enough. This allows Plato to "correct" Socratic ways without marring the image. Plato invites a reaction from interlocutors in the first instance, but from readers in the end. Socrates "bit hard into the individual man," Kierkegaard writes, "continually forcing him and irritating him with his 'universal.' He was a gadfly who provoked people by means of the individual's passion, not allowing him to admire indolently and effeminately, but demanding his self of him."[20] Socrates stood *for* something so assuredly that he got himself killed; whereas Rousseau/tutor comes to sight as a cause—but what that cause *is* is never a matter of consensus. It always awaits a new reading: *Emile* is *never* the contained literary artifact that a Platonic dialogue is.

In his sequel, Rousseau makes the tutor the target of Emile's righteous indignation, accused of precipitating his pupil's ruin: "you loved us, you delighted in us, and you abandoned us! Had you not left, I would still be happy" (200). By this abandonment, Emile cries, "you have caused me more misfortune than any good you had ever done in my entire life."[21] We see a fascinating and powerful literary construct done in by its own author, as Rousseau turns on "genius," in the name of the "victim." To drive Rousseau's bitter turn even further, the sequel recounts the breakdown of that most securely founded of marriages, through a series of events leading to Sophie's adultery and pregnancy.[22] The rhetorician of Rousseau/tutor is subjected to Rousseau's own ressentiment; the allure of uniformity, in which balance is subsumed, proves deadly and produces chaos. The democratic political community lies just around the corner.

3
Democratic America

Five

Surveying Tocqueville

Turning to the contemporary scene of democratic America, we leave behind the edifying stories of the polis and the rhetoric in correlation with the state. The democratic literary form is designated here as "the survey," to indicate that it is as straightforward and "natural" as democracy itself. Tocqueville stands as the preeminent spokesman, because of his deep insights into the situation confronting the democratic writer and his prescience concerning the likely pitfalls ahead. Moreover, Tocqueville is of interest because he does not completely escape these pitfalls himself, for all he penetrates their causes; he is an illuminating example of both "warner" and "casualty" of democracy. The challenge he perceives in respect to balance and political community is unprecedented, and, arguably, it is the most forbidding instance ever faced. If the ancient Greek writers could compensate in their writings for an overvaluation of the public life of the polis, and if the moderns could enforce an equilibrium in their aggressive new constructs, the democratic writer has to struggle merely to suggest the relevance of former times when political thinking reflected two distinct poles of existence. Democracy endorses uniformity, and the survey tells it as it is.

Tocqueville sees democracy as a mighty force, wholly new in its contemporary form, wholly irresistible, sweeping all rivals away, and plunging headlong down a road on which the future is now and the past scarcely more than a swiftly evaporating memory. Democracy is not self-contained in the way of other regimes, for its "basic fact," equality of conditions, "extends far beyond political mores and laws, exercising dominion over civil society as much as over the government" (9). Tocqueville regards equality as a passion stirred relentlessly by the unprecedented disorders of presentism and conformity in the life of the mind. With the advent of democracy, time itself threatens to split asunder: "Have all ages been like ours? And have men always dwelt in a world in which nothing is connected?" (17). The present age is dissociated from all that preceded it: "A new political science is needed for a world itself quite new" (12).

With America's emergence on the world scene, Tocqueville judges, democracy becomes the only choice among regimes. Authoritarian governments would not soon disappear, but a turning point had been reached. From now on, people would suffer an aristocratic regime only when coerced: "An aristocracy cannot last unless it is founded on an accepted principle of inequality, legalized in advance, and introduced into the family as well as into the rest of society—all things so violently repugnant to natural equity that only constraint will make men submit to them" (399). Thus aristocracy was perceived to be a concoction, a contrivance of a special class or interest. Democracy was no longer one option among several choices of forms of governance, but part of Nature itself—and so natural, general, and universal in appeal and application.[1] Set next to universalist democracy, the conventions of aristocracy are repugnant to mankind. Once the love for, and recognition of, the potential for equality takes hold, democracy becomes the sole option for governance. Tocqueville recognizes that democracy's drive for equality cannot be realized in fact, "for among a great people there will always be some very poor and some very rich citizens" (635).[2] But the poor will be relatively few, and the rich will make themselves indistinguishable from the mass of citizens in dress, mannerisms, and opinions. It is democracy's potential for equality that has caused it to drive all contenders from the field.

The phenomenon that Tocqueville describes unsettles him; democracy may be natural, resistless, and inevitable, but it is far from all salutary. To make this clear, Tocqueville structures *Democracy in America* through the dichotomy of aristocracy and democracy. He initiates thereby the novel form of the survey, which is characterized by detailed attention to and contrasts of features of governance, historical points of departure, intellectual movements, sentiments, mores, and attributes of the political society. In doing so, Tocqueville is reminding his readers that when they embraced democracy, they were choosing individual well-being over nobility: "if in your view the main object of government is not to achieve the greatest strength or glory for the nation as a whole but to provide for every individual therein the utmost well-being . . . then it is good . . . to establish a democratic government" (245). He sets out the opposition that most clarifies. No detail is too small and no observation without weight in the recounting of "the gradual and measured advance of equality" (12) and the simultaneous withdrawal of the aristocratic world.

Tocqueville uses an exaggerated demarcation as an effective way of keeping the contrasts salient between the old and new worlds. The constant repetition of now aristocracy, now democracy, contributes to that effect: "Aristocracies produce a few great pictures, democracies a multitude of little ones" (468). With the contrast set firmly before his readers, Tocqueville seeks inventive ways to compensate for losses: "Thus the spread of equality over the earth dries up the old springs of poetry. We must try to show how other springs are revealed" (484). More generally, the sheer weight of the evidence that comes out of this oppositional mode supports Tocqueville's deductions about what is at stake in the emergence of egalitarianism: "I fear that the mind may keep folding itself up in a narrower compass forever without producing new ideas, that men will wear themselves out in trivial, lonely, futile activity, and that for all its constant agitation humanity will make no advance" (645). This adds up to a call for re-energized thinking, as Tocqueville advocates an imaginative understanding for democrats that is capable of holding in balance inclinations that are essentially in conflict. He conjures up the old Aristotelian move of setting out two extremes in order to cultivate a superior intermediary.

Thus two actors—aristocracy and democracy—repeatedly take the stage when the script calls for only one. Democracy always prevails. The aristocracy of Tocqueville's depiction is doomed. It is superfluous and difficult to justify: "It is natural to suppose that not the particular prosperity of the few, but the greater well-being of all, is most pleasing in the sight of the Creator and Preserver of men. . . . Equality may be less elevated, but it is more just" (704). Aristocracy's interest lies solely in its ability to shed light on democracy; it is in its final role, and it is a supporting one. And yet Tocqueville insists on its presence, and along the way he implicates his readers in the same act of accommodating the larger picture. It is a way of thinking that does not come automatically to democrats, whose passion is for unity (439), whose inclination is to accept the ready-made product of public opinion (436), and whose wish is to be unencumbered of their past (508).

Tocqueville's critical corrective to what he sees as democracy's impending disaster is history. Since in his view democracy is an "irresistible revolution advancing century by century over every obstacle" (12), he hopes to ward off its most unsettling consequences. He fears that in a democracy, the population will fall into a stupor unless the memories of the citizenry are activated continuously. Like "dogs in the sun,"[3] democrats are heedless of all that passes by, for as long as their dozing is undisturbed. Tocqueville aims to disturb, but also to instruct in his example of the ways to remembrance. His hope is to deepen the historical consciousness of the democrat.[4] Without history, the democrat is unhinged from all moorings; with remembrance of the past comes the possibility of informed direction. Tocqueville appreciates the need of democrats to see a world not yet in the grip of the egalitarian drive, where the passion for well-being is checked and the impulse for demanding one's due is discouraged. But in the most melancholic moments of *Democracy in America,* he seems to despair of the possibility of American democracy taking any guidance: "The past throws no light on the future, and the spirit of man walks through the night" (703). Nevertheless, Tocqueville makes the supreme effort to conduct his readers through disconnected times by summoning democrats to recollect their past, a past which threatens always to slip from their sight. Tocqueville does not seek to return to, or to restore the past; he does not seek to undermine or undo the present democratic reality. His objective is to demonstrate that without awareness of and attention to the past, democracy becomes dangerously untethered: "Not only does democracy make men forget their ancestors but also clouds their view of their descendants and isolates them from their contemporaries" (508). In compelling snapshots, then, Tocqueville captures the ways of aristocracies over against the ways of democracies. The survey at its best is in touch with ordinary readers without either patronizing them or assuming "the voice of the people." *Democracy in America* is not difficult to understand and is accessible to all; it needs no elaborate explication. It is clear and simple and labeled to the extreme; no one has to untangle it. If Tocqueville titles a chapter "Why American National Pride has a more Restless and Quarrelsome Character than that of the English," readers know what to expect. The author scarcely needs to be heeded at all, for the data seems to gather by itself and to be self-interrogating. For all of his interest in applying his experiences to the benefit of his native France ["I sought (in America) lessons from which we might profit" (18)], Tocqueville self-consciously breaks ties to an earlier world and assumes the posture of a democrat: self-standing and unattached. Tocqueville's survey is both a description of democracy and an effort to point out and try to repair its grave weaknesses.

Tocqueville's effort to highlight the dichotomy between aristocracy and democracy is mirrored in other, less successful contrasts, however. When he turns to perhaps the most distinctive feature of America's own past, its religious tradition, he examines its unique coexistence of the spirit of religion and the spirit of freedom. They are, Tocqueville declares, "perfectly distinct elements which elsewhere have often been at war with one another but which in America it was somehow possible to incorporate into each other, forming a marvelous combination" (46–47). To find ways to sustain that "marvelous combination" becomes Tocqueville's project, yet he cannot maintain his initial exuberance; the memory he seeks to retrieve thins almost beyond reach by the time he concludes his work. Early in Volume One, Tocqueville holds out the hope that the Puritan point of departure will continue to constrain American democrats in their drive for individual independence, but this is before he discerns some of the more extreme tendencies at work in an egalitarian world, including the relentless tendency toward centralization (394). Just five years later writing in Volume Two, Tocqueville is unnerved by the inclination of American democrats toward pantheism, a view of God which extends to all of being and thereby diminishes each individual's sense of accountability to a higher authority. The concept of unity being an "obsession" for the democrat, Tocqueville remarks: "Not content with the discovery that there is nothing in the world but one creation and one Creator, he is still embarrassed by this primary division of things and seeks to expand and simplify his conception by including God and the universe in one great whole" (451). No doubt it was inevitable that the democratic passion for unity would incorporate even religion. "The final achievement of the democratic passion for likeness or unity would thus consist in the obliteration of the only remaining representative of qualitative differentiation, and thus the last ground of human individuality: God."[5]

But because religion for Tocqueville is essential to the thriving of democracy, he clings to a vision represented by the Puritan point of departure. The substance of the original Puritan beliefs is largely immaterial for him ["these ridiculous and tyrannical laws were not imposed from outside—they were voted by the free agreement of all the interested parties themselves"[6] (43)], for it is the form of thinking that is at issue. This is not a simple longing to recreate a situation in the past, then, but an effort to prevent a sameness of views from taking hold in the present. With the appearance of pantheistic beliefs among Americans, Tocqueville worries that democracy will begin to blur into a state of mind rather than a regime; once the egalitarian passion takes on its own momentum, that state of mind resists anything in the way of its immediate claims. Tocqueville reels at the image of the human mind so closed in upon itself, trapped in the locked prison of the present, with no window on the past and no sense of a future. The mentality that Tocqueville aims to recapture is one that balances a strong sense of self and self-direction in the political arena with a humility about the place of mankind in the natural world. The thought is that democrats are mortal, too, and might be brought to apprehend that there are limits to the creed of self-subsistence. He insistently presses the issue: "And what can be done with a people master of itself if it is not subject to God?" (294). Occasions for spirituality are to be preserved at any cost: "Thus, then, when any religion has taken deep root in a democracy, be very careful not to shake it, but rather guard it as the most precious heritage from aristocratic times" (544). Tocqueville urges this even at the risk of appearing to offer pragmatic advice to religious authorities about how to retain their voice in democracy (445). The strategy is close to desperate: "I think that the only effective means which governments can use to make the doctrine of the immortality of the soul respected is daily to act as if they believed it themselves" (546). And the marvelous combination slips away.

Tocqueville cannot be expected to provide the means for preserving the spirit of religion in a disenchanted age, of course. But it is an interesting case for comparative purposes, for our previous writers have had to confront the same elemental concern. The treatment of religion in our polis story ranges from Zeus to *nous,* making generalization difficult, but it may be said fairly that they all combine claims for the indispensability of a sense of the sacred with a delicacy in prescribing how this should be manifested in particular cities. Odysseus hears Zeus's clap of thunder and puts away his warrior gear; the Athenians of the Peloponnesian War have lost this sense of hearing, inspiring Thucydides to end his account with the sly image of the temple of Artemis. Meanwhile Aristotle announces that "the superintendence connected with the divine" is "fifth, and first" of the tasks the city requires (*Pol.* 1328b11–12)—and leaves it to the reader to puzzle out why. Machiavelli and Rousseau are sly but not delicate: Machiavelli rewrites Biblical stories to make them adequate to the brutal reality of politics (his David is armed with a knife against Goliath[7]) and Rousseau asserts as openly that the church must be subsumed under the state (*Soc. Con.*, 220–227), and gives us in the Savoyard Vicar an instance of a purely civil profession of faith (*Emile,* 266–313). Next to these alternatively subtle and brazen accounts, Tocqueville's musings on religion appear to be fatally chained to a historical moment, the Puritan point of departure. That moment having lost its resonance, he is left grasping at air. This suggests to us the inadequacy of a literary form averse to more creative constructions.[8]

If anything, Tocqueville on gender meets with *more* democratic resistance than Tocqueville on the spirit of religion. Kerber concludes that "it is now long past time to dispose of Tocqueville's observations on the condition of American women."[9] He is said to have been so much a product of his times as to neglect what should be foregrounded: "the issue of justice or injustice in the gendered family itself."[10] The sense is that with female roles in the family as with the spirit of religion, Tocqueville is bent on defending inherited and unwarranted hierarchies, but that in this case, he does so at the expense of women's dignity of self and freedom of movement. It is as if he were applauding the sacrifices of half the population for the greater good of the whole: "[American women] seem to take pride in the free relinquishment of their will, and it is their boast to bear the yoke themselves rather than to escape from it" (602). Elshtain concludes that the fact that American equal regard for women did not lead to social or political equality was "glossed over [by Tocqueville] or lost in the midst of his praise for America's success in raising the moral and intellectual level of women."[11]

The pejorative reading is difficult to sustain, however, as Tocqueville's description of American women is not only centered on their dignity, but culminates in a claim for their superiority: "if anyone asks me what I think the chief cause of the extraordinary prosperity and growing power of this nation, I should answer that it is due to the superiority of their women" (603). He describes how Americans "have carefully separated the functions of man and of woman so that the great work of society may be better performed" (601). He neither denies the fundamental equality of the sexes nor promotes the American division of labor as an equitable one. He detects in it the influence of both the Puritan point of departure and the habits of an industrial nation which "demand much abnegation on the women's part and a continual sacrifice of pleasure for the sake of business" (592). He has noted that the Puritans have been known to pass "ridiculous and tyrannical laws." His interest is in speculating about the possible consequences of these inequities, not in perpetuating the American domestic arrangements. And it should go without saying that Tocqueville cherished no illusions about the staying power of the model of America that he describes (and does not prescribe). Few authors believed with more urgency that it is impossible to contain the spirit of egalitarianism.

As a result of the drive for uniformity that characterizes egalitarian times, democrats according to Tocqueville seem especially prone to blurring the line between their political or self-creating dimension and their natural or created one. His provocative suggestion is that the act of separating male and female spheres could be in the service of intellectual liberty for its chastening effect on the dominant principle of democracy. Morton rightly notes that "while the principle of 'self-interest rightly understood' is the foundation of the male education, the female education takes its bearings from sterner notions of virtue and self-discipline reminiscent of a pre-democratic era."[12] Tocqueville describes the unusual sight of the self-sacrificing American female in which a liberated youth is followed by a confined and circumscribed adulthood; this rebuke to democratic claims of homogeneity has the highest political significance for him, and he stands behind the young American wives for choosing to follow a path out of the public domain; "sad and resolute" (594), they have more than a little in common with his own commitments.

Tocqueville finds such potential in women as educators of democracy among other reasons because they are the custodians of mores: "There have never been free societies without mores, and . . . it is woman who shapes these mores. Therefore everything which has a bearing on the status of women, their habits, and their thoughts is, in my view, of great political importance" (590). As Winthrop notes, women are, like the clergy, the only ones in a position to challenge the excesses of American democracy (291).[13] Religion informs mores, mores underlie laws, laws protect freedom—and freedom is needed to offset the evils of unchecked egalitarianism. Thus women have the significant role in supporting the foremost foundation of liberty. The consequence of most interest to Tocqueville concerning the relations between American men and women is that a kind of thinking is encouraged which effectively contravenes the democratic passion for uniformity. He charts another inroad for challenging the monolithic world view of the democrat, with the differences between the male and female worlds serving as the ground for this enterprise, where an almost limitless self-determination is tempered by a realm of gratuitous human attachments.

Yet in the event, the dichotomies of Tocqueville's male-female spheres of action remain unconvincing. The poor transmission of these passages results not from misogynism, however, but from a literary form which cannot sustain his ambitions to counter the homogenizing tendencies of democracy on gender.[14] His style is too imbued with the characteristics of democracy to achieve what he wants to achieve, which is something akin to Rousseau's project in *Emile*. But he provides neither the novelty of a Sophie (or Lucrezia), nor the underdetermined description of Aristotle's "matters that belong to a man's sphere" or "matters suited to a woman" (*NE* 1160b34–35). His orientation again is wholly historical, and a very fragile moment at that: the example of early American households with their strictly demarcated gender roles, where "both are required to keep in step, but along paths that are never the same" (601). He has harsh words for those who would intensify that democratic tendency to regard men and women as "not equal only, but actually similar. They would attribute the same functions to both, impose the same duties, and grant the same rights; they would have them share everything— work, pleasure, public affairs" (601). Those words have lost their sting, and to judge from his critical reception on this topic, Tocqueville comes across as merely nostalgic, not even searing enough to be dangerous. He elicits little of the attention—positive or negative— that Rousseau does, for instance, with *Emile*.

Tocqueville had his reasons for drawing back from the kinds of writing he encountered among the Philosophes. Recognizing (with dismay) the political influence of the literary men of eighteenth-century France,[15] Tocqueville resigns himself to the necessity of constructing a reductionist model: "Generally speaking, it is only simple conceptions which take hold of a people's mind. A false but clear and precise idea always has more power in the world than one which is true but complex" (164). Perhaps he assumed his only hope in reforming democratic tendencies was in promoting simple dichotomies, which, unlike the constructions of the Philosophes, at least had the merit of connecting with actual experience.[16] A disadvantage is that such representations may slip into nostalgic portraits. Tocqueville occasionally exacerbates this effect with maudlin imagery: "Carried away by a rapid current, we obstinately keep our eyes fixed on the ruins still in sight on the bank, while the stream whirls us backward-facing toward the abyss" (13). This is sure to try the patience of democrats, who do not extol the ruins of the past and find ample occasion to busy themselves with projects of the present. Indeed, the binary structure of *Democracy in America* has the deleterious if unintentional effect of highlighting the distance between the extremes in need of balance.

In his habit of trafficking in plain matters of fact, with inescapable conclusions, Tocqueville limits his positive possibilities. He begins his section on the democratic effects on the family, for instance, with the disclaimer that he is "not trying to discover new truths, but to show how known facts have a bearing on [his] subject" (585). His thesis that democracy softens natural relations is supported, as usual, with ground-level evidence ["A perusal of the family correspondence surviving from aristocratic ages is enough to illustrate the difference between the two social states" (588)]. He summarizes the lesson learned, in further testimony to its unequivocal nature: "I may be able to sum up in one phrase the whole sense of this chapter and of several others that preceded it. Democracy loosens social ties, but it tightens natural ones. At the same time as it separates citizens, it brings kindred closer together" (589). There is a finality to all such summaries.

The culmination of Tocqueville's remarks on democracy and the family comes with his chapter "How the American Views the Equality of the Sexes," and here, too, there are repeated emphases on clarity. "But in this [subject of the equality of the sexes,] I need more than ever to make myself clearly understood," he cautions (600), and then remarks that "it is easy to see that the sort of equality forced on both sexes degrades them both" (601). However, the topic is the *American* view of equality, not Tocqueville's, and these Americans of his are unusually reflective on this topic: "In America, more than anywhere else in the world, care has been taken constantly to trace clearly distinct spheres of action for the two sexes" (601). There is no denying the singular nature of the passages to follow, and Tocqueville invites attack by presenting his normally unphilosophic Americans (429–433) deep in thought about the beneficent properties of Nature: "[Americans] think that nature, which created such great differences between the physical and moral constitution of men and women, clearly intended to give their diverse faculties a diverse employment; and they consider that progress consists not in making dissimilar creatures do roughly the same things but in giving both a chance to do their job as well as possible" (601).

The authorial intrusion is noteworthy, as is the care Tocqueville takes not to conflate *his* voice with that of the Americans he features. No doubt Tocqueville attributes to his Americans beliefs that they were unlikely to articulate, on relations that were unlikely to persist, in order to underline the enduring significance of this matter for the democratic regime. But the transparency of the American view as it is asserted and reasserted seems not to have had the effect intended.

Democracy prides itself on its openness and clarity, and these are qualities that penetrate Tocqueville's literary style, to a fault. He worried specifically that a lack of clarity would typify democratic literature, since writers increasingly would show contempt for forms and reject the claims of tradition ["Authors will strive to astonish" (474)]. His counterstrategy is to elicit the plain historical meaning through recurrent contrasts ["So in aristocratic ages the emphasis is on doing things as well as possible, not as quickly or as cheaply as one can. In contrast, when every profession is open to all. . . ." (465)]. His form is *dichotomous,* as he keeps aristocrats and democrats before him in the hopes of educating both, and *neutral,* as he claims not to judge whether democracy's spread is "profitable or prejudicial for mankind" (18). This contributes to Tocqueville's reputation as a fairminded analyst, but it also may well deflate more constructive urges in his writing as the intellectual constraints of his time come across as relentless.

The summary of Tocqueville on literature could stand for his overall attitude about the fate of democracy in America. What if anything could be done to check democracy's headlong career toward chaos? Nothing, if form, purpose, clarity, and experience were all swept out by a vast democratic tide. Tocqueville dreads most that democratic writers will encourage the rampant presentism of Americans. To him it was dismaying that democrats "do not resemble their own fathers, [that] they themselves are changing every moment" (473). His apprehension about the prospects of a vital literature developing in democratic America stems from a number of conditions which discourage intellectual pursuits, including the ubiquitous expression of the desire for comfort on the part of Americans, and the unrelenting industry required to procure it. Both encourage "a taste for the useful more than the love of beauty" (465). In 1840, when Tocqueville published his ruminations about the influence of democracy on intellectual life in the United States, he conjured up the image of individuals "narrowly shut up" in themselves, from which position they "[make] the pretension to judge the world" (430). He goes on to predict that "this turn of mind soon leads them to a scorn of forms, which they take as useless, hampering veils put between them and truth" (430). Tocqueville wonders then what might serve as the source of poetic inspiration, and concludes that such sources will range from trivial items from "the actual, visible world" (483) to the oversized pictures of nations acting as single citizens, as a consequence of ready-made notions of one vast democracy (486). Finally, Tocqueville is alarmed at the possibility of writers in a democratic age becoming altogether disconnected from the actual world, indulging in "too many immense, incoherent images, overdrawn descriptions, bizarre effects, and a whole fantastic breed of brainchildren who will make one long for the real world" (489).

Here Tocqueville seems to overstate the need for unambiguous language, as he is uncharacteristically closed-minded on the subject. Regarding the democratic innovation of giving words double meanings, Tocqueville asserts that "writers hardly ever appear to stick to a single thought, but always seem to envisage a group of ideas," pronouncing this "an annoying feature of democracy." He goes on to assert "you cannot have a good language without clear terms" (480). But clear terms might also be implicated in the extremes of an untutored democracy, one that celebrates only spontaneity and the immediacy of talk. There are reasons to be more wary than Tocqueville was of writing that retains the surface dimension of ordinary speech, and to search for the means to maintain a distance from the everyday. Significantly, it was unimaginable to Tocqueville that in

America literary genius was soon to arise ("Tocqueville simply did not bank on anyone like Emerson occurring"[17]). It might be true that the richness of American literature comes about precisely through the attentiveness of its writers to how clear terms may obstruct and *not* clarify, as in the Emersonian-pragmatic tradition that Poirier describes: "language, if it is to represent the flow of individual experience, ceases to be an instrument of clarification or of clarity and, instead, becomes the instrument of a saving uncertainty and vagueness."[18]

In the end, the unparalleled brilliance of *Democracy in America* as an analysis and depiction of its titular subject cannot overcome the reality of Tocqueville's failure to solve the problem he apprehends in his work. If it is true that the test of a powerful culture is the extent to which it shapes each and every endeavor under its sway, then *Democracy in America* is a tribute to the force of democracy itself. For Tocqueville adapts to the reigning egalitarian spirit in his writing style. The question remains about whether democratic writers can call forth a thoughtful response in the reader, allowing for more interpretation than does the dualistic writing of Tocqueville. At its least successful, Tocqueville's style binds him to the back-and-forth litany of lost causes (public over private, materialistic over spiritual, democratic over aristocratic) and comes across in the main as a series of increasingly grim assertions of fact. It seems possible to answer him constructively on one important front: the possibilities for new democratic forms to take hold which invite and do not impose thinking. This would contribute significantly to inspire more hopeful remedies for democratic ills. The survey may tell it "as it is," but democrats might benefit more from a literary form that would suggest "what might be."

Six

Gertrude Stein's Socrates

At first glance, Tocqueville's famous predictive powers would seem to have forecast accurately a Gertrude Stein as the exemplar of American democracy's baneful effect on literature: presentist, insidiously weakening any and all stays against incoherence and chaos, overbearing in its ambition to encompass the masses of people. But Gertrude Stein, in *The Autobiography of Alice B. Toklas,* engages past and present, masculine and feminine, speaking and writing into new perspective and balance. In doing so she takes on a corrective role for democracy in the way that Plato's Socrates did for the polis and Rousseau/tutor did for the state. As we find in Plato's "Socrates" a revolutionary effort to transform a warrior culture into a civic culture, so we may also detect in Gertrude Stein's "Gertrude Stein" an attempt to set forth precepts for balancing a political system that strains ceaselessly against balance.

Miss Stein Replies (to Alexis)

In her early writings every degenerative aspect Tocqueville catalogues emerges in Stein's work, as she shows signs of seeking the indiscriminate novelty that Tocqueville set out in *Democracy in*

America. She celebrates the American way "not to need that generations are existing."[1] She announces virtually as a first principle her
efforts at "making what I know come out as I know it, come out not as
remembering" (*LIA*, 181). The "business of Art" as she describes it is
"to live in the actual present, that is the complete actual present"
(*LIA*, 104–105). Inherited forms *were* conceived by her as "useless,
hampering veils" between the writer and the truth. To her mind, even
the basic elements of grammar needed to be rethought. Stein held to
this stance throughout her life, in works which range from her epic
American history to poetry and plays to operas and children's books.
In the early work *The Making of Americans,* she attempts nothing
less than to describe everything, to "finally describe really describe
every kind of human being that ever was or is or would be living"
(*LIA*, 142), and this even as she drew the characters from her own
past. "Everyone is a real one to me, everyone is like some one else
to me."[2]

Quite apart from her grammatical innovations, the early Stein
aims for a history without action and characters without identities,
in a time sequence without definition. In one of many elaborations of
the "continuous present," she experiments in *The Making of Americans* with dehumanized referents ("such a one") in combination with
a series of more or less rhythmical gerunds in an attempt to suspend
the influence and closure of historical time. Her verbs are ordinary,
her sentences anything but: "Sometime it takes many years of knowing some one before the repeating in that one comes to be a clear
history of such a one. Sometimes many years of knowing some one
pass before repeating of all being in such a one comes out clearly from
them, makes a completed understanding of them by some one listening, watching, hearing all the repeating coming out from such a one"
(*MOA*, 292). Leon Katz identifies in this work the emergence of two
problems that long preoccupy Stein—dissociation and anonymity:
"the conscious feeling of dissociation from the cosmos (in her phrase,
the loss of the 'feeling of everlastingness') and that contemporary
description of men as bundles of 'factors' and causative patterns
which leads to a loss of one's sense of uniqueness (in her phrase, that
'each one is one')."[3]

If consistent intentions can be traced in Stein's writings across her lifetime, however, her literary forms continue to change radically. Stein maintained that *The Making of Americans* put her in the company of Marcel Proust (*Remembrance of Things Past*) and James Joyce (*Ulysses*) ["the three . . . important things written in this generation" (*LIA*, 184)]; she never stopped grappling with challenges that emerged in the writing of that work. And though *The Making of Americans* drew more memorable attacks than critical acclaim, she persisted in thinking the project a sound one; a generation later she acknowledges that "now I am trying to do it again to say everything about everything."[4] She immediately left behind the striking features of the continuous present in *The Making of Americans* to experiment anew in *Tender Buttons*. There she sought to represent the ordinary in a fresh way by extracting from objects any of their customary associations, to objectify her perceptions alone. The results are uneven, and always startling: "A dog"—"A little monkey goes like a donkey that means to say that means to say that more sighs last goes. Leave with it. A little monkey goes like a donkey." Bridgman calls *Tender Buttons* her most "original and cohesive work"—if also "unusually resistant to interpretation."[5] Soon afterwards, Stein undertook portraits in which she attempted to convey how people "are existing" without in any way "remembering" them. This, too, could be problematic for her readers, as in "Preciosilla" ("Please be please be get, please get wet, wet naturally, naturally in weather. Could it be fire more firier. Could it be so in ate struck"[6]) or "Jean Cocteau" ["Needs be needs be needs be near. Needs be needs be needs be" (*WM*, 53)]. Her plays similarly push the outermost limits: "I wanted to write a drama where no one did anything where there was no action" (*EA*, 283).[7] And so her late return to discursive writing in her various "autobiographies" may be the biggest wonder of all. Beginning with *The Autobiography of Alice B. Toklas* but including also *Everybody's Autobiography, Paris France,* and *Wars I Have Seen,* Stein assumes in her late writing a distinctive but eminently understandable voice.

In terms of content as well, Stein's path prior to the *Autobiography* had hardly seemed to veer from the one foreseen grimly by Tocqueville several generations earlier. He had predicted that the sources of inspiration for a democratic writer would range from trivial objects of the visible world to grand generalizations. Stein's narrator in *The Making of Americans* professes an interest "in simple firm ordinary middle class traditions, in sordid material unaspiring visions, in a repeating, common, decent enough kind of living, with no fine kind of fancy ways inside us" (*MOA*, 37–38). Throughout her work, she plays with notions of national character ["the French were the only ones who really knew (the ground) was still there, even though it was in France that twentieth century art and literature is made"][8] and national writing ["the disembodied way of disconnecting something from anything and anything from something was the American one" (*LIA*, 53)]. And the American way is formed in turn by geography: "After all anybody is as their land and air is. Anybody is as the sky is low or high. Anybody is as there is wind or no wind there. That is what makes a people."[9]

The further Tocquevillian charge that democratic writers would become untethered from the actual world and produce incoherent images and bizarre effects also fits the popular image of Gertrude Stein prior to her best-selling work. Some of her flights from the "actual world" had the effect of sheltering her from criticism, as they appealed to something beyond understanding. When she rejected all forms of discursive writing, her writing could be both impenetrable and self-indulgent; she later regretted what she called her "lyric turn." In *Lectures in America*, she admits that she became carried away with her powers to entrance, letting the melody "rather [get] the better of me." Conceding that she "was rather drunk with what [she] had done" and that she preferred sobriety, Gertrude Stein set out to pursue a more controlled writing. "I like to be sober so I began again" (*LIA*, 197–199).[10]

The Decentering Turn: *The Autobiography of Alice B. Toklas*

The constructive achievement of *The Autobiography of Alice B. Toklas* bears directly upon Tocqueville's project, in the first case since Stein succeeds in opening up unforeseen literary possibilities. The conundrum Tocqueville faced remains with us today: democracy's way of encouraging self-reliance and individual thinking is threatened always by its obverse, its stimulation of a despotic public opinion. But in a formal device of a deceptively simple nature, the writer Stein combats this tendency towards the uniform perspective and sustains a complex and decentered view. Striding into postures of literary authority, she withdraws again, always before the game is up. Neither philosophical nor allegorical, "Gertrude Stein" is genius incarnate, or so Alice B. Toklas affirms on numerous occasions. "I may say that only three times in my life have I met a genius and each time a bell within me rang and I was not mistaken."[11] Is this for real? It turns out that Alice is "in character" when she makes these judgments, not rendered by the real Alice but by Gertrude Stein herself, whose real interest is—Gertrude Stein herself. "About six weeks ago Gertrude Stein said, it does not look to me as if you were ever going to write that autobiography. You know what I am going to do. I am going to write it for you. I am going to write it as simply as Defoe did the autobiography of Robinson Crusoe. And she has and this is it" (913). The distancing mechanism of the *Autobiography* serves to disarm and provoke the audience; its possibilities are intriguing if one is true to form.

The *Autobiography* elaborates upon the Tocquevillian project also in historiographical terms, and for this reason critical reactions to the *Autobiography* are of interest. One of the most memorable re-actions—contained in the document *Testimony Against Gertrude Stein*—reveals how *not* to pigeonhole the *Autobiography*. This special issue of Transition consists of individual responses by several individuals named in Stein's work: Henri Matisse, Georges Bracque, André Salmon, Tristan Tzara, Eugene Jolas and Marie Jolas. All six contributors imply that factual inaccuracies disqualify *The Autobiography of Alice B. Toklas* as a legitimate composition; for example, Matisse calls it a harlequin's costume, "the different pieces of which, having been more or less invented by herself, have been sewn together without taste and without relation to reality."[12] André Salmon corrects her story of his drunken antics at the infamous Rousseau banquet: "I did not climb onto the table, as Miss Stein would have had me do" (*Testimony,* 15). The tone is remarkably strident, as when Tzara denounces her "baby style" which "[simpers] at the interstices of envy" (*Testimony,* 13). Critics have long noted since then that these artistic figures were not just miffed, but scandalized, by Stein's rendition: "The fact that they respond to her book with testimony, as if she were a criminal on trial, and the fact that their responses became known as a manifesto suggest more than the usual anger at being misquoted or misrepresented."[13] All of this has the effect of highlighting Stein's sophistication over their naivete concerning remembrance. For her part Gertrude Stein pronounces the testimony of this avant-garde collection "a scream," and attributes their ire to jealousy of Picasso and of Picasso's centrality in her account.[14] She might have added that the vehemence of their objections suggests their recognition that *her* account would prevail over their combined voices. It has done so precisely because she is more attuned to the kind of insight that will count in regard to the past, versus the literal translation that likely will not. Bracque may complain that "she never knew french really well" and that therefore she "understood nothing of what went on around her" (13), but it seems that her sense of the acceptable democratic story has had considerably more staying power than his.

By the time Stein wrote the *Autobiography* in 1932, her commitment is evident to certain core principles regarding the nature of creative activity, and she develops a distinctive brand of commentary as a consequence of her flexible handling of these same principles. Without precisely intending to do so, Gertrude Stein performs in the *Autobiography* an exquisite balancing act between historical *identity* and the creative *entity*. She presents herself as the unproblematic ally of Picasso: "I was alone at this time in understanding him," Stein writes later, "perhaps because I was expressing the same thing in literature."[15] Each was striving for intellectual exactitude beyond identity. The portrait clinches the relation. "Gertrude Stein" speaks of eighty or ninety sittings for this portrait before Picasso announces one day in irritation, "I can't see you any longer when I look" (*ABT*, 706, 713). He paints out the whole head, and "everybody goes away" from Paris for the summer. Picasso's struggle "enacts a progression from identity to entity," as Merrill observes, "the accumulated memories of those eighty or ninety sittings interfere with Picasso's immediate perception, bring in identity, and destroy creation."[16] During that summer "Gertrude Stein" works feverishly and returns to Paris "full of excitement." At the same time, Picasso had returned from

Spain and "out of his head" finished the head of Gertrude. It was 1907. "And when she saw it he and she were content" (717). This was an anchoring of her character in real historical time— no small concession on the part of the fifty-eight-year-old "writer's writer." In unexpected ways her commitment to certain principles of creative activity release her from a writer's inhibitions concerning her historical situation. In an obvious sense, the historical orientation is "avant-garde" Paris of the early decades of the twentieth century; less obviously, it is oriented specifically towards a work of art, Picasso's *Portrait of Miss Gertrude Stein*. Moreover, at the same time that Stein secures the *Autobiography of Alice B. Toklas* to time, place, and historical figures, she also transforms this given into an innovative and refined literary form. If the *Autobiography* is aligned at the start with Picasso's portrait, it gradually becomes established as a unique and self-standing competitor.

In Stein's later formulation, though the human mind "lives alone," there are these chance encounters of genius. Many years afterwards, according to the account in the *Autobiography*, "Gertrude" decides to have Alice cut off all her hair, before then having worn it "as a crown on top of her head as Picasso had painted it" (717). When Picasso spies the newly shorn Gertrude some days later at a social event, he approaches her: "Gertrude, what is it, what is it?" he asks, provoked. Gertrude removes her hat. "And my portrait, said he sternly." And then: "his face softening, he added, mais, quand même, tout y est, all the same it is all there" (717). "Miss Gertrude Stein" remains, and *that* is the entity to which the *Autobiography* is aligned.

Considered in the alternate mode—that is, with "identity" foremost—Stein and Picasso are rivals in portraiture. In this context, "Gertrude Stein" asserts herself as one not to be enclosed or appropriated by another; she reveals herself on *her* terms. As Berthoff observes, "the finer the novelist's art, the more the characters will be seen to give form to their own history."[17] Stein's ego has to be constructed in a world which insists on labeling her as a personality; her way is through carefully crafted anecdotes. For it is clear enough how it goes for Stein the writer: "most of them did not even know that I did write" (*ABT,* 729). If Picasso had to pay the price for being ahead of his contemporaries in recognizing new ways of seeing, he did not pay the same price that Stein did, as a female who was not taken seriously in terms of her work. For it was her salon and her personality that attracted attention, and in this state of frustration in regard to her writing, Stein may have seen more deeply than others. "It always did bother me that the American public were more interested in me than in my work" (*EA,* 50). She schemes in daily life to honor her calling, to be amused and not disheartened by the successes of her compatriots. Hosting a lunch for "all the painters"—who are all male—she strategically places each opposite his own picture: "and they were happy so happy that we had to send out twice for more bread" (672). No one notices "her little arrangement" until they break up and Matisse pronounces it proof of her wickedness: "Mademoiselle Gertrude, the world is a theatre for you" (672). But as stage manager, "Gertrude Stein" is somewhat removed from the scenes she is famed for assembling.

Eventually she would deepen her characterization of the creative process in terms of "entity" (the creative writer who "sees") over against "identity" (one whose self-awareness depends upon being seen). "I am not I any longer when I see," she writes in *Four in America,* and continues: "This sentence is at the bottom of all creative activity. It is just the opposite of I am I because my little dog knows me" (*FIA,* 119). The term *identity* is used pejoratively throughout her late writings: it is the person who knows herself because her little dog recognizes her, the writer who feeds off popular taste, the self who is validated through the eyes of others. Alternatively, identity is "human nature" as opposed to the "human mind," and "human nature now is not at all interesting."[18] In contrast, as entity or human mind, the writer has no external dependencies, no linkages to time and place. "The human mind lives alone . . . the human mind . . . can write but not speak . . . the human mind writes what there is and what has identity got to do with that" (*GHA,* 458, 465, 423). Adhering to this dichotomous view of entity-identity or human mind-human nature is a liberating device for Stein not only in the sense meant by Harold Bloom (who notes that her "rugged distinction" is "a ruthless strategy for subverting any author's sense of belatedness, of coming after Shakespeare"[19]), but also in impelling her constantly to juggle the two realms of her lived experience, literary and historical. There is a certain reckless agility to her posture, no doubt cultivated by her years of literary isolation, which, when applied to historical issues, generates a unique narrative power. In *Four in America* Stein utilizes her "rugged distinction" to excellent effect. There she uses her distinction between entity and identity in a provocative comment on her own writing as well as that of Shakespeare and Henry James. She takes the common observation about the deadening effects of popularity on artistic invention to an absorbing level when she identifies two distinct kinds of writing in Shakespeare, the "real" sounds of his plays and the "smooth" sounds of his sonnets. Stein recalls that she had always been struck by how unlike were the sounds produced by Shakespeare in his two literary capacities, and she wondered how the same author could compose so differently. By coincidence, she informs us, she recreates the effect of the smooth sound when she began to translate George Hugnet's poem "Enfances"; she concludes that the smooth sound of the words captures a certain detachment of the writer.[20] Smoothness, in other words, is a mark of the corrupting effects of human nature. And so she ascertains the matter: "Shakespeare's plays were written as they were written. Shakespeare's sonnets were written as they were going to be written" (*FIA,* 120). The dramatic plays show the author's true expression, the sonnets, his responses to external inducement. "You write what you intend to write." Or, "you write what some one has intended to write" (*FIA,* 124).

The important feature of Stein's entity-identity distinction is its expressly hermeneutical status, for she proceeds to violate the boundaries of her terms as needed. She claims, for instance, that Henry James combines two forms of writing, her "inside" and "outside"—as she herself does, too ["I did not choose to use either one of two ways but two ways as one way" (*FIA,* 123)]. The "two ways as one way" is the theme that informs her reinvention of Henry James as "general" in one of her thought experiments in *Four in America:* "Everything that could happen or not happen would have had a preparation. Oh yes you know you know very well how Henry James had had to do this" (*FIA,* 137). Like her hero Ulysses S. Grant who really *was* a general, the thinker who integrates the two types of writing (who both "intended" and responded to "someone else's intention") would be an extraordinary judge and witness of the human condition. She evokes the crucial overlap in the writer's originality and his connectedness to his world; the writer and the general are disclosed as one, each motivated and guided from within while anticipating and recognizing claims from without. For the moment, Stein's entity and identity lose their sharp contours; an indefinite space is evinced in which it makes sense for her to claim "while I am writing I am most completely," or that the meaning of genius is "entirely and completely listening and talking, the two in one" (*LIA*, 180).

The egotism for which "Gertrude Stein" is notorious is also tied in with her identity/entity maneuvers. Accused of inordinate pride, she replies "yes of course. She realises that in english literature in her time she is the only one. She has always known it and now she says it" (*ABT*, 738). Bernard Faÿ is reported to have remarked that he had encountered in his life three people "of first rate importance"— Picasso, Gertrude Stein, and André Gide, "and Gertrude Stein inquired quite simply, that is quite right but why include Gide" (905). Commentators most disturbed by her assertions ["Think of the Bible and Homer think of Shakespeare and think of me" (*GHA*, 407)] often come across as humorless, but this is not to deny that this is a basic component of "Gertrude Stein." Reid, who characterizes the *Autobiography* as largely "chitchat," is correct that the one conviction insisted upon in all of the autobiographical works is the "preeminent genius of their author."[21] But her genius is asserted and reasserted in tribute to her gift for writing, a gift, it is true, which gives meaning to her own life—but which fundamentally points *beyond* her personal identity. "Genius," remarks Poirier, "describes those moments when language and the person using it reach a point of incandescence. It marks the disappearance of individuality on the occasion of its triumph."[22] In terms established by Stein, her writing is not in the service of her ego; her ego is in the service of writing. So long as Stein adheres to those rules, the world is her sport.

Conscious of her calling, "Gertrude Stein" could show an indifferent acceptance of the demands of the historical moment. Any number of conditions existed that the contemporary writer was not free to ignore, beginning with the "death" of the ways of the nineteenth century. Realism may have been viable in the nineteenth century which "believed in progress and permanence," but in the twentieth century the writer and the painter had come to share the same predicament: "there is no realism now" (*WIHS*, 144, 44). Stein pronounces the novel obsolete, except for detective stories, "where the only person of any importance is dead" (*EA*, 102). Stories with a beginning, middle, and end could not compel belief; thus does Stein "liberate herself and her writing from the certainties of all totalizing systems of knowledge and [celebrate] difference and discontinuity."[23] Strong characters had to be relinquished, for they falsified contemporary conditions by glorifying an unrealistic heroic model. They also condoned passivity in the reader, by encouraging the belief in a saving figure. Such a hero, Stein contends, is an imposition to which the contemporary writer has no access. The twentieth century had its own injunctions: "The characteristic thing of the 20th century was the idea of production in a series, that one thing should be like every other thing, and that it should be made alike and quantities of them" (*PF*, 61).

Redressing the Balance

As compelling as the novelty of *The Autobiography of Alice B. Toklas* is the way in which Stein reconfigures issues of gender and balance. There is nothing as indelicate as explicit denunciation in the *Autobiography;* groundless authority is unmasked with a wink, by the one who sees further. The first significant hold on "Gertrude Stein" that must be released is familial, in the person of her older brother. Leo Stein directs the education, travel, social, and intellectual life of his younger sister until she imperceptibly extracts his hold and claims her self as writer. Leo is then immortalized as "Gertrude Stein's brother," as she finds her own soul mate in Picasso. The dismissal of Leo occurs in a whisper. During one Saturday evening at 27 Rue de Fleurus, Leo presents to Picasso "portfolio after portfolio" of Japanese prints. Picasso, who "solemnly and obediently looked at print after print," confides to "Gertrude Stein" under his breath: "he is very nice, your brother, but like all americans, like Haviland, he shows you japanese prints. Moi j'aime pas ça, no I don't care for it. . . . Gertrude Stein and Pablo Picasso immediately understood each other" (705). In *Everybody's Autobiography,* Stein is pictured reclining on her terrace in the south of France with her dogs Pépé and Basket as she remarks: "It takes a lot of time to be a genius, you have to sit around so much doing nothing" (EA, facing 37, 70). This is not a simple matter of her self-satisfaction. During the Second World War, she and Alice lived in considerable danger as Jewish lesbians in occupied France, with Germans not only posted in Bilignin but actually quartered in their home for some time. Here is the "Gertrude Stein" from those times: "you think how nice it will be to have those happy days come back when vegetables grew not in the ground but in tins. A vegetable garden in the beginning looks so promising and then after all little by little it grows nothing but vegetables" (WIHS, 39). She kept this work un-typed "as long as there were Germans around" (her handwriting would not betray her to most native speakers of English), but what is remarkable in this account is how easily she distances the scene: "Even now I always resent it when in a book they say they sat down to a hearty meal and they do not tell just what it was they ate" (WIHS, 229, 16). "Not since the mid-nineteenth century," Saunders writes, "has an American writer asserted with such optimism our ability to shape our own destiny and to balance 'somewhere between . . . the Actual and the Imaginary.'"[24]

"Gertrude Stein" is there among the painters, dealers, and buyers to record just what the great revolution in modern art amounts to, and far from offering grand narrative, she specializes in the shaggy dog story. The Steins' first purchase of a Cézanne in their earliest days in Paris is paradigmatic. Gertrude and Leo go to Vollard's picture gallery, the contents of which are seemingly unprepared to be divulged: "Inside there were a couple of canvases turned to the wall, in one corner was a small pile of big and little canvases thrown pell mell on top of one another, in the centre of the room stood a huge dark man glooming" (686). Vollard, glooming, is yet cheered by their request to see some Cézanne landscapes. The dealer lumbers about, disappears, then "was heard heavily mounting the steps" (687). A long wait ensues, whereupon he returns with a canvas which is mostly unpainted, except for a tiny picture of an apple. The Steins view the apple appreciatively but they persist: they had come to see landscapes. "Ah yes, sighed Vollard," as he ascends and then returns with a picture of a human figure, in the form of a back. This the Steins judged to be quite beautiful but still not the landscape they requested. The third effort does produce a landscape, but a very small landscape on a very large canvas. The Steins explain further: they would like to see a landscape that fully covers the canvas. "They said, they thought they would like to see one like that" (687). Meantime, the sun was setting, and down the stairs came "a very aged charwoman" bidding them good evening; she was soon followed by a second woman, who also murmured "bon soir" as she departed. "Gertrude Stein" began to laugh. She laughed harder and harder, finally deducing that "there is no Cézanne." She explains to her brother: "Vollard goes upstairs and tells these old women what to paint and he does not understand us and they do not understand him and they paint something and he brings it down and it is a Cézanne" (688). Now both Steins laugh, barely recovering to repeat to Vollard one more time what it is they wish to see. Vollard returns with the desired painting: "It was lovely, it covered all the canvas, it did not cost much and they bought it" (688).

The understatement of this story does not prevent it from asserting the significance of women as markers for the new reality. "The only thing that is different from one time to another is what is seen and what is seen depends upon how everybody is doing everything" (*WM*, 26).

When Gertrude and Leo had become regular and welcome visitors to Vollard's picture gallery [he had "found out that when they laughed most they usually bought something so of course he waited for them to laugh" (688)] and had become accomplished in their purchases, they conceived the desire for a "big Cézanne" ["After that they would be reasonable" (689)]. They are shown narrowing down the choice to two, one a portrait of a man, the other of a woman. They select the latter. This was important, "Gertrude Stein" says, "because in looking and looking at this picture [she] wrote *Three Lives*" (690), her stories of "The Good Anna," "Melanctha," and "The Gentle Lena." In the same year, Matisse painted his "La Femme au Chapeau," Woman with a Hat, the painting that so scandalized the viewing public that people scratched at it with their fingernails. It found its home at 27 Rue de Fleurus. Finally, hovering along the edges is the great modernist icon, Picasso's *Les Demoiselles d'Avignon,* all part of a remarkable coincidence of artistic breakthrough which occurred in Paris in 1907.[25]

Stein deflects aggression on the way to a retaking of terrain; though she is not a specific advocate for women's rights or part of a movement, her pen is a potent force. The character "Gertrude Stein" is too much her own 'destiny' to figure in the details of other people's causes. When she was facing difficulties as a young woman in medical school, her good friend Marion Walker pleads with her to finish, and to "remember the cause of women"—to which "Gertrude Stein" responds: "you don't know what it is to be bored" (*ABT,* 743). This is not complacence about the obstacles women faced but a protectiveness about the writer's space that is beyond identity and gender. "Not, as Gertrude Stein explained to Marion Walker, that she at all minds the cause of women or any other cause, but it does not happen to be her business" (743). She carves out a realm in which the outside world cannot penetrate: in the good days, this was her all-night writing (699); in bad, this was time snatched for writing in the automobile, in between visits, anywhere at all (861). Once again, her retreat to her creative activity shields her from attachments to the more ordinary causes of her contemporaries, and provides an occasion for thinking beyond the historical moment.[26]

In rivaling Picasso, Stein faces down "the fathers."[27] Her strategy is to allow masculine aggressiveness to reveal itself through anecdote, and then, in all mildness, to deflect that assertiveness. So in speaking of "the first times" together, Alice recounts an evening with Picasso and Fernande: "He was sitting next to Gertrude Stein at dinner and she took up a piece of bread. This, said Picasso, snatching it back with violence, this piece of bread is mine" (705). The comeback? "She laughed." Hints of imperiousness surround the motif of the Picasso portrait. Though Stein and Picasso may meet each other on equal terms ["They sit in two little low chairs up in his apartment studio, knee to knee and Picasso says, expliquez-moi cela" (738)], the larger world takes no such view, and Picasso himself, "every inch a chief," seems to be oblivious to the contrast of their positions: "Picasso was more than ever as Gertrude Stein said the little bullfighter followed by his squadron of four . . . Napoleon followed by his four enormous grenadiers" (Derain, Braque, Apollinaire, Salmon,

718). And Picasso's portrait may well contribute to the trivialization of Stein's work, as Caramello argues, by his establishing her as the "created icon" of Cubism rather than as a creative agent in her own right. Relatedly, Schmitz formulates the preeminent question of this autobiography as "how to shine" next to Picasso: "Only two geniuses matter in *The Autobiography of Alice B. Toklas,* and their relation is the problem of the text."[28] Picasso's long struggle with Stein's portrait is relived, and when it is finally finished, nobody admires it "except the painter and the painted" (669). Early on, Alice recounts Picasso's famous quip: when people said that Gertrude Stein doesn't look like that, he answered, don't worry, she will. The presumption of that remark still startles. His appropriation appears complete; his version of her takes pride of place, and henceforth, the Picasso portrait *is* Gertrude Stein. Painting here, as in Plato's *Republic,* provides a once-and-for-all time basis, an assertive masculine declaration of interpretive authority. Stein responds with her own creative tools: in writing, and in full partnership with Alice. Stein struggles, too, in composing her portrait, but in her case there is no single conquering hero to celebrate at the close. For behind every articulated, typed, and published word lurks Alice B. Toklas. That "Gertrude Stein" is a joint effort is communicated in the fantastic mixture of voices and identity. Genius is expressed lovingly, in shared consciousness—and in full recognition of the balance being inventively prescribed.[29]

Stein's writing aspires to a balance unavailable to painting. As in Plato, a dialogue strategy keeps her from being didactic, imperious, dictatorial—and does so ironically through the creation of a written character who incessantly discourses and interrogates the text: "Gertrude Stein."

The Socratic "Stein"

Like Socrates in the *Phaedrus,* "Gertrude Stein" is emended by the model of writing in which she is contained. The talking that is shown is ennobled by the account that is written: "Gertrude Stein of course talked to them all, wanted to know what state and what city they came from, what they did, how old they were and how they liked it" (*ABT,* 838). Upon meeting Charlie Chaplin, someone who loved to talk as much as she, "Gertrude Stein" relates that "each one had to

stop to be polite and let the other one say something" (*EA*, 283).
Walking the streets of Paris, she stops to ask the workmen "what are
they doing and why" (*EA*, 11), or pauses to observe someone with a
satchel of a funny shape: "I always ask anybody who is carrying
anything what they are carrying" (*EA*, 203). "Who is in there I asked
Kahnweiler I always like to know who is anywhere and I always ask"
(*EA*, 35). This inquisitiveness and receptivity elides into the province
of the writer: "Of course I am interested in any one . . . or else I must
betake myself to some entirely different occupation and I do not
think I will" (*LIA*, 183).

Writers might, on occasion, take their leave of such a world, and
accordingly, Stein insisted on sharpening the distinction between
"writing" and "speaking." She observed that the distance between
them was becoming more and more extreme: "talking and writing
have gotten more and more separated" (*EA*, 46), and in consequence
she believed that resorting to a conversational banter was as false a
step for the writer as was clinging to outmoded traditions. Writers
should beware the tendency to immerse themselves in what is ready
at hand ["everybody keeps saying and writing what anybody feels
that they are understanding" (*EA*, 122)] and rather seek the means to
enter "right into things" (*Primer*, 33). Readers of her day were bringing the expectations of conversation to books; she counters that writing is more elevated than speaking and that writers should emphasize
that distance, not seek to close it. This was no idle matter, as she was
asked time and again why she did not write as clearly as she spoke
["And, why, she wondered, do you not think as I write?" (*EA*, 171,
292)]. That to her would have been an intolerable capitulation to the
desires of the audience. "Talking is not thinking or feeling at all anymore" (*EA*, 46). Better to follow her example: "My writing is clear
as mud, but mud settles and clear streams run on and disappear"
(*EA*, 123).

The authorial detachment of the *Autobiography* in general elaborates upon Stein's devotion to writing. The literary device of Gertrude
Stein writing the "autobiography" of Alice is Platonic in its ingenuity;
as in the opening of the *Symposium* or the *Theatetus*, the innocent
historical nature of what is to follow is made suspect. This perspective
of "Gertrude Stein" ever shifts as we assess and reassess the life being

revealed: "the reader struggles to see her through Alice's eyes while realizing . . . that it is really Gertrude pretending to be Alice and thereby contemplating herself and compelling readers to contemplate her through the eyes of an imagined (but not fictitious) other." It is because Gertrude Stein can imagine that "other" so affectionately that the device succeeds as well as it does.[30] The intimacy of the two confirms the standing of the one, sometimes with the most extraordinary comedic effect. Schmitz captures the tone in his ingenious linking of "Alice" and "Huck Finn," both speaking from excluded positions: "Huck and Alice, those elusive figures of speech, these reluctant writers, enable Mark Twain and Gertrude Stein to slip away from the cramped and smothery intention of serious writing . . . [their] spacious anti-Aristotelian, anti-patriarchal sense of the world . . . does not fall discursively into the trap of counter-statement."[31] The wry and indirect expression exemplifies an alternative to what it is attacking.

The laughter of "Gertrude Stein" resounds throughout the pages of the *Autobiography* and takes its distinctive coloring, again, in accordance with an almost absent-minded appeal to hard-headed principles. When all can be catalogued, much is amusing. Early in the work, Alice and a friend inadvertently seat themselves in a vernissage directly in front of the most controversial paintings (a Braque and a Derain), causing "Gertrude Stein" to roar with laughter as she explains: "right here in front of you is the whole story" (674). To Alice and her friend, still uncomprehending, "Gertrude Stein" is as remarkable a presence as any other component of the vie de Bohème, as she goes off "with a great shout of laughter" (675). Nor is "Gertrude Stein" only mirthful at the trials and tribulations of the art world and at the expense of others. When she arranges to print *Three Lives* herself from lack of interest on the part of any publishers, the director of her vanity press sends an assistant to Paris to meet with her. "You see, he said slightly hesitant, the director of the Grafton Press is under the impression that perhaps your knowledge of English" (727). She responds laughing: "everything that is written in the manuscript is written with the intention of its being so written" (727). Through her humorous composure, "Gertrude Stein" spurns the status of cultural latecomer and remains quite untouched by that legacy which marks the modernist spirit. "I was bored with the hopelessness of

painters and poetry" (*EA,* 31). In the *Autobiography,* Alice writes
that Pablo Picasso was always trying to persuade "Gertrude Stein"
that she was as unhappy as he was. "But are you, [Alice asks]. Well I
don't think I look it, do I, and she laughs" (*ABT,* 738). The only
somber conversation that Stein reports in that work is with T. S.
Eliot: "Eliot and Gertrude Stein had a solemn conversation, mostly
about split infinitives and other grammatical solecisms and why
Gertrude Stein used them" (857). And "Alice" reports the words by
"Gertrude Stein" that caused the break with Ezra Pound: "I am so
sorry . . . but Miss Toklas has a bad tooth and besides we are busy
picking wild flowers" (858).[32]

Reactions to Stein's *Autobiography* reveal a gap between judgments of "high" and "low" culture, as if the work must be either
sophisticated or popular. When the *Autobiography* became a best-
seller, avant-garde painters accused Stein of pandering (Marie Jolas
speaks of her "final capitulation to a Barnumesque publicity"); meanwhile, her serious critics expressed disappointment ("It was a public
work, written for an audience and not for the sake of writing"), and a
prominent biographer claimed that she "suppressed her scruples"
and "set out to satisfy the public appetite for entertaining and understandable anecdotes."[33] But Stein's creation is both sophisticated
and popular, and despite all appearances, the exchanges that occur
in the *Autobiography* cannot be dismissed as everyday discourse.
Here Gertrude Stein's long interest in reproducing the *distinctive* in
speech patterns serves her well; in language reminiscent of *The Making of Americans,* Thornton Wilder observes to the point that "even
up to her last years she listened to all comers, to 'how their knowing
came out of them.' "[34] Though her compositions often provoked imitations, she was "funnier in every way than the imitations, not to say
much more interesting" (*ABT,* 828). Her artifice is entrenched, all the
more so when it looks commonplace. In the *Autobiography,* the talk
is as "democratic" and "American" as could be, but it is mediated and
nearly inimitable. An example (which is daffy, but not exceptionally
so) occurs when "Gertrude and Alice" appear before the head of the
American Fund for French Wounded to ask how they may best volun-
teer: "and she said, get a car. But where we asked. From America she
said. But how, we said. Ask somebody, she said, and Gertrude Stein

did" (826). The utmost simplicity in the telling belies the authorial complexity, for Stein's imitation of Alice's delivery makes contact both with the predilections of Toklas' actual speech and her own; furthermore, it replicates patterns familiar in Stein's writing.[35] Her anecdotes give the appearance of being ready-made and on the surface, and her character of being of almost transparent openness. But "Gertrude Stein" is not so easily procurable. Stein's snapshots of herself intrigue by their very flatness. Many stylized glimpses are offered, all without depth and without pointing to a centered identity. Thus does the *Autobiography* give "the inside by way of the outside; it plays down psychology and sticks to the surface, recording externals (objects, acts, dialogues) in a way that clearly manifests deliberate and idiosyncratic acts of selection and stylization."[36] Through such means "Gertrude Stein" proclaims herself a democrat—and is transparently so: "Now as for herself she was not efficient, she was good humored, she was democratic, one person was as good as another, and she knew what she wanted done. If you are like that she says, anybody will do anything for you. The important thing, she insists, is that you must have deep down as the deepest thing in you a sense of equality. Then anybody will do anything for you" (*ABT*, 831).

The Inexplicable "Gertrude Stein"

And yet, Gertrude Stein failed to see the magnitude of what she had done: to create stories that moderns could live with. Though Stein recognized the trivial nature of the complaints about her veracity ["Matisse said that Picasso was not the great painter of the period that his wife did not look like a horse" (*EA,* 32)],[37] she still doubted the legitimacy of her enterprise. Elsewhere she put the dilemma in the following terms: it is only through the skill of the writer that the "existing" of character could be conveyed, but then the character belongs to the writer rather than the outside world: "the more a writing is a writing the more no outside is outside outside is inside."[38] To the degree that the character "Gertrude Stein" appeals as a written creation, she appears to be false historically. Stein characterizes the historian's problem (and, analogously, the autobiographer's) as insoluble, for if the writer is true to her creative principles, the result will be unacceptably fictional to the audience that brings to bear its own remembrances. "The historian is bound to have with him all the audience that has known every one about whom he is writing" (*N*, 61). Writers must make considerable contact with the audience in order to remain credible, but to be credible to themselves they must leave behind that influence. Accordingly, she insists on the impossibility of history as literature. "[H]ow can the historian lose [the audience]," she asks, "how can he how can he lose any of them and how can he lose all of them and if he does not how can history be writing that is be literature. How can it. Well I am sure I do not know" (*N*, 61). "Gertrude Stein" was inexplicable even to Gertrude Stein.

The hermeneutical tools with which Gertrude Stein writes the *Autobiography* could withstand anything but too much earnestness on her part; her imaginative construct only loses power when the scheme becomes determinative, when she conforms too rigidly to her own terminology. In a strange turn, this woman with "one of the great egos of all time," an ego both "monumental" and "heroic,"[39] comes to underrate the greatness of her late writing, by overdrawing the poles of entity versus identity, human nature and human mind. The result is that she disparages autobiography: "And yet autobiographies have nothing to do with the human mind" (*GHA*, 389). She insists too far on the reality of her distinctions, and thus classifies the *Autobiography* as secondary writing. "The words ran with a certain smoothness" (*Primer*, 102), she recounts, thus delegating it to the realm of compromised writing—compromised with the audience, compromised by mammon, indirect, untrue. So her sudden success at the age of 58 precipitated a personal crisis: "It was a strange year that year and it is a strange year this year. The blue of the sky looks rather black to the eye" (*EA*, 65). For the first time in her life, she was unable to write: "All this time I did no writing. I had written and was writing nothing. Nothing inside me needed to be written. Nothing needed any word and there was no word inside me that could not be spoken and so there was no word inside me" (*EA*, 64).

Stein's artful controlling of material has more historical legitimacy than she was prepared to grant. Only rarely did she acknowledge in retrospect that she had achieved something decidedly new and important in *The Autobiography of Alice B. Toklas*. Then she left behind

the irrelevant standards of objectivity and described herself as having unconsciously managed to create a viable continuous present.
She had generated the sense of an immediate voice even as she related a history of her era: "I described something momentous happening under my eyes and I was able to do it without a great sense of
time" (*WM*, 102). Neuman explains: "The present moment exists in
her writing as an entity to which the past is admissible only insofar as
it is not recalled or relived, but recreated."[40] The stories recounted
are of people and events of undeniable historical interest, but these
accounts are primarily in the service of illuminating that abiding
creation, "Gertrude Stein," such that the claim on us is in the present
tense. In this instance, Gertrude Stein captured a truer state of affairs. "And when one has discovered and evolved a new form," she
explains, "it is not the form but the fact that you are the form that is
important."[41]

The magnificent accomplishment of *The Autobiography of Alice
B. Toklas* is the comedic invention "Gertrude Stein," who inspires us
to think more deeply about the characters we allow to define us. "I
certainly do know all about knowing everything," Gertrude Stein
confides (*GHA*, 482), in a voice that is a prompt in that direction.
Stein's integration of historical markers of her era signifies an advance and not a regression in her writing. When she takes full measure of her historical situation, she does so without succumbing to its
presentist dictates. Tocqueville's investigations had suggested that
democrats require *some* anchoring in the past, and that they are in
need of *more* than the transparent truth. In the *Autobiography*, Stein
creates this called-for form which is grounded *and* critical, offering a
solution to the problem of writing in a democratic America.

Conclusion: Redressing the Balance

"Lopsidedness is a fact of human history and therefore a fact of human nature."[1]

—Stuart Hampshire

Agreed, that lopsidedness *is* a fact of human history, but human nature, in the best political community, can gyroscopically act to bring human history into a more balanced state. There are ways to determine the self-definition and even geographical extent of the political community,[2] but we are not so sure about the nature of political reality. This book offers a new look at the nature of political reality as a contribution toward the pursuit of the best political community.

Democratic political discourse addresses this question through the "master themes" of the individual and the community, libertarianism, and utilitarianism, "a sharp dichotomy that threatens to become one of the banalities of the age."[3] The seemingly unresolvable tensions are perpetuated by the accompanying lack of confidence (at least among "the cognitive elite") of any normative or natural foundations for our common political life. Able to agree only that people's views on the good life and the nature and purpose of the political community will differ, attention has devolved to procedure, to a focus on the importance of an open, neutral process of consideration of contending views about what may constitute acceptable provision of the core attributes of justice. Thus procedure itself—legal, political, social, philosophical—becomes a core attribute of justice.[4] The assumption is that the democratic process will empower one version or another of the good life and that the nonselected versions will accept this outcome while awaiting and preparing to enter the process again.

Political positions in this process, couched in terms of the individual or the community, the one or the many, diversity or unity, fragmentation or centralization, are spread across a wide spectrum, left and right. Some surprising cross associations and shifts can occur. Right-wing Nobel laureates in economics appear to accept a Marxist view of human beings as solely economics-determined. A philosopher reformulates the "leftist, anti-capitalist political project" to reassert a largely disowned Cartesian subjectivity.[5]

The master themes of the individual and the community contending over the concepts of liberty, equality, and justice are permanent concerns of political philosophy. This book's contention, however, is that a fresh look at the classic texts reveals an additional theme or paradigm, rooted in human nature, and essential to the understanding and achievement of a sound political community—and that this theme has been largely forgotten or discounted by contemporary thought. Political principles, qualities, and characteristics tend to cluster around one of two poles. For simplicity's sake, these can be thought of as a balancing of masculine and feminine principles, but gender is irrelevant to a person's political inclination, allegiance, or leadership on either side. When a society leans heavily to one side, to the neglect of the other, it does indeed become "lopsided." Within this context, the works analyzed in this book provide the occasion for taking a new or renewed angle of vision on four topics: the depth of our present political discourse, the place of time and history in political life today, a more comprehensive approach to contemporary statecraft, and assessing the comparative successes of democracies and their party systems in the light of a masculine-feminine paradigm.

Enormous attention has been given in our time to the paradigm of "communicative action," to the idea that the communicative practice of everyday life is inextricably bound up with the use of reason and to claims of validity for any political argument.[6] This philosophical-theoretical stance has been inundated by the reality of interpersonal and transglobal electronic communication now taking place ceaselessly and on a scale of previously unimaginable magnitude. Yet the more communicative action there is, the more evanescent it seems, conveying thoughts as thin as the computer screens that project them. This is a problem, paradoxically, for democratic politics. The huge increase in popular participation and expression is democratic in the extreme, but as our classic texts show, if democratic opinion is untrammeled, the results surely will be chaotic. The speed and volume of communication made possible by electronic technology can make political polls resemble the direct democracy that undid Athens.

A crucial question of political reality is how political views are formed in the public sphere. How are policies formulated and presented? How can a requisite depth of understanding be generated? The texts examined in this book take many forms, but all share the power to draw the reader into an extended, nondidactic engagement with the ideas presented. There is the epic depiction of the vagaries of power and war; the history that almost silently subverts its own ostensible message; the comedy that "underscores the power of language to create something out of nothing";[7] the diatribe conveyed in perhaps the longest letter ever devoted to a political cause; and that most protean form, the novel. Each form, in its unique way, has the capacity to draw the mind of the reader into substantive engagement with a kaleidoscopic progression of ideas. The outcome cannot be programmed or predicted; a depth of field can be achieved, of a kind far beyond that possible through today's daily media.

In several of these works, the theater is used as metaphor and example: Herodotus' Gyges story; Plato's Cave; Machiavelli's play. Burke's letter returns again and again to references and images from the stage. The political significance of the theater metaphor lies in its insistent demand that we bring our minds, emotions, experiences, and judgment to bear on what lies behind and ahead of the scene we are witnessing at the moment. In the drama unfolding before us the actors of course know they are being watched, but the play's characters do not. The audience in one sense endeavors to block out awareness of the actors in order to accept the characters portrayed, and then, in another sense, appreciates and evaluates the actor's performance, the script, and the playwright. And as theater critics we observe the reactions of others in the audience, reactions that cannot help but influence us to some extent. Beneath this come questions about the cost of production, the sets, theater maintenance, ticket prices, actors' pay and benefits, the mix of the theater-going population, the provenance and prospects for this and like productions.[8] There are profound leads herein for analysts of contemporary political theater.

Memory, remembrance, and a sense of time in depth are important counteractives to the dominance of time present in today's politics. Presentist politics are largely oblivious or dismissive of how, and why, things have come about in history, and glibly unconvincing about commitments to "our children's children." When a deep, balanced, comprehensive view of past, present, and future as a continuum is lacking, politics, raw and rootless, will take command in every field. Our ancients, Thucydides most notably, constantly challenge the tendency to overvalue a presentist, masculine politics, to demonstrate that a unipolar politics proceeding in disregard of its stabilizing counterpart principle will carry a polity into serious trouble. Thucydides induces our recognition that direct democracy, swift and single-minded, is highly likely to fail to attend to the need to balance the modes of political life.[9]

Remembrance is important for Tocqueville, but its prospects are dim. In his epic effort to understand and give guidance to democracy in America, Tocqueville tries to convince the reader that there once was, or should be, two poles, two principles to keep in balance if democracy is successfully to endure. He tries to make us remember and to repopulate our democratic world with a feminine antidote to masculine presentism, for he senses that the vitally important female dimension is fading. But despite Tocqueville's best efforts, he cannot persuasively bring that other sphere to life. He holds up the image of an early American, New England past. By pinning all his hopes on a narrow band of historical time, Tocqueville's argument weakens as the example of the Puritan errand into the wilderness ceases to resonate, with no other solution on offer. Tocqueville is too finely attuned to the insistence of his audience on facts to be able to provide them with new perceptions in depth.

Gertrude Stein, however, succeeds precisely in the sense that Tocqueville fails. She draws us toward a weightier understanding of political reality, using history buoyantly so that it is continually present, informing and stabilizing, yet not didactic. Stein fashions history to fit democratic requirements even as she lures democracy from its anti-historical bias. The power of Stein's achievement is revealed in the extent to which she has been attacked for letting in some history. She created a history to which democrats can respond, a history populated by created characters. Works such as these, when fully engaged, can lead us to address practical problems of contemporary democracy as encapsulations of time past, present, and future. Study of the "unfolding" of a core practice, law, or institution can sweep away the self-deceptions of the present and shape the agenda for a more balanced politics to come.

The frontispiece to Hobbes' 1629 translation of Thucydides' *Peloponnesian War* vividly depicts the polarization of Hellenic society. Archidamus, a Spartan king, stands before a Doric column, an order characterized as "male." The Spartan is a grizzled, hierarchical figure in a society ruled oligarchically. Settled, slow, and manly, in warfare Sparta is almost exclusively a land power. Sparta's weakness, paradoxically, eventually will be revealed to be the incorporation, at the heart of its society, of a distorted femininity, of Spartan women virtually unchecked in the expression of extreme versions of their womanly inclinations, to the ultimate detriment of Spartan society as a whole. Athens, of course, is represented by Pericles, a far more stylish figure, posed before an Ionic column, the "female" counterpart to the Doric order. As Onian notes, Pericles' Funeral Oration "is a thinly veiled assertion that the Athenians have an interest in luxury and philosophy—the two things for which the Ionian cities were most famous—yet still can match the physical and moral capacities for which the Dorians were renowned. . . . [It is] likely that the use of Doric for exteriors and Ionic for interiors was an approximate expression of the ways of life of the two races, the one fond of manly exercise in the open and the other given to a gentler and more feminine indoor life."[10]

Athens is a sea power and a democracy, both identifiable with the feminine, yet Thucydides repeatedly if subtly points his readers toward indications that Athens has become "lopsided," emphasizing the masculine in its imperial rise, to the neglect of its feminine aspect. Athens has become too exclusively a sea power, and Pericles' policy of simply ceding land to the Spartan invaders leads to disastrous consequences. Similarly, Athens has become all too democratic. The single-chamber assembly to which Pericles points with pride proves disastrous in its unchecked ability to turn impulse into action almost instantaneously, making ill-considered decisions that a bicameral system, i.e., an oligarchic, "male" chamber and a democratic "female" house, might have avoided. Mirroring Sparta's flaw of imbalance, Athens cannot succeed in its Periclean form. Under the pressure of impending war, Pericles took a pragmatic position that undermined the people's respect for religion. Like Sparta, Athens becomes so unbalanced as to take up the most unbridled attributes of the opposite gender. Athens adopts sheer power as the sole principle of political life.

Athens and Sparta each fails to grasp that the unbalanced character of their statecraft has led them to the edge of catastrophe. At Sphacteria the Spartans lose their identity; at Syracuse the Athenians lose theirs. Strangely, only the seemingly unbalanced Alcibiades, rash military genius and reckless playboy, seems to perceive, and to act on through his defections, the necessity of bringing all Greeks into a larger, balanced whole, Sparta and Athens together with land and sea power, martial and philosophical arts, pleasure and austerity in equipoise.[11]

Machiavelli's *Prince* is of course a manual for statecraft, but in a far deeper way than the popular image of an advocate for ruthlessness and immorality as necessary rungs on the ladder of power. The "realist" reading of Machiavelli regards him as the ultimate masculine figure, ready to seize "Fortune" as a woman, to hold her down and beat her. But Machiavelli's statecraft is more balanced than that, more understanding of the need for, and significance of, for example, remembrance. Time, for Machiavelli's statesman, is the awareness and employment of past, present, and future all in the critical moment at hand. Guidelines for doing so are set out across chapters 14, 15, and 16 through 23 of *The Prince*. Examples of great princes in action in the past are available, but the "case studies" never quite bear out the point for which Machiavelli cites them. The facts of the situation immediately at hand must be addressed. Greene observes that the "text begins with gestures ostensibly grounding precepts in past experience and then goes on essentially to unground them, to demonstrate as it were in spite of itself the difficult struggle of the precept to stem directly from experience."[12] The statesman then must take a generally applicable yet imperfect precedent and assess it in the context of eleven paired qualities ("justice" being notably absent), which amount to "do's" and "don'ts" and "cautions." Success is possible for the prince best able to apply this approach when the need for action is immediate and imperative and yet when all the facts of the present situation are impossible to know. The model is utterly dynamic, yet capable of achieving balance[13] and stability by means of, paradoxically, ceaseless shifting.

In Thucydides, Machiavelli, Burke, and others, the essence of statecraft is rhetoric,[14] a rhetoric that displays the dangers of imbalance and, either directly or indirectly, contains the required correctives. Democratic rhetoric in America, once ornate, exfoliating, and comprehensive, has come to be clear and simple, direct, and unadorned. These are attractive qualities, but easily misappropriated for single-minded, unipolar, presentist advantage. The true statesman's rhetoric in a balanced democracy will be Lincolnian in its capacity to hold past, present, and future in continuing equilibrium.

Attempts to identify and comprehend the basic configurations, or patterns, of conflict and cooperation across political community or international boundaries must confront basic questions about human nature. Here, most famously, stands Thomas Hobbes with his denial that altruism is natural, his conviction that man is by nature rapacious, and that human nature unchecked is war of all against all.

The view of classic texts presented in this book suggests that a more productive question might be, "What aspects of human nature, when recognized and kept in some basic form of balance, provide the strongest foundations for the agreements and arrangements that a flourishing political community needs?"

As do many of the political thinkers studied here, Aristotle at a key point supplements his reasoned argumentation—about the best regimes—with an unexpected illustration, or analogy. Book 4, chapter 3 of *The Politics* "has been much disputed"[15] with its references to the musical modes, Dorian and Phrygian. What does seem undeniable is that the Dorian embodies masculine, and Phrygian the feminine characteristics.[16] There are two "finely constituted" regimes (*Pol.* 1290a24), and the ideal is a harmonious blending of the two. Well-blended harmony is the completeness and perfection that emerges from different qualities placed compatibly, in equipoise rather than exact equality, to produce a better whole. Aristotle's *Politics* moves steadily toward this perceived truth. The regime that is best under conceivable circumstances is "polity," a combination which employs the strengths and curtails the weaknesses of oligarchic and democratic regimes in their isolated forms. Aristotle's pointed references to musical modes provide insight into what the best possible regime requires: balance. Harmony can be achieved when counterparts come together in mutual recognition of their differences and positive potential interplay. For Aristotle, one side, the male Doric, comprises such metaphoric concepts and characterizations as north wind, a warlike nature, a settled temperament, liberty, oligarchy, secularism, the sciences, politics, and "the Good." The other is represented by the south wind, a peaceful temperament, equality, democracy, religion, the arts, statecraft, and "the Just." And there are indications in *The Politics* of the dangers and distortions when imbalances become severe. When that happens, as suggested in the reading of Thucydides offered here, one side may be driven to adopt and drive to an extreme the worst qualities of the other, as Periclean-, Ionic-, luxury-and philosophy-loving Athens turned to raw power as its sole purpose, justification, and objective. So also, in Aristotle as elsewhere, we hear hints of the Phrygian feminine turning frenzied and warlike, and the image of Delacroix's "Liberty Leading the People" appears before us.

Such conceptions can inform investigations of politics today, as in the question of whether a two-party system is better than a multi-party democracy, or whether a bicameral or unicameral assembly is best. There is also the larger, even civilizational, scene to consider, for the global culture that is emerging around us seems increasingly lopsided as well.[17]

Democratic self-government is a complicated and potentially precarious form of political community which must not neglect organic forms and foundations based in human nature. Chief among these are two principles addressed in this book. Our first task is the necessity to redress the balance.

Afterword

The Ship of State

The Political Metaphor and Its Fate

Horace usually gets credit for the "ship of state" image.[1] For his contemporaries in Augustan Rome comparing *res publica* to a seagoing vessel, as in Ode I.14, *O navis, referent,* would not have been strange; a long line of such references stretched back to the early Hellenic world. Horace took pride in drawing from Alcaeus, whose fragments of six centuries earlier employ the ship of state metaphor.[2]

From the ancient world to admiralty law today, ships invariably are referred to as feminine.[3] If the state is a ship and the ship is female, then the polis and state are female as well. But sailors are male; women on board are bad luck. Seafaring under sail calls for ship and crew to interact constantly in productive tension, rudder and rigging, sails and ballast incessantly adjusted to manage and make the most of ever-shifting winds and seas to keep the vessel on course.

Odysseus sets sail homeward from Troy after the war has been won. He seems, however, to have forgotten the mission of restoring the abducted Helen to her royal home in Sparta. In the most grave of many challenges, Odysseus' sailors, in violation of their oath, slaughter and eat the oxen of the Sun. In anger Zeus blasts Odysseus' ship with a thunderbolt. Odysseus lashes keel, mast, and some remaining timbers into a makeshift vessel which eventually drifts to Calypso's isle, where the nymph detains him for years until, Zeus having relented, she provides Odysseus with the materials and tools to construct a new craft and put out to sea again, only to go aground again on the island of the Phaecians. Once again a woman, this time Nausicaa, arranges for yet another ship which, despite being turned to stone by Poseidon, carries him home to Ithaca. A story of ships and sailors often out of phase with each other and on the edge of forgetting their purpose and destination, is kept on course only by acts of cooperation by male and female at decisive moments. It is a tale that would be retold as the epic voyage to transport the polity that would found the world's greatest empire and its successors.[4]

In the Persian war against the Greeks as recounted by Herodotus, the polis, as ship, behind its "walls of wood," remains in being even when Athens as city has been sacked and occupied by the invaders. Themistocles alone has fathomed this in the enigmatic prophecy of the oracle at Delphi (7.141). Adimantus, the Greek general from Corinth, taunts Themistocles with the charge that: "You have no country" (8.61). But the polis of Athens remains in being so long as its fully manned ships remain in service. In power, legitimacy, and political essence, Athens *is* its ships, and its sailors under Themistocles throw back the Persian threat to Greek freedom.[5]

Thucydides' *Peloponnesian War* opens with the "Archaeology" (1.1–17), tracing the steps to wealth and power: the suppression of piracy creates security which enables trade; thus wealth is generated which on the one hand requires protection and on the other provides the means to pay for it. Ships are the essence of this progression and a great naval empire is the result. What follows through the bulk of Thucydides' account describes a progressively deteriorating connection between ship and state. In contrast to Themistocles' awareness of the importance of the ship-as-state in the Persian war is Pericles' decision in the Peloponnesian war to concentrate the population in Athens, and his failure to carry through energetically on his pledge to the people that "if they march against our country we will sail against theirs" (1.143).

The people of Athens are manipulated by demogogues to vote to send the fleet under Alcibiades on the Sicilian expedition (6.29), even as it was planned to recall him for trial on charges of scheming to overthrow the democracy. The ceremonial trireme *Salaminia,* named for the polis' greatest victory at sea, is sent to Sicily to bring him back for trial and execution (6.61). The disruption of the bond between state and ship is accompanied by indications that the Athenian national character is sharply deteriorating under the pressures of the expeditionary campaign. The once-swift Athenians now procrastinate, and "the length of the time we have now been in commission," Nicias declares, "has rotted our ships and wasted our crews" (7.12). The Athenians meet with "total destruction, their fleet, their army—everything was destroyed and few out of many returned home" (7.87). And throughout, signs accumulate that the Syracusans are acquiring a feel for the connection between their ships and the success of the state.

Aristotle seems to begin again, to think through the fundamental essence of the image. When Aristotle takes up the ship of state, he posits a proper measure of growth for the city, as if it were a living animal: "A ship that is a foot long, for example, will not be a ship at all, nor one of twelve hundred feet, and as it approaches a certain size it will make for a bad voyage, in the one case because of smallness, in the other because of excess" (1326a40–1326b1). A principle of exclusion rests at the heart of this concept, for unlike an animal, a city will not stop growing when it has reached its natural limit, and yet an unchecked growth will efface it.

This recognition that the proportions of the polis are critical would become central when the massive reality of "America" imposed itself on the consciousness of political thinkers. "Thus in the beginning all the world was *America,* " declared John Locke,[6] and in sprinkling his treatise with the word "America," he made the fact of America a concept of political theory. Locke's concern is with the ship of state captained by a tyrant or slaver. When the power of governance is "employed contrary to the end for which it was given," then action by the individual to rebel is justified. Locke's vivid image is of the passenger who comes to realize that the captain of the ship is "carrying him, and the rest of the company, to Algiers," that is, into slavery. One does not have to wait until the deed is accomplished; it is enough to perceive that the captain always returns to that course "as soon as the wind, weather, and other circumstances would let him" (XIX.210), for action to be justified.

The American Revolution produced political theorists alive to the need to address the dangers of direct democracy portrayed by Thucydides and the limitations on the size of the polis set forth by Aristotle. Their solution lay in "the ENLARGEMENT of the ORBIT" (Federalist 9),[7] the encouragement of faction to check faction (Federalist 10) and in the design of a "compound republic" of divided and separated powers (Federalist 51). The result would be representative democracy on a continental scale. Could such a state find any use in perceiving itself in the metaphor of a ship?

Henry Adams declared that the physical symbol of the nation's best qualities was created in the War of 1812—the American sloop-of-war, or privateer, the most efficient vessel afloat: "If the privateer could sail close to the wind, and wear or tack in the twinkling of an eye; if she could spread an immense amount of canvas and run off as fast as a frigate before the wind; if she had sweeps to use in a calm, and one long-range gun pivoted amidships, with plenty of men in case boarding became necessary—she was perfect."[8] Under a chapter headed "American Character," Adams asserted that "the American invention of the fast-sailing schooner or clipper was the more remarkable because, of all American inventions, this alone sprang from direct competition with Europe. . . . Americans instantly made improvements (surpassing centuries of ship construction) which gave them superiority and which Europeans were unable immediately to imitate even after seeing them. . . . the Americans resorted to expedients that had not been tried before, and excited a mixture of irritation and respect in the English service, until Yankee smartness became a national misdemeanor."[9]

Quite another representation of America was presented in 1851 by the *Pequod* of Herman Melville's *Moby Dick*. "Long seasoned and weather-stained in the typhoons and calms of all four oceans, her old hull's complexion was darkened like a French grenadier's, who has alike fought in Egypt and Siberia. Her venerable bows looked bearded. Her masts—cut somewhere on the coasts of Japan, where her original ones were lost overboard in a gale—her masts stood stiffly up like the spines of the three old Kings of Cologne. Her ancient decks were worn and wrinkled. . . . She was a thing of trophies. A cannibal of a craft, tricking herself forth in the chased bones of her enemies."[10]

Banal as it may be to call Melville's whaling-ship a state, and society, in microcosm, it is nonetheless so, for "even at sea we are constantly reminded of the sites and institutions which men build in their attempts to live and work together, of the signs and structures of their attempts at corporate, communal existence"; the *Pequod* is "a parliament, a guildhall, a fortress, and perhaps most notably, a factory."[11]

Pequod, like America, is noted for its "Isolatoes" and presents a tension between the extremes of a sailor's self-reliance and a ship's insistence on connectedness and close cooperation.[12] "What Melville is showing is that the apparently opposing elemental powers and drives which go to make up life—good and evil, light and dark, love and hate, potency and negation, Osiris and Typhon—are not absolutely separable or starkly opposed. Rather, they are reciprocal, mutually constitutive, 'interweavingly' mixed."[13] At stake is democracy itself, and the ship's destruction is the result of a lack of balance brought about by Ahab's monomania.

As Melville was writing *Moby Dick*, Tocqueville was producing his own thoughts on ships and America. As Thucydides did for the Athenian empire, so Tocqueville did for America: set down an "Archaeology" of ways by which this democracy would rise to national greatness and world power. The steps traced by Thucydides and Tocqueville are similar: by suppressing troublesome elements (pirates in the former case; Indians in the latter) trade will take place, producing wealth which must be safeguarded and the naval power to do so. And that power, in turn, can gain an empire. "Reason suggests and experience proves that there is no lasting commercial greatness unless it can, at need, combine with military power. . . . if all the trading states of the Union were combined in one coherent nation, then for them trade would become a national interest of the first importance; they would then be disposed to make great sacrifices to protect their ships and there would be nothing to stop their following their inclinations in this respect . . . Seeing how energetically the Anglo-Americans trade, their natural advantages and their success, I cannot help believing that one day they will become the leading naval power on the globe. They are born to rule the sea, as the Romans were to conquer the world" (406–407). The challenge of Tocqueville's prediction was met by Alfred Thayer Mahan, Captain, U.S. Navy, in his instant classic of 1890, *The Influence of Sea Power Upon History*,[14] arguably the most significant work of naval strategic thought ever written.[15] In seeking to redefine the principles of sea power for the revolutionary technological transformation from sail to steam, Mahan concluded that acquisition and control of oceanic lines of communication could only be obtained by a great sea battle bringing a decisive outcome. Forty-two years later such a battle was fought, at Midway, between carriers of The Imperial Japanese and United States navies, a battle in which the opposing ships were never in sight of one another and the outcome was decided by weapons delivered from the air or undersea; perhaps the last major sea battle ever.

The sailing ships of the "ship of state" image were coherent arrangements of opposing tensions set in a constantly adjusting dynamic. The contemporary steam, diesel, or nuclear-power ship, like democracy in the electronic age, seems able to be easily and quickly directed to go wherever and whenever you want it to go. The fate of Athens revealed that democracy, like a sailing vessel, needs ballast, constraints, and balance; indirection may often prove better than direct action. The "ship of state" metaphor is needed, but today's automated vessels, with crews of women as well as men, pose a barrier to the imagination. All the same, loving reconstructions and sailings of such history-making ships as *Amistad,* whose course at sea recalls Locke's "ship to Algiers," and *Bonhomme Richard,* "the most illustrious ship to fly the American flag during the Revolutionary War," may give continued life to this most ancient and informative political image.[16]

Tell me a story.
In this century, and moment, of mania,
Tell me a story.
—Robert Penn Warren

Notes

Introduction

1. Alexis de Tocqueville, *Democracy in America*, trans. by George Lawrence, ed. by J. P. Mayer (New York: Harper Collins Publishers, 1969), p. 704.

2. Diana Coole, *Women in Political Theory: From Ancient Misogyny to Contemporary Feminism*, 2nd ed. (Hemel Hempstead: Harvester Wheatsheaf, 1993), p. 2. And see Jacques Derrida, *Dissemination*, trans. with intro. and notes by Barbara Johnson (Chicago: University of Chicago Press, 1981), p. 4.

3. Richard Rorty writes, for instance: "It is not evident that [democratic institutions] are to be measured by anything more specific than the moral intuitions of the particular historical community that has created those institutions." Richard Rorty, "The Priority of Democracy to Philosophy," in *The Virginia Statute for Religious Freedom: Its Evolution and Consequences in American History*, eds. Merrill D. Peterson and Robert C. Vaughan (New York: Cambridge University Press, 1988), p. 269.

4. Arneil contends that the real problem as seen by contemporary ("third-wave") feminists is that "most texts reflect the reality of only one gender. The goal of equality does not fully recognize the extent to which every aspect of western societies within which we live [is] masculine, and

therefore alienating to women." Barbara Arneil, *Politics and Feminism* (Oxford: Blackwell Publishers, 1999), p. 4. Cavarero writes: "Inevitably, the roles played by female figures have their meaning in the patriarchal codes that constructed them. . . . [I]n the large range of samples available within the tradition, one cannot find a single figure that adequately meets the declared needs of female subjectivity." Adriana Cavarero, *In Spite of Plato: A Feminist Rewriting of Ancient Philosophy,* trans. Serena Anderlini-D'Onofrio and Áine O'Healy, foreword by Rosi Braidotti (Cambridge: Polity Press, 1995, 1990), pp. 2, 4. The "French feminist" school (including Luce Irigaray, Julia Kristeva, and Hélène Cixous) is often associated with the strongest claims along this line; in *Speculum,* Irigaray titles one section "Any Theory of the 'Subject' Has Always Been Appropriated by the 'Masculine,' " and instead of an index on the final page, one finds the line "[the woman] does not have to conform to the codes theory has set up for itself." Luce Irigaray, *Speculum of the Other Woman,* trans. by Gillian C. Gill (Ithaca: Cornell University Press, 1985, 1974), pp. 133, 365.

5. Rorty claims that "logocentrism is simply essentialism as applied to sentences and beliefs." Richard Rorty, "DeMan and the American Cultural Left," in *Essays on Heidegger and Others* (Cambridge: Cambridge University Press, 1991), p. 130. It has been Rorty's project to discredit essentialism since his earliest work; see *Philosophy and the Mirror of Nature* (Princeton: Princeton University Press, 1979), pp. 361–363, and see *Contingency, irony, and solidarity* (Cambridge: Cambridge University Press, 1989).

6. "Anti-foundational" would come to mind as a pejorative association of constructivism, except that it is a term of praise in our times—indicating how much more "indigenous" constructivism is to democracy than essentialism. According to Benjamin Barber, "democracy both requires and entails an immunity to its own foundations in order to flourish" ["Misreading Democracy: Peter Euben and the *Gorgias,* " in *Dēmokratia: A Conversation on Democracies, Ancient and Modern,* eds. Josiah Ober and Charles Hedrick (Princeton: Princeton University Press, 1996), p. 370. The idea is that democracy at its most flourishing is self-absorbed, free from metaphysical and historical hangovers, and encouraged perpetually through debate to create itself anew. Democracy, Barber likes to repeat, "is the debate about what democracy is." Ibid., p. 373. See also his "Foundationalism and Democracy," in *Democracy and Difference: Contesting the Boundaries of the Political,* ed. Seyla Benhabib (Princeton: Princeton University Press, 1996), p. 355.

Diana Fuss is an example of someone who negotiates the middle terrain when she exposes the "hidden essentialism" that characterizes all radical constructionist projects. By making the important distinction between "lapsing into" essentialism and "deploying" it self-consciously, she suggests an overlap in the two terms that is more profound than the terms are in isolation. She stresses that "essentialists" since Plato and Aristotle have always been mindful of the instability of the essence/accident distinction: "The entire history of metaphysics can be read as an interminable pursuit of the essence of essence, motivated by the anxiety that essence may well be accidental, changing and unknowable. . . . the repeated attempts by these philosophers to fix or to define essence suggest that essence is a slippery and elusive category." Diana Fuss, "The 'Risk' of Essence," in *Feminisms,* eds. Sandra Kemp and Judith Squires (Oxford: Oxford University Press, 1997), pp. 255, 257. And see her *Essentially Speaking: Feminism, Nature and Difference* (New York: Routledge, 1989).

7. Quoted by Lewis Mumford in *Herman Melville* (New York: The Literary Guild of America, 1929), p. 190.

8. Niccolò Machiavelli, *Mandragola*, trans., intro., and notes by Mera J. Flaumenhaft (Prospect Heights, Illinois: Waveland Press, 1981), p. 34.

9. My claim that Socrates is a literary character is in contradistinction to attempts to delineate the "historical Socrates," as detailed below. Gregory Vlastos asserts, for instance, that we can have no doubt about the allegiance of the historical Socrates to the Athenian constitution, since in the *Crito* "he tells his friend in the privacy of his prison cell, where he could have no other motive for dissembling, that he prefers the laws of Athens to those of any other state known to him" [Gregory Vlastos, "The Historical Socrates and Athenian Democracy," *Political Theory* 11, 4 (November 1983): 511]. The false move here is to mistake the apparent artlessness of the Socratic figure for his historical embodiment. It is Plato who places Socrates in that cell with Crito and has him impersonate the Laws of Athens. And the question that "the Laws" put to Socrates—"could you, in the first place, deny that you are our offspring and servant?"—perhaps hangs heavily for those readers unaccustomed to viewing Socrates as a natural outgrowth of the city [Plato, *Crito,* in *Five Dialogues,* trans. G. M. A. Grube (Indianapolis: Hackett Publishing Company, 1981): 50e].

An alternative view is presented by Alexander Nehamas, who argues that with the completion of the early dialogues, "Plato abandons his project of presenting Socrates simply as he saw him and makes instead an effort to explain the phenomenon Socrates constitutes." *The Art of Living: Socratic Reflections from Plato to Foucault* (Berkeley: University of California Press, 1998), p. 88.

10. The notes reveal my substantial debts, though it must be recognized

how selective I have had to be in citing works across this range of primary material. If there is a single criterion behind my positive citations, it is something like the critic's unabashed love of the text; negative citations usually reveal the critic's knack for ruining a good story.

11. Friedrich Nietzsche, "On the uses and disadvantages of history for life," in *Untimely Meditations,* trans. by R. J. Hollingdale, intro. by J. P. Stern (New York: Cambridge University Press, 1983), pp. 60, 105.

Chapter One: Stories at the Limits

1. As Sommerstein notes, "the history of the Dionysian genres is almost coextensive with the history of the polis." Alan H. Sommerstein, "Introduction," *Tragedy, Comedy and the Polis,* eds. Alan H. Sommerstein, Stephen Halliwell, Jeffrey Henderson, and Bernhard Zimmermann (Bari, Italy: Levante Editori, 1993), p. 19.

2. The term is used reservedly, of course; in order to frame my own inquiry, I bypass controversies about the "who" and "how many" of Homer and the "when" of the poem's transcription.

3. Donald Kagan's monumental multivolume work on the Peloponnesian War has been correctly characterized by George Steiner as one of the great intellectual achievements of our time. But Thucydides, even when refuted on the facts, does not relinquish his possession of the war in the realm of the imagination or in its practical influence on statecraft.

4. David Harvey, "Women in Thucydides," *Arethusa* 18 (1985): 73.

5. "Ithaca the polis, as opposed to Ithaca the island, is only once described by epithet in the whole of the *Odyssey.*" Stephen Scully, *Homer and the Sacred City* (Ithaca: Cornell University Press, 1990), p. 5.

6. I support Scully's conclusion that the Homeric polis "is still a group of co-inhabitants, an aggregate of oikoi, the sum of its parts qualitatively different from each part perceived independently." Ibid., p. 15. Consult pages 105–113 and endnotes 34–35 for his rendition of opposing views, and see Raaflaub, "Homer to Solon," *The Ancient Greek City-State,* ed. Mogens Herman Hansen, *Historisk-filosofiske Meddelelser* 67 (Commissioner: Munksgaard Copenhagen, 1993): 41–59.

7. Homer, *The Odyssey,* trans. Robert Fagles, intro. and notes by Bernard Knox (New York: Penguin Books, 1996): 6.200–202.

8. The breakdown in the sanctity of oaths in the fifth-century polis becomes thematic in Thucydides' *Peloponnesian War*. The urgency of this topic for the *Odyssey* is recognized by Dobbs, who argues that the central location of this episode of the cattle of the Sun is meant to highlight the "dawn of reverence in Odysseus." Dobbs suggests that the epic stature of Odysseus

is justified in his replacing of a "reckless heroic competitiveness" with a sense of the sacred. Darrell Dobbs, "Reckless Rationalism and Heroic Reverence in Homer's *Odyssey,*" *American Political Science Review* 81, 2 (June 1987): 494, 502.

9. As Victoria Josselyn Wohl reminds us in "Standing by the Stathmos: Sexual Ideology in the *Odyssey,*" *Arethusa* 26 (1993): 35, n. 49.

10. In the case of Penelope, Beye points out, the suitors make animals of themselves. Charles Rowan Beye, "Male and Female in the Homeric Poems," *Ramos* 3,2 (1974): 98.

11. James Redfield, "*Homo Domesticus,*" in *The Greeks,* ed. Jean-Pierre Vernant (Chicago: University of Chicago Press, 1995), p. 183.

12. Homer, *The Iliad,* trans. Robert Fagles, intro. Bernard Knox (New York: Penguin, 1990): VI.424–426.

13. Schein writes that she is "a victim of the inevitability of her situation. . . . Just as Achilles, though responsible for the destruction of Troy, is not morally blameworthy, so with Helen: she simply is who and what she is, simultaneously more-than-human and all-too-human." Seth L. Schein, *The Mortal Hero: An Introduction to Homer's Iliad* (Berkeley: University of California Press, 1984), p. 23. Redfield concurs: "Helen is no villainess; she does harm passively, it is not her fault." James R. Redfield, *Nature and Culture in the Iliad: The Tragedy of Hector* (Chicago: The University of Chicago Press, 1975), p. 122.

14. "Andromache is the faithful wife who completes and motivates the hero; Helen is woman as source of danger and social disorder (III.156–60)." Redfield, *Nature and Culture,* 122. And Austin: "We might even interpret Penelope as the revision of Helen . . . with Helen's shamelessness almost canceled out by Penelope's higher sense of shame." Norman Austin, *Helen of Troy and Her Shameless Phantom* (Ithaca: Cornell University Press, 1994), p. 85, n. 22.

15. S. Douglas Olson, "The Stories of Helen and Menelaus," *American Journal of Philology* 110 (1989): 391.

16. As noted by Lillian Eileen Doherty, *Siren Songs: Gender, Audiences, and Narrators in the Odyssey* (Ann Arbor: The University of Michigan Press, 1995), p. 58.

17. Seth L. Schein, "Female Representations and Interpreting the *Odyssey,*" *The Distaff Side,* ed. Beth Cohen (New York: Oxford University Press, 1995), p. 23.

18. Helene P. Foley, "'Reverse Similes' and Sex Roles in the *Odyssey,*" *Arethusa* 11, 1–2 (Spring and Fall 1978): 20.

19. This is Dobbs' suggestion in "Reckless Rationalism," p. 503. Austin

writes that Odysseus and Penelope reflect "a ceaseless effort to build with hand and mind a world that the gods may—no will—sooner or later destroy." Norman Austin, *Archery at the Dark of the Moon* (Berkeley: University of California Press, 1975), p. 252.

20. *The Landmark Thucydides: A Comprehensive Guide to The Peloponnesian War,* revised edition of the Richard Crawley translation, ed. Robert B. Strassler, intro. by Victor Davis Hanson (New York: Touchstone, 1998): 7.69.2.

21. Hunter R. Rawlings III details the interrelations of Thucydides' Books 2 and 7 in *The Structure of Thucydides' History* (Princeton: Princeton University Press, 1981), pp. 126–175.

22. W. Robert Connor, *Thucydides* (Princeton: Princeton University Press, 1994), p. 34.

23. As Hanson writes, "Athens and Sparta are states in a real war, but they are also metaphysical representations of opposite ways of looking at the universe, whose corollaries are often emphasized in a variety of contexts." Hanson, "Introduction," *The Landmark Thucydides,* xi.

24. Paul Cartledge, "Spartan Institutions in Thucydides," Appendix C in *The Landmark Thucydides,* p. 589.

25. Adam M. Parry, "Thucydides' Historical Perspective," in *The Language of Achilles and Other Papers* (Oxford: Clarendon Press, 1989), p. 299.

26. As Orwin notes, Thucydides is thought to have "remained entirely sympathetic to [Pericles'] goals and program." Clifford Orwin, *The Humanity of Thucydides* (Princeton: Princeton University Press, 1994), p. 15. In the historicist vein, Immerwahr, for instance, writes that "Thucydides conceived of his own ideas not as private thoughts, but as common ideas of the period." Henry R. Immerwahr, "Pathology of Power and the Speeches in Thucydides," in *The Speeches in Thucydides,* ed. Philip A. Stadter (Chapel Hill: University of North Carolina Press, 1973), p. 23.

27. Gregory Crane, *The Blinded Eye: Thucydides and the New Written Word* (Lanham, Maryland: Rowman and Littlefield Publishers, 1996), p. 129. Earlier he claims that "even within the misogynist tradition of Greek literature, Thucydides stands out" (76). The second citation is from Harvey, "Thucydides and Women," p. 71, and the final one from Simon Hornblower, "The Religious Dimension to the Peloponnesian War, Or, What Thucydides Does Not Tell Us," *Harvard Studies in Classical Philology,* 94 (1992): 170. In contrast to these literal readings, Nicole Loraux offers fascinating thoughts about the historian's possible motives: "Thucydides' care not to involve women in the bloodiest episodes of the *stasis* has already led to the

supposition that he endowed them (or at least desired to do so) with inherent wisdom and reserve." Nicole Loraux, *The Experience of Tiresias: The Feminine and the Greek Man,* trans. Paula Wissing (Princeton: Princeton University Press, 1995), p. 240, and "Conclusion: Feminine Nature in History," pp. 227–248.

28. The scholarship on Thucydides is voluminous and unusually rich, and I am far from claiming any originality on the matter of his literary acumen; here I note the particular influence of W. Robert Connor's work. I have arrived at the Herodotus-Thucydides accord (elaborated below) on my own, however, after many years of seeking to detail the nature of their "quarrel," without satisfaction. I am pleased enough with this emendation to refrain, on principle, from apologizing for any future reversals.

29. My own approach is similarly fashioned to accommodate the literary and historical, as here where I argue that even as Thucydides is "in Athenian character" in the Methodology, he articulates a historiographical position that transcends that role. His great literary innovations bring no discredit to him as historian; this is the highest possibility inherent in the act of writing that I trace throughout this book.

30. See my *Herodotus and the Origins of the Political Community: Arion's Leap* (New Haven: Yale University Press, 1996), pp. 31–36, for a further account.

31. Westlake is particularly useful on this point: "Thus on a point of detail, which is of some historical importance, the excursus on Pausanias is in accord with the normal practice of Herodotus and not with that of Thucydides." H. D. Westlake, "Thucydides on Pausanias and Themistokles—A Written Source?" *Classical Quarterly* 27 (1977): 100. And see Charles Forster Smith, "Traces of Epic Usage in Thucydides," *Transactions and Proceedings of the American Philological Association* XXXI (1900): 69–81.

32. Arguably, it is Herodotus who retains more distance in his portrayal, he being neither Athenian nor Persian. Thucydides the Athenian may step more fully into his part.

33. Herodotus, *The History,* trans. David Grene (Chicago: University of Chicago Press, 1987): 1.4.

34. Connor, *Thucydides,* p. 26.

35. Gomme, for one, finds cause to wonder whether this custom was restricted to men. A. W. Gomme, *A Historical Commentary on Thucydides,* Vol.1 (Oxford: Clarendon Press, 1971, 1945), p. 102.

36. Artemisia being the fascinating exception. See my "Public or Private? An Artemisian Answer," *Arion* 7, 2 (Fall 1999): 49–63.

37. Many consider the Archaeology to be a puzzle unsolved: "It is a pecu-

liar fact that Thucydides' method of identifying the beginnings of wars has never been adequately explained." Rawlings, *Structure,* p. 13.

38. I find little support in the critical literature for my view here, but Marc Cogan [in *The Human Thing: The Speeches and Principles of Thucydides' History* (Chicago: University of Chicago Press, 1981), p. 37] makes the following relevant observation: "What we must recognize in Pericles' speech, and what is most peculiar and most revelatory of Athens' orientation at the beginning of the war, is that Pericles proposed *no war aims.* . . . As far as this Thucydidean Pericles is concerned, the totality of Athenian intentions at the beginning of the war was to be mere endurance." I would add that "mere endurance" is the derogatory restatement of "a possession for all time."

39. Virginia Hunter, *Past and Process in Herodotus and Thucydides* (Princeton: Princeton University Press, 1982), p. 45.

40. Wiedemann pronounces the ending "ironic," and I concur: irony permits the responsible self-concealment of Thucydides. Thomas E. J. Wiedemann, "Thucydides, Women, and the Limits of Rational Analysis," *Greece and Rome* XXX, 2 (October 1983), n. 2, p. 170.

41. Wolfgang Kullman, "Man as a Political Animal in Aristotle," in *A Companion to Aristotle's Politics,* eds. David Keyt and Fred D. Miller, Jr. (Cambridge: Basil Blackwell, Inc., 1991), p. 109. M. H. Hansen, "Introduction," *Ancient Greek City-State,* pp. 16–17. Murray, "Polis and *Politeia* in Aristotle," in ed. Hansen, *Ancient Greek City-State,* p. 203. And the "natural" component itself is not a simple concept. See note 45 in Fred D. Miller, Jr., *Nature, Justice and Rights in Aristotle's Politics* (Oxford: Clarendon Press, 1995), p. 45, and Mary P. Nichols, *Citizens and Statesmen: A Study of Aristotle's Politics* (Savage, Maryland: Rowman and Littlefield Publishers, 1992), p. 18.

42. "[The polis] is a paradigm case of a mode of the distribution of power on which environmental pressure has the effect of generating maladaptive responses," W. G. Runciman writes, but this is not the polis of Aristotle: "Nor does it have to be small enough for a Stentorian herald to be heard by all its members" ["Doomed to Extinction: The Polis as an Evolutionary Dead-End," in *The Greek City: From Homer to Alexander,* eds. Oswyn Murray and Simon Price (Oxford: Clarendon Press, 1990), pp. 355, 348]. David Keyt, "Three Basic Theorems in Aristotle's *Politics,*" in Keyt and Miller, eds., *Companion,* p. 128. The Aristotle that Keyt "refutes" is sometimes unrecognizable. See Cary J. Nederman, "The Puzzle of the Political Animal: Nature and Artifice in Aristotle's Political Theory," *Review of Politics* 56, 2 (Spring

1994): 296. On the objectivity charge, see Saunders, *Aristotle: Politics Books I and II,* trans. and commentary by Trevor J. Saunders (New York: Clarendon Press, 1995), p. 56.

43. Mortimer H. Chambers, "Aristotle's Historical Method," in *Panhellenica: Essays in Ancient History and Historiography in honor of Truesdell S. Brown,* eds. Stanley M. Burstein and Louis A. Okin (Lawrence, Kansas: Coronado Press, 1980), p. 62.

44. Plutarch, *The Rise and Fall of Athens: Nine Greek Lives,* trans. with intro. by Ian Scott- Kilvert (New York: Penguin Books, 1960), p. 55.

45. Fr. 36.18–20W. Quoted by Steiner, who comments: "There is no mistaking that emphatic Ἔγραγχ" [*I wrote* them *down*]. Deborah Tarn Steiner, *The Tyrant's Writ: Myths and Images of Writing in Ancient Greece* (Princeton: Princeton University Press, 1994), p. 230.

46. Plutarch, *Athens,* pp. 60, 57.

47. Kurt A. Raaflaub, "Homer to Solon: The Rise of the Polis. The Written Sources," in *The Ancient Greek City-State,* p. 42.

48. Lord, *The Politics,* n. 98, p. 253.

49. *Plutarch on Sparta,* trans. with intro. and notes by Richard J. A. Talbert (New York: Penguin Books, 1988), p. 8.

50. Aristotle, *Nicomachean Ethics,* trans. H. Rackham (Cambridge: Harvard University Press, 1982): 1180a25–27.

51. Plutarch, *Sparta,* p. 22.

52. Eckart Schütrumpf, "Aristotle on Sparta," in *The Shadow of Sparta,* eds. Anton Powell and Stephen Hodkinson (New York: Routledge, 1994), pp. 335–336.

53. As in the Carnes Lord translation of Aristotle's *Politics.*

54. Oswyn Murray, "Polis and *Politeia* in Aristotle," in *The Ancient Greek City-State,* p. 201. Aristotle also presents, as the "simply best" regime, that of rule by "philosopher kings," an ideal beyond the reach of practical politics. See Liz Anne Alexander, "The Best Regimes of Aristotle's *Politics,* " *History of Political Thought* XXI, 2 (Summer 2000): 216.

55. Michael Davis, *The Politics of Philosophy: A Commentary on Aristotle's Politics* (Lanham, Maryland: Rowman & Littlefield, 1996), p. 87.

56. Stephen G. Salkever, *Finding the Mean: Theory and Practice in Aristotelian Political Philosophy* (Princeton: Princeton University Press, 1990), p. 198. Saxonhouse concludes: "The city of Aristotle's dreams exalts the feminine virtue of constraint." Arlene Saxonhouse, *Women in the History of Political Thought: Ancient Greece to Machiavelli* (New York: Praeger Publishers, 1985), p. 90.

57. The literature on natural slavery is substantial and more detailed than it is possible to reproduce here. Among several excellent works, see especially Wayne Ambler, "Aristotle on Nature and Politics: The Case of Slavery," *Political Theory* 15 (1987): 390–410; Mary Nichols, *Citizens and Statesmen;* and Darrell Dobbs, "Natural Right and the Problem of Aristotle's Defense of Slavery," *The Journal of Politics* 56, 1 (1994): 69–94, with bibliographies.

58. Diana Coole, *Women in Political Theory,* p. 29. Note Horowitz's opening (my emphasis): "*A conventional Greek,* Aristotle limited his perspective of women's service to the state to her fulfillment of functions within the family." Maryanne Cline Horowitz, "Aristotle and Woman," *Journal of the History of Biology* 9, 2 (Fall 1976): 208. Arneil sums up "feminist scholarship" in an unintentionally devastating indictment: "What ultimately distinguishes Aristotle from Plato, according to feminist scholarship, is not simply his acceptance of 'natural differences' but the tying of this to defending his present day status quo; that is, the existing functions of each of the parts of Greek society." Arneil, *Politics and Feminism,* p. 83.

59. This refrain comes most influentially from Okin: "Aristotle has established a philosophical framework by which he can legitimize the status quo. . . . Every person, therefore, is naturally suited to his or her existing role and position in society." Her Aristotle "starts from a basic belief that the *status quo* in both the natural and social realm is the best way for things to be." Susan Moller Okin, *Women in Western Political Thought* (Princeton: Princeton University Press, 1979), pp. 80, 74.

60. "The male's more thymotic nature *relative to his natural mate* ensures that he will be the one better fit to lead their partnership. Likewise, the female proceeds in accord with nature when she rejects as a mate any male endowed with less *thymos* than herself." Darrell Dobbs, "Family Matters: Aristotle's Appreciation of Women and the Plural Structure of Society," *American Political Science Review* 90, 1 (March 1996): 83.

61. Masugi writes that "the most striking instances of female inferiority prove to be not only ambiguous but affirmative of the opposite—in given instances women can be the equals and indeed the superiors of even exceptional men." Ken Masugi, "Another Peek at Aristotle and Phyllis: The Place of Women in Aristotle's Argument for Human Equality," p. 282. I resist the temptation here to elaborate on these literary allusions, since they are so well-established in the critical literature—even if resolutely ignored by the feminist scholars cited above. See the bibliography in Dodds, "Aristotle's Appreciation of Women."

62. Dobbs, "Family Matters," p. 80, citing *GA,* 736b27–28.

Chapter Two: Plato's Socrates

1. Generals of the "old guard" were Leo Strauss and Gregory Vlastos, whose legacies are to be traced, respectively, in the following *Republic* translations: *The Republic of Plato,* 2nd edition, trans. with notes and intro. by Allan Bloom (New York: Basic Books, 1968), and Plato, *Republic,* trans. G. M. A. Grube, revised by C. D. C. Reeve (Indianapolis: Hackett Publishing Company, 1992). Strauss insisted on taking as paramount the fact that Plato does not stand behind any theory in his own name and offers no encouragement for readers to take Socrates as his mouthpiece. Bloom reproduces the view that the integrity of the dialogue must be respected if readers are to approach anything like a Platonic teaching. (Citations from the *Republic* are from Bloom's translation.) On the other side, Gregory Vlastos theorized that the dialogues reflect Plato's own development as a philosopher such that initially he reproduces the teachings of Socrates, then experiments with his own theory of Forms in his middle phase, and finally grows into his own in his late dialogues. Along this line, Reeve refers casually to "what Plato believes" or to "Plato's ideal city," and in his revision of the Grube translation, he includes a bibliography which recognizes only variations of the blueprint view.

The battle lines are slowly being redrawn. Press refers to "the gradual realization that [attention to literary and dramatic characteristics, contextualism, and a less doctrinal orientation] do belong together in a satisfactory interpretation of the dialogues." Gerald Press, "The Dialogical Mode in Modern Plato Studies," in *Plato's Dialogues: The Dialogical Approach,* eds. Richard Hart and Victorino Tejera (Lewiston, New York: Edwin Mellen Press, 1997), p. 29. As the sheer number of "dialogical" readings becomes overwhelming, some convergence of views is inevitable. Nevertheless, a knee-jerk hostility to Straussian readings still remains acceptable "scholarly" behavior, as in Rutherford's remark: "I have read only one of Strauss's works (*The City and Man*), and have been unable to finish any of the books by his epigoni." R. B. Rutherford, *The Art of Plato: Ten Essays in Platonic Interpretation* (Cambridge: Harvard University Press, 1995), x. Cited by Charles L. Griswold, Jr. ["'E Pluribus Unum?* On the Platonic 'Corpus,'" review of Charles H. Kahn, *Plato and the Socratic Dialogue: The Philosophical Use of a Literary Form* (Cambridge: Cambridge University Press, 1996) in *Ancient Philosophy* 19, 21 (1999): 363]; he also notes that the current convergence of views frequently takes place without attribution to Strauss or his "epigoni." No doubt Strauss and Bloom will continue to be vilified in the secondary literature—at the same time that their ideas are becoming mainstream.

2. Plato's *Phaedrus*, trans. with intro. and commentary by R. Hackforth (New York: Cambridge University Press, 1982): 275d.

3. "The female and the philosopher live apart from the political world. They both satisfy their erotic desires independently of the needs or demands of the city, though they both may need the security that the city offers." Arlene W. Saxonhouse, "The Philosopher and the Female in the Political Thought of Plato," in *Feminist Interpretations of Plato,* ed. Nancy Tuana (University Park: Pennsylvania State University Press, 1994), p. 79. The erotic desires of the *city,* meanwhile, come to light in this work and others as in need of instruction. See David M. Halperin, "Plato and the Erotics of Narrativity," in *Methods of Interpreting Plato and His Dialogues, Oxford Studies in Ancient Philosophy,* suppl. vol., eds. James C. Klagge and Nicolas D. Smith (Oxford: Clarendon Press, 1992): 93–129.

4. Elena Duvergès Blair, "Women: The Unrecognized Teachers of the Platonic Socrates," *Ancient Philosophy* 16 (1996): 333. Blair rightly notes that Plato seems to be saying something about *Socrates* rather than about *women.*

5. Jacques Derrida, *Dissemination,* trans. with intro. and notes by Barbara Johnson (Chicago: University of Chicago Press, 1981), p. 137.

6. Christopher Norris, *Derrida* (Cambridge: Harvard University Press, 1987), p. 34.

7. Hackforth, *Plato's Phaedrus,* 157, n. 2.

8. Plato, *Timaeus,* trans. Benjamin Jowett, in *The Collected Dialogues of Plato,* eds. Edith Hamilton and Huntington Cairns (Princeton: Princeton University Press, 1961): 21d.

9. *The Laws of Plato,* trans. with notes and essay by Thomas L. Pangle (New York: Basic Books, 1980): 656e.

10. *Plato's Phaedo,* trans. with intro. and commentary by R. Hackforth (Cambridge: Cambridge University Press, 1955): 80c-d.

11. Ronna Burger, *Plato's Phaedrus: A Defense of a Philosophical Art of Writing* (Tuscaloosa: University of Alabama Press, 1980), pp. 98, 93.

12. "Phaedrus' desire to memorize a text illustrates perfectly Thamus' critique of the written word." Charles L. Griswold, Jr., *Self-Knowledge in Plato's Phaedrus* (New Haven: Yale University Press, 1986), p. 24.

13. And the legend continues in our own times: in 1996, two writers proclaimed that they "think it possible that the Sphinx and the three great Pyramids may offer knowledge of the genesis of civilization itself." Robert Bauval and Graham Hancock, *Keeper of Genesis: A Quest for the Hidden Legacy of Mankind* (London: Heinemann, 1996), p. 6. Other New Age versions of the

Sphinx's "coded messages" are more bizarre. Alexander Stille details the coded messages in "Perils of the Sphinx," *New Yorker* (February 10, 1997): 60; 54–66.

14. Mary Lefkowitz, *Not Out of Africa: How "Afrocentrism" Became an Excuse to Teach Myth as History* (New York: Basic Books, 1996), p. 81.

15. John Herman Randall, Jr., *Plato: Dramatist of the Life of Reason* (New York: Columbia University Press, 1970), p. 5. Randall directs his comments to Platonic dialogues in general, whereas I believe his words are especially apt for the *Phaedrus*.

16. Cropsey, "Phaedrus," p. 233.

17. See, for example, *Ion* 534c, 536c; *Apology*, 22c; *Meno*, 86bc.

18. E. N. Tigerstedt, "Plato's Idea of Poetical Inspiration," *Commentationes Humanarum Litterarum* 44, 2 (1969): 56. And Hackforth notes: "Amongst the eschatological myths that of *Phaedrus* is exceptional in being attributed directly to Socrates: the palinode is 'all his own work' (257a)." Hackforth, *Phaedrus*, p. 14.

19. Tigerstedt, p. 58.

20. As Berger notes: "textuality proclaims its difference from, its independence of, its superiority to, the conversation it pretends to represent." Harry Berger, Jr., "Levels of Discourse in Plato's Dialogues," in *Literature and the Question of Philosophy*, ed. Anthony J. Cascardi (Baltimore: Johns Hopkins University Press, 1987), p. 95.

21. Cropsey's suggestions about the Plato-Socrates relation are to the point: "A man who knew both Plato and Isocrates, and was capable of acknowledging Isocrates as his favorite, could not be a first-rate judge of human quality." Cropsey, "Phaedrus," p. 233. And see G. R. F. Ferrari, *Listening to the Cicadas: A Study of Plato's Phaedrus* (Cambridge: Cambridge University Press, 1987, 1990), p. 283, n. 33.

22. His anonymity is his way of criticizing Socrates' insistence on immediacy. Berger notes that Plato "shares with Heidegger and Derrida a critical view of the metaphysics of presence." Berger, "Levels of Discourse," p. 78.

23. Ferrari, *Listening*, p. 53, and Burger, *Plato's Phaedrus*, p. 97. Ferrari distances his reading from Burger's, however, as he sees no warrant for the extreme irony behind the claim that "Plato is covertly claiming that his kind of writing, as opposed to philosophic conversation, is in fact the best way forward in philosophy" (214).

24. Norris, *Derrida*, p. 30.

25. See Cropsey, "Phaedrus," p. 249.

26. This is an appropriate moment to note that I am not putting forth a theme of painting *per se* in the *Republic*, much less across the dialogues. My

subject is "the painting of kallipolis" and how Socrates' feminine strategies in Book 5 wear down the egotistic and misogynist assumptions that inhere in that painting. Already by the end of this book, Socrates gains assent to a more sophisticated idea: "Do you suppose a painter is any less good who draws a pattern of what the fairest human being would be like and renders everything in the picture adequately, but can't prove that it's also possible that such a man come into being?" Glaucon answers: "No, by Zeus, I don't" (472d).

I do not deny the far-ranging implications of Aristotle's criticisms; I simply emphasize how circumscribed is his direct attack. I agree with Dobbs' conclusion that "Aristotle points toward a genuine and important disagreement with Plato's Socrates regarding the conditions of a philosophical education and their compatibility with political concerns." Darrell Dobbs, "Aristotle's Anticommunism," *American Journal of Political Science* 29, 1 (February 1985): 44.

27. Most feminist criticism of the *Republic,* Book 5, remains on this level. In Bluestone's *Women and the Ideal Society,* for instance, she delineates "seven types of hostility" toward women in a century of Platonic scholarship, all premised on a literal equation of what Socrates says in Book 5 with what "Plato believes"; she persists in characterizing any dialogical views as an assertion that "Plato wasn't serious." Natalie Harris Bluestone, *Women and the Ideal Society: Plato's Republic and Modern Myths of Gender* (Amherst: University of Massachusetts Press, 1987), pp. 12, 21. In *Feminist Interpretations of Plato,* however, the previously mentioned article by Saxonhouse goes against this grain; as the editor Nancy Tuana claims, Saxonhouse adds a welcome note of diversity to what otherwise would appear to be a uniform and unitary feminist view (10). Unfortunately this tolerant note is all-too *rare* in feminist collections: see the appallingly politicized comments about Saxonhouse in Bluestone (101), and the imperious dismissal: "Her approach is different from all others, however, and I think few would describe her own argument as feminist" (99). For good measure, Bluestone misspells her name.

28. It is true, as Forde claims, that "the first wave of argument raises but cannot definitively settle the question as to what human nature really is and which of its parts is essential or inessential." Steven Forde, "Gender and Justice in Plato," *American Political Science Review* 92,3 (September 1997): 660.

29. There are other reasons, to be sure, for readers to respect the studied ways of Socrates, and to expect to have to qualify whatever first impressions he makes. Socrates, of course, is presented from the start as *coerced* accom-

plice in this discussion (327c); the suggestion is that the discussion is for the sake of the interlocutors and on their terms. The scene of mock violence that opens the *Republic* recurs in Book 5 with unmistakable signs of physical restraint (449b). And force or no force, there is the "habitual irony" of Socrates that should make readers wary of surface meanings (337a) and that suggests his manipulation of the twists and turns of the argument. Already (early) in Book 1, as Bloom notes, "Socrates takes command of the little community, forces Cephalus to leave, and makes the nature of justice the problem of the discussion." Allan Bloom, "Interpretive Essay," p. 314.

30. Saxonhouse, "Philosopher and the Female," p. 76.

31. *Plato: Five Dialogues,* trans. G. M. A. Grube (Indianapolis: Hackett Publishing Company, 1981): *Phaedo,* 60b.

32. Joseph Cropsey, "The Dramatic End of Plato's Socrates," *Interpretation* 14, 2 & 3 (1986): 159.

33. Jacob Klein, *A Commentary on Plato's Meno* (Chapel Hill: University of North Carolina Press, 1965), p. 125.

34. Loraux, *Experience of Tiresias*, p. 5.

35. Hayden W. Ausland, "On Reading Plato Mimetically," *American Journal of Philology* 118 (Fall 1997): 376.

36. David Sedley, "The Dramatis Personae of Plato's *Phaedo,* " in *Philosophical Dialogues: Plato, Hume, Wittgenstein,* ed. Timothy Smiley (Oxford: Oxford University Press, 1995), p. 20 and n. 20.

37. Ibid., pp. 4–5.

Chapter Three: The Rhetoric of the State

1. Loraux writes that "the feminine realm is revealed to be essential, for it is there to modulate and at the same time support the necessary virility of the *andres* " (Loraux, *Experience of Tiresias,* p. 9). Among the many critics who have contributed important insights on this issue, I single out for particular mention Stephen Salkever, *Finding the Mean* (see, for example, p. 178) and Mary Nichols, *Citizens and Statesmen* (pp. 33–34).

2. J. G. A. Pocock, *The Machiavellian Moment: Florentine Political Thought and the Atlantic Republican Tradition* (Princeton: Princeton University Press, 1975), p. 158.

3. Niccolò Machiavelli, *The Prince,* trans. with intro. by Harvey C. Mansfield, Jr. (Chicago: University of Chicago Press, 1985), pp. 5–6. Hereafter, *P.*

4. Hanna Fenichel Pitkin, *Fortune Is a Woman: Gender & Politics in the Thought of Niccolò Machiavelli* (Berkeley: University of California Press, 1984), p. 285.

5. Victoria Kahn, "Virtù and the Example of Agathocles in Machiavelli's

Prince," in *Machiavelli and the Discourse of Literature,* eds. Albert Russell Ascoli and Victoria Kahn (Ithaca: Cornell University Press, 1993), p. 205.

And Mansfield writes: "The young men who master Lady Fortune come with audacity and leave exhausted, but she remains ageless, waiting for the next ones. . . . One might go so far as to wonder . . . whether Machiavelli, who has personified fortune, can impersonate her in the world of modern politics he attempted to create." Harvey C. Mansfield, Jr., "Introduction," *Prince,* xxiv.

6. Harvey C. Mansfield, "Machiavelli's *Stato* and the Modern State," in *Machiavelli's Virtue* (Chicago: University of Chicago Press, 1996), p. 291.

7. Robert Hariman, "Composing Modernity in Machiavelli's *Prince,"* *Journal of the History of Ideas* 50 (January, March 1989), p. 27.

8. Mona Ozouf, *Women's Words: Essay on French Singularity,* trans. Jane Marie Todd (Chicago: University of Chicago Press, 1997), p. 246. The Burke quotations are from Edmund Burke, *Reflections on the Revolution in France,* ed. J. G. A. Pocock (Indianapolis: Hackett Publishing Company, 1987), p. 66, and *Philosophical Enquiry into the Origin of Our Ideas of the Sublime and Beautiful,* ed. with intro. by Adam Phillips (New York: Oxford University Press, 1990), p. 58. Hereafter, *Reflections* and *Enquiry.*

9. Mary Wollstonecraft, *A Vindication of the Rights of Men and A Vindication of the Rights of Woman,* eds. D. L. Macdonald and Kathleen Scherf (Orchard Park, New York: Broadview Press, 1997), p. 96. Unless otherwise noted, references to Wollstonecraft's *Vindication* is to *Vindication of the Right of Men,* her direct response to Burke's *Reflections.*

10. George Levine, "The Ambiguous Heritage of *Frankenstein,"* in *The Endurance of Frankenstein: Essays on Mary Shelley's Novel,* eds. George Levine and U. C. Knoepflamacher (Berkeley: University of California Press, 1979), p. 15; and Sandra M. Gilbert and Susan Gubar, "Mary Shelley's Monstrous Eve," in *Mary Shelley: Frankenstein,* ed. J. Paul Hunter (New York: Norton & Company, 1996), p. 232.

11. William Veeder, "Gender and Pedagogy: The Question of *Frankenstein,"* in *Approaches to Teaching Shelley's Frankenstein,* ed. Stephen C. Behrendt (New York: The Modern Language Association of America, 1990), p. 47.

12. Livy, *The Early History of Rome: Books I-V of The History of Rome from Its Foundation,* trans. by Aubrey De Sélincourt, intro. by R. M. Ogilvie (New York: Penguin Books, 1960, 1971), p. 98.

13. Contrary to common portrayals, Lucretia is not the paradigmatic victim. If she succumbs to the rape because of her concern for reputation, she also *triumphs* through that same concern: her suicide absolves her of any complicity in the act. Her resolve is heroic and is certainly recognized as

such by Livy. See the careful treatments by Ronald L. Martinez in "The Pharmacy of Machiavelli: Roman Lucretia in *Mandragola,*" *Renaissance Drama* New Series XIV (1983): 1–43, especially p. 18, and Ian Donaldson, *The Rapes of Lucretia: A Myth and Its Transformations* (Oxford: Clarendon Press, 1982), especially pp. 21–23.

14. Nancy S. Streuver, *Theory as Practice: Ethical Inquiry in the Renaissance* (Chicago: University of Chicago Press, 1992), p. 166. Again, this feature does not set moderns apart from ancients so much as it does from contemporary democrats, who guard their genre boundaries with more concern.

15. Niccolò Machiavelli, *Discourses on Livy,* trans. by Harvey C. Mansfield and Nathan Tarcov (Chicago: University of Chicago Press, 1996): III.2, p. 213.

16. Harvey C. Mansfield, Jr., *Machiavelli's New Modes and Orders: A Study of the Discourses on Livy* (Ithaca: Cornell University Press, 1979), p. 306.

17. "Machiavelli suggests that true memory allows one to experience the past as one would the present, through one's senses." Jack D'Amico, "Machiavelli and Memory," *Modern Language Quarterly* 50, 2 (June 1989): 106.

18. "Perhaps intelligent adaptability is more important for establishing hegemony than glorious self-sacrifice." Frank Fata, "Machiavellian Strategies in *Mandragola,*" *Machiavelli Studies* 2 (1988): 94.

19. Streuver, *Theory as Practice,* p. 175.

20. Jack D'Amico, "The Virtù of Women: Machiavelli's *Mandragola* and *Clizia,*" *Interpretation* 12, 2 & 3 (May and September 1984): 261.

21. Niccolò Machiavelli, *Mandragola,* trans., intro., and notes by Mera J. Flaumenhaft (Prospect Heights, Illinois: Waveland Press, Inc., 1981), p. 10.

22. Fata, "Machiavellian Strategies," p. 92.

23. Theodore A. Sumberg, "*La Mandragola:* An Interpretation," *The Journal of Politics* 23 (1961): 334. An implausible mixture of ancient and modern is stipulated in the name Callimaco Guadagni. The Greek derivation of the first name brings together *kalos* (noble) and *machê* (battle), whereas the surname is Italian for 'gains' or 'earnings.' See Mera J. Flaumenhaft, "The Comic Remedy: Machiavelli's *Mandragola,*" *Interpretation* 7,2 (May 1978): 57.

24. Martinez, "The Pharmacy of Machiavelli," p. 15.

25. D'Amico, "Virtù of Women," p. 264.

26. She is *not* depicted as "falling in love with Callimaco," as Pitken claims (*Fortune Is a Woman,* 30); that would indeed make the Livy connec-

tion incoherent. From first to last, Lucrezia is a woman without illusions, which is what makes her "new case" widely applicable.

27. D'Amico, "Virtù of Women," p. 268.

28. Sumberg, *La Mandragola,* " p. 320. "If Machiavellian history had a single purpose," Smith writes, "it was to cultivate the deed." Bruce James Smith, *Politics and Remembrance: Republican Themes in Machiavelli, Burke, and Tocqueville* (Princeton: Princeton University Press, 1985), p. 37. And see Carnes Lord, "On Machiavelli's *Mandragola,* " *Journal of Politics* 41 (August 1979): 806–827.

29. James Boyd White, *When Words Lose Their Meaning: Constitutions and Reconstitutions of Language, Character, and Community* (Chicago: University of Chicago Press, 1984), p. 218.

30. Michael A. Mosher, "The Skeptic's Burke: *Reflections on the Revolution in France,* 1790–1990," *Political Theory* 19, 3 (August 1991): 400.

31. Capitalism "was precisely expected and supposed to repress certain human drives and proclivities and to fashion a less multifaceted, less unpredictable, and more 'one-dimensional' human personality." Albert O. Hirschman, *The Passions and the Interests: Political Arguments for Capitalism Before Its Triumph* (Princeton: Princeton University Press, 1977), pp. 132, 12.

32. Hannah Arendt, *The Origins of Totalitarianism* (New York: Harcourt Brace Jovanovich, 1973), p. 300.

33. Letter of Philip Francis to Edmund Burke, February 19, 1790, in *The Correspondence of Edmund Burke,* vol. VI, ed. Alfred Cobban and Robert A. Smith (Chicago: University of Chicago Press, 1967), pp. 85–87.

34. Tom Furniss, *Edmund Burke's Aesthetic Ideology: Language, Gender, and Political Economy in Revolution* (Cambridge: Cambridge University Press, 1993), p. 154. Furniss goes on to charge that "it is Burke's text, rather than the revolutionary 'mob,' which exposes the queen to 'the last disgrace' in order to activate its rhetorical resonance" (155).

35. Isaac Kramnick, *The Rage of Edmund Burke: Portrait of an Ambivalent Conservative* (New York: Basic Books, 1977), p. 195. In *Signifying Woman: Culture and Chaos in Rousseau, Burke, and Mill* (Ithaca: Cornell University Press, 1994), Linda Zerilli writes: "We can discern moments when Burke's hysterical defense of moderation exceeds the terms of his own rhetorical strategy of figurative excess, and when Burkean political discourse is swept up by the revolutionary play of signification that the *Reflections* would contain with the pleasing illusion of woman as proper femininity" (p. 62). And Mitchell summarizes: "At the level of rhetorical and aesthetic effect, however, it is generally acknowledged that [in the *Reflec-*

tions] his habitual moderation gave way to extremism and excess. His reliance on detailed analysis of the circumstances surrounding any political event gave way to the very sort of imaginative excess he deplored in the French." W. J. T. Mitchell, *Iconology: Image, Text, Ideology* (Chicago: University of Chicago Press, 1987), p. 143.

36. Mitchell, *Iconology,* p. 130. In *The Rage of Edmund Burke,* Kramnick poses the question of whether in the *Reflections,* Burke will be "so partial to the masculine principle" as he was in the *Enquiry* (98).

37. Burke does not press the issue of "how far" that might be. Compare Adam Smith's careful differentiation by gender between "humanity" and "generosity": "Humanity is the virtue of a woman, generosity of a man. . . . Humanity consists merely in the exquisite fellow-feeling which the spectator entertains with the sentiments of the persons principally concerned. . . . We never are generous except when in some respect we prefer some other person to ourselves, and sacrifice some great and important interest of our own to an equal interest of a friend or of a superior." Adam Smith, *The Theory of Moral Sentiments,* intro. by E. G. West (Indianapolis: Liberty Classics, 1976), p. 313.

38. Richard M. Weaver, *The Ethics of Rhetoric* (Davis, California: Hermagoras Press, 1953, repr. 1985), p. 58; Leo Strauss, *Natural Right and History* (Chicago: University of Chicago Press, 1953), pp. 294, 316; Ronald Paulson, *Representations of Revolution (1789–1820)* (New Haven: Yale University Press, 1983), p. 59.

39. Burke is of course writing before the execution of the royal family, but it is a noteworthy point that in later events, the king was never vilified in the way Marie Antoinette was. Hunt writes: "The queen's body, then, was of interest, not because of its connection to the sacred and the divine, but because it represented . . . the possible profanation of everything that the nation held sacred." This would seem to be in keeping with Burke's insight that the desired movement by the revolutionaries was from "a king is but a man, a queen is but a woman; a woman is but an animal, and an animal not of the highest order" (67). But Hunt steps back from that position in her conclusion and, citing Carole Pateman, decides that the different treatments of king and queen came about because the revolutionaries "wanted to separate mothers from any public activity." In my view, the former direction is more plausible. Lynn Hunt, "The Many Bodies of Marie-Antoinette: Political Pornography and the Problem of the Feminine in the French Revolution," in *The French Revolution in Social and Political Perspective,* ed. Peter Jones (New York: St. Martin's Press, 1996), pp. 271, 282.

40. Furniss, *Edmund Burke's Aesthetic Ideology,* p. 153.

41. Ibid., p. 152.

42. Plutarch's collection of stories on the virtue of women (*Mulierum virtutes*) provides a series of examples of the "bravery of women" as distinctively feminine, rather than emulative of courageous men, and as inseparable from the imperative of modesty. "Once upon a time," Plutarch says, the women of Miletus were afflicted by an insane desire for suicide and many hanged themselves. The arguments and tears of parents and friends had no effect. But when an ordinance was passed that the body of any woman who committed suicide would be carried naked through the marketplace to burial, the women immediately lost the desire to hang themselves. Women who had no fear of pain and death "yet could not abide nor bear the thought of disgrace which would come after death." *Plutarch's Moralia*, vol. III, trans. Frank Cole Babbitt (London: William Heinemann, 1931), p. 509.

43. Stephen K. White, *Edmund Burke: Modernity, Politics, and Aesthetics* (Thousand Oaks, California: Sage Publications, 1994), p. 48. And see Reid: "The sentimental discourse of the *Reflections* is Burke's tribute to this 'feminine' principle which permeates the whole sphere of manners." Christopher Reid, "Burke's Tragic Muse: Sarah Siddons and the 'Feminization' of the *Reflections*," in *Burke and the French Revolution: Bicentennial Essays*, ed. Steven Blakemore (Athens, Georgia: University of Georgia Press, 1992), p. 20.

44. Zerilli, *Signifying Woman*, pp. 62–63.

45. As summarized by David Bromwich, "Wollstonecraft as a Critic of Burke," *Political Theory* 23,4 (November, 1995): 619–620.

46. Mary Poovey, *The Proper Lady and the Woman Writer* (Chicago: University of Chicago Press, 1984), pp. 59–60. Gatens faults her for arguing "that women are as free as men to occupy the public sphere as 'disembodied' rational agents [given the character of liberal social organization]." Moira Gatens, "'The Oppressed State of my Sex': Wollstonecraft on Reason, Feeling, and Equality," in *Feminist Interpretations and Political Theory*, eds. Mary Lyndon Shanley and Carole Pateman (University Park: Pennsylvania State University Press, 1991), p. 121.

47. Poovey, *Proper Lady*, p. 64. Boulton notes: "Her style, however, does not invariably constitute proof of her fervent belief in the 'sovereignty of reason,' that reason she insists must discipline merely instinctive emotions." James T. Boulton, *The Language of Politics in the Age of Wilkes and Burke* (Toronto: University of Toronto Press, 1963), p. 173.

48. Myers argues that Wollstonecraft's dual commitments—her socio-economic and moral-aesthetic arguments against the manifold prevailing codes of authority—are interwoven "contrapuntally" and thus form a co-

herent "humane" whole. My point is that Wollstonecraft's didacticism in each mode is too overbearing for any such reconciliation to be viable. Mitzi Myers, "Politics from the Outside: Mary Wollstonecraft's *First Vindication,*" *Studies in Eighteenth-Century Culture,* ed. Ronald C. Rosbottom (Madison: University of Wisconsin Press, 1977), pp. 121–122.

49. Bloom writes, for instance, that *Frankenstein* "is only a strong, flawed novel with frequent clumsiness in its narrative and characterization," but he also judges it "one of the most vivid versions we have of the Romantic mythology of the self." Harold Bloom, "Introduction," *Modern Critical Views: Mary Shelley* (New York: Chelsea House Publishers, 1985), p. 4. Levine comments that "of course, *Frankenstein* is a 'minor' novel, radically flawed by its sensationalism, by the inflexibly public and oratorical nature of even its most intimate passages. . . . but that novel has qualities that allow it to exfoliate as creatively and endlessly as any important myth." George Levine, "The Ambiguous Heritage of *Frankenstein,*" *The Endurance of Frankenstein: Essays on Mary Shelley's Novel,* eds. George Levine and U. C. Knoepflmacher (Berkeley: University of California Press, 1979), pp. 3–4.

50. Johnson identifies the central transgression in Shelley's novel as "the desire for resemblance, the desire to create a being like oneself—which is the autobiographical desire par excellence. . . . What is at stake in Frankenstein's workshop of filthy creation is precisely the possibility of shaping a life in one's own image . . . *Frankenstein,* in other words, can be read as the story of the experience of writing *Frankenstein.*" Barbara Johnson, "My Monster/My Self," in *Frankenstein,* ed. Hunter, p. 248.

51. Anne K. Mellor, *Mary Shelley: Her Life, Her Fiction, Her Monsters* (New York: Routledge, 1988), p. 115.

52. "All the interesting, complex characters in the book are male, and their deepest attachments are to other males. The females, on the other hand, are beautiful, gentle, selfless, boring nurturers and victims who never experience inner conflict or true desire." Johnson, "My Monster/My Self," p. 248. Johnson recognizes in her excellent article that the portrayals are not so simple.

53. Veeder comments without too much exaggeration that this reference to a "summer bug" entails that "woman is ephemeral, or at least can be made so." William Veeder, "Gender and Pedagogy," p. 41.

54. William Veeder, *Mary Shelley and Frankenstein: The Fate of Androgyny* (Chicago: University of Chicago Press, 1986), pp. 184–185.

55. Veeder continues: "Victor sees the daughter-as-future-wife destroying the older mother-as-rival in order to possess him exclusively." "Gender and Pedagogy," p. 41.

56. Paul A. Cantor and Michael Valdez Moses, "Teaching *Frankenstein* from the Creature's Perspective," in *Approaches to Teaching,* ed. Behrendt, p. 130.

57. Lipking writes, for instance: "*Emile* already adumbrates the two most powerful imaginative feats of Mary Shelley's novel: the hero's crazed longing to surpass his species, and the monster's pathetic account of his frustrated self-education." Lawrence Lipking, "*Frankenstein,* the True Story: or Rousseau Judges Jean-Jacques," in *Frankenstein,* ed. Hunter, p. 322.

58. Veeder, "Gender and Pedagogy," p. 47.

59. Lawrence Lipking, "*Frankenstein,*" p. 317.

60. Anne Mellor, *Mary Shelley,* p. 114.

61. Ellen Moers, "Female Gothic: The Monster's Mother" in *Frankenstein,* ed. Hunter, p. 217. In the same edition (294), Susan Winnett wonders dubiously whether Shelley *really* "set out to write a 'horror story of maternity.'" See her "Coming Unstrung: Women, Men, Narrative, and Principles of Pleasure."

62. "*Frankenstein* as a modern metaphor implies a conception of the divided self, the creator and his work at odds. . . . The angel in the house entails a demon outside it." George Levine, "Ambiguous Heritage," p. 15.

Chapter Four: Rousseau/Tutor

1. Jean-Jacques Rousseau, *Essay on the Origin of Languages,* ed., trans., and annotated by Victor Gourevitch (New York: Harper and Row, 1986), p. 248.

2. As Bloom notes, this might be translated as 'novel.' See his *Emile,* note 41, page 493.

3. Arthur M. Melzer, *The Natural Goodness of Man: On the System of Rousseau's Thought* (Chicago: The University of Chicago Press, 1990), p. 247. And see J. H. Broome, *Rousseau: A Study of His Thought* (London: Edward Arnold Publishers, 1963), p. 80, and Kelly, who connects the *Second Discourse, Emile* and the *Confessions* under a shared theme ("the development of artificial passions out of natural desires") as seen from different perspectives. Christopher Kelly, *Rousseau's Exemplary Life: The Confessions as Political Philosophy* (Ithaca: Cornell University Press, 1987), pp. 38–39.

4. Joel Schwartz, *The Sexual Politics of Jean-Jacques Rousseau* (Chicago: University of Chicago Press, 1984), p. 47.

5. "At the end of the 'age of nature,' Emile is said to be twelve; at the end of the 'age of reason,' fifteen; at the end of the 'age of force,' twenty; and at the end the 'age of wisdom,' twenty-five." Kelly, *Rousseau's Exemplary Life,* p. 78.

6. For example, see Judith Shklar, "Rousseau's Images of Authority," in *Hobbes and Rousseau: A Collection of Critical Essays,* eds. Maurice Cranston and Richard S. Peters (Garden City, New York: Doubleday & Company, 1972), p. 342.

7. Jimack has studied the manuscripts of *Emile,* and argues from them that Rousseau only gradually developed the self-standing characters of Emile and the tutor, and that the jarring quality of the narrator role is a result of Rousseau failing to integrate the later with the earlier stance. This view is plausible, yet does not detract from the Rousseau/tutor that I set forth here. Peter Jimack, "La Genèse et la rédaction de *l'Emile* de Jean-Jacques Rousseau," *Studies on Voltaire and the 18th Century* 13 (1960). DeJean writes: "Because Rousseau radically changed his conception of the work in the course of its composition, *Emile* is riddled with strange, Ur-passages where the narrative flow is as troubled as in the hysterical narrative Freud describes." DeJean, *Literary Fortifications,* p. 124. Paul de Man's response to Derrida seems to be to the point: "Rousseau's text has no blind spots: it accounts at all moments for its own rhetorical mode." Paul de Man, *Blindness and Insight: Essays in the Rhetoric of Contemporary Criticism,* intro. by Wlad Godzich, second edition (Minneapolis: University of Minnesota Press, 1983), p. 139.

8. Robert J. Ellrich, *Rousseau and His Reader: The Rhetorical Situation of the Major Works* (Chapel Hill: The University of North Carolina Press, 1969), pp. 99, 76.

9. According to Ellrich, "the little dance he performs succeeds in confusing the fiction-reality issue far more effectively than the conventional claim of documentary reality could conceivably have done." Ibid., p. 42.

10. "In the case of the child as in the case of a people," Grant observes, "the development of both freedom and virtue depend on a ruse that disguises the fact that they are being led, guided, indeed ruled." Ruth W. Grant, *Hypocrisy and Integrity: Machiavelli, Rousseau, and the Ethics of Politics* (Chicago: University of Chicago Press, 1997), p. 126.

11. Victor Gourevitch, "Rousseau on Lying: A Provisional Reading of the Fourth Rêverie," *Berkshire Review* 15 (1980): 94.

12. In the *Social Contract,* "The People" is created when "each gives all to all." The attribute of The People is Sovereignty, exercised as the General Will and expressed as the Law. All this is general in nature, and acts upon the particular affairs of day to day life, conducted by a government and in which law (small "l") address specific cases involving people (small "p"). Thus a person has a dual role: as a "subject," and as "citizen," an undifferentiated component of The People.

13. As Weiss argues, "the sexes are intended by Rousseau, rather than by nature, to be perfect complements." Penny Weiss, "Rousseau, Antifeminism, and Woman's Nature," *Political Theory* 15,1 (February 1987): 95; and see her *Gendered Community: Rousseau, Sex, and Politics* (New York: New York University Press, 1993).

14. Allan Bloom, *Love and Friendship* (New York: Simon & Schuster, 1993), p. 130.

15. Among many others, Christenson concludes: "In his system of ideas, [Rousseau] employs most of the familiar disparaging stereotypes of women in building his argument that since women are by nature different (read inferior), they should be kept in their proper role, as man's helpmate with no political power." Eisenstein claims that Rousseau is revealing his nostalgia for the social arrangements as proposed by ancient thinkers, and primarily their sharp distinctions between public and private spheres: "Rousseau wishes to reestablish the separate spheres of classical antiquity to aid in the development of the moral male citizen." Ron Christenson, "The Political Theory of Male Chauvinism: J. J. Rousseau's Paradigm," *The Midwest Quarterly* Volume XIII, Number 3 (April, 1972): 291. Zillah R. Eisenstein, *The Radical Future of Liberal Feminism* (Boston: Northeastern University Press, 1981, 1993), p. 66. And see Okin: "The ancient two-fold demands made of woman—that she be both the inspiration of romantic, sexual love, and the guardian of marital fidelity—are seen at their most tragic in Rousseau." *Women in Western Political Thought*, p. 176.

16. One successful example is proposed by Ann Charney Colmo, "What Sophie Knew," in *Finding a New Feminism: Rethinking the Woman Question for Liberal Democracy*, ed. Pamela Grande Jensen (Lanham, Maryland: Rowman & Littlefield, 1996), pp. 83–84.

17. As DeJean writes, out of an initial triad of narrator, tutor, and pupil, a strange blend evolves: "In *Emile*, three souls are meant to share the same 'body.' The hybrid creature inhabiting *Emile's* narrative voice reveals through this vision its desire to take over all the principal roles in this pedagogical drama." Joan DeJean, *Literary Fortifications: Rousseau, Laclos, Sade* (Princeton: Princeton University Press, 1984), p. 138. DeJean adds, to the point, that "the tutor even replaces the mother."

18. Schwartz writes that "Rousseau can philosophize successfully only insofar as he can somehow combine the mental abilities of both males and females . . . [Rousseau] is sexually double in practice as well as in theory, in that at different times he exemplifies both the male principle of manifest rule and the female principle of hidden rule." *Sexual Politics*, p. 172, n. 60.

19. "The tutor claims a place both at the center of love's rapture and outside it. He knows both the rapture of contact and the freedom of total disengagement. He enjoys and renounces simultaneously. He abandons himself to feeling but immediately withdraws into reflection." Jean Starobinski, *Jean-Jacques Rousseau: Transparency and Obstruction,* trans. Arthur Goldhammer, intro. by Robert J. Morrissey (Chicago: University of Chicago Press, 1988), p. 177.

20. Søren Kierkegaard, *Stages on Life's Way,* quoted in *The Socratic Enigma: A Collection of Testimonies Through Twenty-Four Centuries,* ed. Herbert Spiegelberg, with Bayard Quincy Morgan (Indianapolis: Bobbs-Merrill, 1964), p. 12.

21. Jean Jacques Rousseau, *Emile and Sophie, or Solitary Beings,* trans. Alice W. Harvey in *Finding a New Feminism,* p. 200.

22. Thus I believe that the outrage is misplaced when readers object to what is taken to be an incriminating portrait of Sophie: "Rousseau displaces the blame for Sophie's crime and punishment on the victim herself. It is not Emile who is held responsible." Nicole Fermon, *Domesticating Passions: Rousseau, Women, and Nation* (Hanover, New Hampshire: University Press of New England, 1997), p. 121. Keohane concurs: "the blame for disrupting Emile's happiness rests squarely on Sophie's shoulders." Nannerl O. Keohane, " 'But for Her Sex . . .': The Domestication of Sophie," *University of Ottawa Quarterly* 49, 3–4 (July and October 1979): 396.

Chapter Five: Surveying Tocqueville

1. Pierre Manent, *Tocqueville and the Nature of Democracy,* foreword by Harvey C. Mansfield, trans. John Waggoner (Lanham, Maryland: Rowman and Littlefield Publishers, Inc., 1996), p. 71.

2. Tocqueville deduces that as the distance between the poor and the rich diminishes, the aversion between them actually may grow: "the breakup of fortunes . . . seems to have provided them with new reasons for hating each other" (15).

3. As in the title of the work by Erhart Kästner, quoted by Wilhelm Hennis, "In Search of the 'New Science of Politics,' " in *Interpreting Tocqueville's Democracy in America,* ed. Ken Masugi (Savage, Maryland: Rowman and Littlefield, 1991), p. 62.

4. "Tocqueville's most fundamental teaching regarding political memory is this," Smith writes, "to live in the present alone is to be made ready for servitude. The vessel of all that is cherished, remembrance is also the foundation of political liberty." Smith, *Politics and Remembrance,* p. 163.

5. Ralph C. Hancock, "The Uses and Hazards of Christianity in Tocqueville's Attempt to Save Democratic Souls," in *Interpreting Tocqueville,* ed. Masugi, 387.

6. Tocqueville refers to a law forbidding the use of tobacco.

7. Sullivan writes on this passage in the *Prince* (56) and also discusses Machiavelli's "sly equation of himself and Christ." Vickie B. Sullivan, *Machiavelli's Three Romes: Religion, Human Liberty, and Politics Reformed* (DeKalb, Illinois: Northern Illinois Press, 1996), pp. 144–146.

8. Perhaps Tocqueville's closest predecessor in his dependence on real-life historical exemplars is Thucydides, but Thucydides supplements *his* Athenian and Spartan material with speeches containing what was "in [his] opinion demanded of them by the various occasions" (1.22.1).

9. Linda K. Kerber, "Separate Spheres, Female Worlds, Woman's Place: The Rhetoric of Women's History," *The Journal of American History* 75,1 (June 1988): 10, n. 1.

10. Susan Okin, "Reason and Feeling in Thinking about Justice," in *Feminism and Political Theory,* ed. Cass Sunstein (Chicago: The University of Chicago Press, 1982), p. 17.

11. Jean Bethke Elshtain, *Public Man, Private Woman: Women in Social and Political Thought* (Princeton: Princeton University Press, 1981), p. 129.

12. F. L. Morton, "Sexual Equality and the Family in Tocqueville's *Democracy in America,"* *Canadian Journal of Political Science* 17, 2 (June 1984): 315. But Mathie observes that in choosing the path that the American female does, she also expresses the doctrine of self-interest properly understood, "even if Tocqueville carefully avoids identifying [it] as such." William Mathie, "God, Woman, and Morality: The Democratic Family in Tocqueville," *Review of Politics* 57,1 (Winter 1995): 25.

13. Delba Winthrop, "Tocqueville's American Women and 'The True Conception of Democratic Progress,' " *Political Theory* 14, 2 (May 1986): 253.

14. The truth of this claim is reflected in the fact that Tocqueville is simply bypassed in the vast majority of accounts which presume to trace the influence of misogynism in the history of Western political thinking. He is not a subject for Arneil, *Politics and Feminism;* Clark/Lange, *The Sexism of Social and Political Theory;* Coole, *Women in Political Theory;* or Okin, *Women in Western Political Thought,* among many others that could be listed.

15. Alexis de Tocqueville, *The Ancien Régime,* trans. by John Bonner, intro. by Norman Hampson (London: J. M. Dent & Sons, 1988), pp. 110–111. See James W. Caeser, "Political Science, Political Culture, and the Role of the Intellectual," in *Interpreting Tocqueville,* ed. Masugi, pp. 287–325.

16. Tocqueville, *Ancien Régime,* p. 112.

17. David Bromwich, quoted by Richard Poirier in *Poetry and Pragmatism* (Cambridge: Harvard University Press, 1992), p. 33.

18. Poirier, *Poetry and Pragmatism*, p. 3.

Chapter Six: Gertrude Stein's Socrates

1. Gertrude Stein, *Lectures in America*, intro. by Wendy Steiner (Boston: Beacon Press, 1935, repr. 1966), p. 166. Hereafter, *LIA*.

2. Gertrude Stein, *The Making of Americans* (New York: Something Else Press, 1925, repr. 1966), p. 289. Hereafter, *MOA*.

3. Leon Katz, "Weininger and *The Making of Americans*," in *Twentieth Century Literature* 24, 1 (Spring 1978): 15. Harold Bloom calls Gertrude Stein "the greatest master of dissociative rhetoric in modern writing." Harold Bloom, "Introduction," in *Modern Critical Views: Gertrude Stein*, ed. Harold Bloom (New York: Chelsea House Publishers, 1986), p. 1.

4. Gertrude Stein, *Everybody's Autobiography* (New York: Random House, 1937), p. 99. Hereafter, *EA*.

5. Gertrude Stein, *Tender Buttons*, in *Gertrude Stein: Writings 1903–1932*, eds. Catharine R. Stimpson and Harriet Chessman (New York: Library of America, 1998), p. 325. Hereafter, *TB*. Richard Bridgman, *Gertrude Stein in Pieces* (New York: Oxford University Press, 1970), p. 125.

6. Gertrude Stein, *What Are Masterpieces*, foreword by Robert Bartlett Haas (New York: Pitman Publishing Corporation, 1940, repr. 1970), p. 40. Hereafter, *WM*.

7. Kate Davy quotes Richard Foreman in 1969: "Gertrude Stein obviously was doing all kinds of things we haven't even caught up to yet." Kate Davy, "Richard Foreman's Ontological-Hysteric Theatre: The Influence of Gertrude Stein," *Twentieth Century Literature* 24,1 (Spring 1978): 109. Stein found room to discriminate herself from the best of her generation: "You see it is the people who generally smell of the museums who are accepted, and it is the new who are not accepted . . . it is much easier to have one hand in the past. That is why James Joyce was accepted and I was not. He leaned toward the past, in my work the newness and difference is fundamental" [Quoted in *A Primer for the Gradual Understanding of Gertrude Stein*, ed. Robert Bartlett Haas (Los Angeles: Black Sparrow Press, 1971), p. 29]. Hereafter, *Primer*.

8. Gertrude Stein, *Paris France* (New York: Charles Scribner's Sons, 1940), p. 62. Hereafter, *PF*.

9. Gertrude Stein, *Wars I Have Seen* (New York: Random House, 1945), p. 258. Hereafter, *WIHS*.

10. Or so goes the retrospective account. Bridgman rightly observes that

"Gertrude Stein habitually educated herself before the reader's eyes," and adds that readers should be cautioned against taking too literally her accounts of her progress as a writer, especially in *Lectures in America:* "the actual record is much more disheveled." Bridgman, pp. 103, 264. Whether or not Stein exaggerates her self-consciousness at this moment is unimportant to me, however, since the disjunction between her autobiographical writings and her earlier work is not in dispute.

11. Gertrude Stein, *The Autobiography of Alice B. Toklas,* in *Gertrude Stein: Writings 1932–1942,* Vol. 1, eds. Catharine R. Stimpson and Harriet Chessman (New York: Library of America, 1998), pp. 660–661. Hereafter, *ABT*.

12. *Testimony Against Gertrude Stein,* Transition Pamphlet No.1, Supplement to *Transition* (The Hague: Servire Press, 1935), p. 8. Hereafter, *Testimony*.

13. Timothy Dow Adams, *Telling Lies in Modern American Autobiography* (Chapel Hill: University of North Carolina Press, 1990), p. 18. Gertrude's brother Leo chimed in with "God what a liar she is!" The force of this accusation is notably diminished when Leo fills in the nature of these lies: "So she speaks of her memories of Paris 'when she was three.' She was four and a half when she went there and five and a half before she came way." Leo Stein, *Journey Into the Self,* ed. Edmund Fuller, intro. Van Wyck Brooks (New York: Crown Publishers, 1950), p. 134.

14. Quoted by Charles Caramello, *Henry James, Gertrude Stein, and the Biographical Act* (Chapel Hill: University of North Carolina Press, 1996), p. 120.

15. Gertrude Stein, *Picasso* (New York: Dover Publications Inc., 1938, repr. 1984), p. 16.

16. Cynthia Merrill, "Mirrored Image: Gertrude Stein and Autobiography," *Pacific Coast Philology* 20, 1–2 (November 1985): 15, 16.

17. Warner Berthoff, *The Ferment of Realism: American Literature, 1884–1919* (New York: The Free Press, 1965), p. 25.

18. Gertrude Stein, *The Geographical History of America,* in *Gertrude Stein: Writings 1932–1946,* Vol. 2, eds. Catharine R. Stimpson and Harriet Chessman (New York: The Library of America, 1998), p. 379. Hereafter, *GHA*.

19. Bloom, "Introduction," in *Modern Critical Views,* pp. 2–3. Stein highlights the experience of being dissociated from her physical surroundings in these moments of "absorbed intellectual activity," in Allegra Stewart's formulation: *Gertrude Stein and the Present* (Cambridge: Harvard University Press, 1967), p. 36.

20. George Hugnet objected to more than the "smoothness" of her lan-

guage in the resulting product, for after the first line, Gertrude Stein left the original far behind. Hugnet and Stein quarreled about whether her contribution was a "free translation" or a "reflection," resulting in yet another "friendship faded." See the account in Bridgman, pp. 201–202.

21. B. L. Reid, *Art by Subtraction: A Dissenting Opinion of Gertrude Stein* (Norman: University of Oklahoma Press, 1958), p. 186.

22. Richard Poirier, *The Renewal of Literature: Emersonian Reflections* (New York: Random House, 1987), p. 45.

23. Jayne L. Walker, "History as Repetition: *The Making of Americans,*" in ed. Bloom, *Modern Critical Views,* p. 199. We note in passing that "Gertrude Stein" does admit to *adoring* "the beginning and middle and end of a story" (*ABT,* 858), suggesting that she had at least an instinctive sense that storytelling of the right sort might answer twentieth-century needs.

24. Judith P. Saunders, "Gertrude Stein's *Paris France* and American Literary Tradition," in Bloom, ed. *Modern Critical Views,* p. 129. Saunders also sees Stein's genius in "the discovery of fruitful tension between opposites" (124).

25. More or less, that is; if Stein fudges the dates for effect, her overall story is unobjectionable. Dydo seeks to add precision to this lineup in a review of Schmitz's *Of Huck and Alice:* "*Three Women* and *Three Lives* are not parallel. The Picasso/Stein analogies are soft at the edges and wobble because they are not supported by facts." Ulla E. Dydo, "Must Horses Drink," *Tulsa Studies in Women's Literature* 4, 2 (Fall 1985): 277. But facts are not simply self-standing, and Schmitz's reading of Stein is certainly defensible: "Cubism begins with a male deconstruction of the female form as it preexists in the eyes of Picasso and Matisse. Gertrude Stein also begins a deconstruction of how women are known, but that work is overlooked . . . Picasso's masculine authority is a congenial Spanish translation of Leo Stein's inflexible paternalism." Neil Schmitz, *Of Huck and Alice: Humorous Writing in American Literature* (Minneapolis: University of Minnesota Press, 1983), p. 216.

26. Chessman addresses Stein's effort "both to extend her dialogic intimacy to male as well as female figures and to create a safe space within her writing where the differences between the masculine and the feminine can be addressed." Harriett Chessman, *The Public Is Invited to Dance: Representation, the Body, and Dialogue in Gertrude Stein* (Stanford: Stanford University Press, 1989), p. 4.

27. This formulation comes from *Everybody's Autobiography,* p. 133. My assumption is that "Gertrude Stein" is the same persona in all of Stein's autobiographical works. The difference is that only in *ABT* is "Gertrude

Stein" seen through the eyes of Alice. That form "self-destructs" after a single use, as Bloom notes. Lynn Z. Bloom, "Gertrude is Alice is Everybody: Innovation and Point of View in Gertrude Stein's Autobiographies," *Twentieth Century Literature* 24 (1978): 82.

28. Caramello, *Biographical Act,* p. 162, and Schmitz, *Of Huck and Alice,* p. 211.

29. "Stein constructed these images of Toklas and herself, so that the couple could regain control of their representations and, thus, reputations." So concludes Caramello in *Biographical Act,* pp. 167–8. Couser remarks: "More important than Stein's relationship with Picasso, her relationship with Alice Toklas stands as an example of an ideal, mutually fulfilling relationship between writer and reader, artist and audience." Thomas G. Couser, *American Autobiography: The Prophetic Mode* (Amherst: University of Massachusetts, 1979), p. 153. I concur with these readings which stress the equal dignity of Alice in this partnership; Alice and Gertrude are the epitome of the complementary unit: "while Stein stares at the sun," Merrill observes, "Toklas sits with her back toward the view." "Mirrored Image," p. 14. These complementary motifs are sprinkled throughout. "Gertrude Stein never likes her food hot," and Alice always does; Alice gets her way on this issue save for the exceptional moment when she is called upon—just as dinner is ready—to share "Gertrude Stein's" writing: "Finally I read it all and was terribly pleased with it. And then we ate our supper" (*ABT,* 777). In matters that really matter, they are as one.

30. Paul K. Alkon, "Visual Rhetoric in *The Autobiography of Alice B. Toklas,"* *Critical Inquiry* 1,4 (June 1975): 862. And Couser writes that "*The Autobiography of Alice B. Toklas* . . . expressed the possibilities of self-transcendence, by its recognition of the strong bond between Alice Toklas and Gertrude Stein and the looser bonds between Gertrude Stein and the artists and writers she knew." G. Thomas Couser, "Of Time and Identity: Walt Whitman and Gertrude Stein as Autobiographers," *Texas Studies in Literature and Language* 17 (Winter 1976): 802.

31. Schmitz, *Of Huck and Alice,* p. 12. Chessman captures the amiable spirit informing Stein's critique when she suggests that for Stein "language is an open field, marked by previous usage but not owned or structured wholly by a patriarchy." *The Public Is Invited to Dance,* p. 73.

32. "All of which was literally true," Alice continues, "like all of Gertrude Stein's literature, but it upset Ezra, and we never saw him again." It was not that Gertrude Stein did not *like* Ezra Pound; it was just that she did not find him *amusing:* "She said he was a village explainer, excellent if you were a village, but if you were not, not" (856).

33. See *Testimony*, p. 11; Ulla E. Dydo, "*Stanzas in Meditation:* The Other Autobiography," in *Gertrude Stein Advanced: An Anthology of Criticism,* ed. Richard Kostelanetz (Jefferson, North Carolina: McFarland and Company, Inc., 1990), p. 122; and Richard Bridgman, *Gertrude Stein in Pieces,* p. 215.

34. Thornton Wilder, "Introduction" to Gertrude Stein, *Four in America* (New Haven: Yale University Press, 1947): xxvii.

35. Sutherland writes that "she had about the same way with an anecdote or a sly observation in talking as Miss Toklas has . . . it is part of the miracle of this little scheme of objectification that she could by way of imitating Miss Toklas put in writing something of her own beautiful conversation. So that, aside from making a real present of her past, she re-created a figure of herself, established an identity, a twin." Donald Sutherland, *Gertrude Stein: A Biography of Her Work* (New Haven: Yale University Press, 1951), pp. 148–149; cited by Bloom, "Gertrude is Alice," p. 83. And compare *EA,* 61, for a similarly stylized example in Stein's writing: "I said well and she said yes and she said Jean is always like that . . . What I said. Blood on the dining room floor she said." On the subject of Stein imitators, I nominate W. H. Auden's "All about Ida" as one of the very best, in *Critical Essays on Gertrude Stein,* ed. Michael J. Hoffman (Boston: G. K. Hall and Co., 1986), pp. 82–83.

36. James E. Breslin, "Gertrude Stein and the Problems of Autobiography," in *Critical Essays,* ed. Hoffman, p. 153. See also Meyer's discussion of Stein's "resistance to subjectivity," in "Stein and Emerson," *Raritan* 10, 2 (1990): 102.

37. For the record, Madame Matisse *is* described as having "a long face and a firm large loosely hung mouth like a horse" (*ABT,* 694). Henri Matisse counters in *Testimony Against Gertrude Stein* that "Madame Matisse was a very lovely Toulousaine" (3).

38. Gertrude Stein, *Narration: Four Lectures,* intro. by Thornton Wilder (Chicago: University of Chicago Press, 1935), p. 39. Hereafter, *N.*

39. Reid, *Art by Subtraction,* p. 168.

40. Shirley C. Neuman, *Gertrude Stein: Autobiography and the Problem of Narration* (Victoria, British Columbia, English Literary Studies, University of Victoria, 1979), p. 27.

41. Quoted by John Hyde Preston in Linda Simon, *Gertrude Stein Remembered* (Lincoln: University of Nebraska Press, 1994), p. 165.

Conclusion: Redressing the Balance

1. Stuart Hampshire, *Innocence and Experience* (Cambridge: Harvard University Press, 1989), p. 134.

2. Thompson, *Herodotus and the Origins of the Political Community.*

3. Bruce Ackerman and Anne Alstott, *The Stakeholder Society* (New Haven: Yale University Press, 1999), p. 43.

4. Lon Fuller, *The Morality of Law* (New Haven: Yale University Press, 1969); Charles Larmore, *The Morals of Modernity* (Cambridge: Cambridge University Press, 1996); Mark Bauerlein, *The Pragmatic Mind* (Durham: Duke University Press, 1997), p. 101: "To Pierce, pragmatism is a method, not a morality."

5. Slavoj Žižek, *The Ticklish Subject: The Absent Centre of Political Ontology* (London: Verso, 1999), p. 4.

6. Jürgen Habermas, *The Philosophical Discourse of Modernity,* trans. Frederick Lawrence (Cambridge: The MIT Press, 1987).

7. Wayne A. Rebhorn, *Foxes and Lions: Machiavelli's Confidence Men* (Ithaca: Cornell University Press, 1987), p. 67.

8. See Charles L. Griswold, Jr., *Adam Smith and the Virtues of Enlightenment* (Cambridge: Cambridge University Press, 1999), pp. 65–70, on "the impartial spectator."

9. Memory, as Augustine perceived it, is a feminine quality. In this sense, it is "not accurate to speak of past, present, and future as 'three times' at all. The 'three times' were rather: a time present of things past; a time present of things present; and a time present of things future." The first is memory, the second direct experience, the third expectation. Speech was for Augustine the most revealing example, for the very transient essence of the sentence, if rightly understood, provides continuity and makes communication possible. The sound uttered at any given moment is part of a cumulative continuity, as is the best political community. The discourse "passes on, until the present intention carries the future over into the past. The past increases by the diminution of the future until, by the consumption of all the future, all is past." Jaroslav Pelikan, *The Mystery of Continuity: Time and History, Memory and Eternity in the Thought of Saint Augustine* (Charlottesville: University Press of Virginia, 1986), citing *The Confessions,* 11.27.36. And see Allen Tate, *Memoirs and Opinions, 1926–1974* (Chicago: The Swallow Press, 1975), p. 12. "Saint Augustine tells us that memory is like a woman. The Latin *memoria* is properly a feminine noun, for women never forget; and likewise the soul is the *anima,* even in man, his vital principle and the custodian of memory, the image of woman that all men both pursue and flee." Also see Robert S. Dupree, *Allen Tate and the Augustinian Tradition* (Baton Rouge: Louisiana State University Press, 1983).

10. John Onians, *Bearers of Meaning: The Classical Orders in Antiq-*

uity, the Middle Ages, and the Renaissance (Princeton: Princeton University Press, 1988), p. 16.

11. Steven Forde, *The Ambition to Rule: Alcibiades and the Politics of Imperialism in Thucydides* (Ithaca: Cornell University Press, 1989).

12. Thomas M. Greene, "The End of Discourse in Machiavelli's *Prince,*" *Yale French Studies* 67 (1984): 65.

13. "Balance" in the sense intended here should not be confused with, or considered attainable by, some version of the classical "balance of power" in international power. Statecraft must comprehend a far more complex set of factors—diplomatic, financial, cultural—and hold them in dynamic equipoise.

14. There is a rich field for study here. Francis A. Beer and Robert Hariman's *Post-Realism: The Rhetorical Turn in International Relations* (East Lansing: Michigan State University Press, 1996) illuminates the extent to which cold war strategy, under the label of "realism," and considered the inheritor of a Thucydidean-Machiavellian "realism," is being superseded by a different rhetorical strategy of how statecraft works. My argument is that cold war "realists" misunderstood Thucydides and Machiavelli [and their differences—see Steven Forde, "Varieties of Realism: Thucydides and Machiavelli," *Journal of Politics* 54,2 (May 1992): 381.]

15. Carnes Lord, trans., *The Politics,* p. 257, n. 14.

16. Warren D. Anderson, *Ethos and Education in Greek Music: The Evidence of Poetry and Philosophy* (Cambridge: Harvard University Press, 1968), p. 90.

17. "The precarious, but necessary, balance between scientific capitalism and Judeo-Christianity has been lost . . . the former has subsumed, co-opted and superseded the latter to our current detriment and future moral peril." David Bosworth, "The Spirit of Capitalism, 2000," *The Public Interest* 138 (Winter 2000).

Afterword: The Ship of State—The Political Metaphor and Its Fate

1. Hans Blumenberg, *Shipwreck with Spectator* (Cambridge: The MIT Press, 1997), p. 11. Horace, *The Odes and Epodes,* trans. by C. E. Bennett (Cambridge: Harvard University Press, 1968), pp. 42–43. See also I.14 translated by the British statesman William Ewart Gladstone (1809–1898) in D. S. Carne-Ross and Kenneth Haynes, eds., *Horace in English* (New York: Penguin, 1996), pp. 228–229.

2. Alcaeus, closely associated with Sappho, was born about 620 B.C. at Mytilene, on Lesbos. See James S. Easby-Smith, *The Songs of Alcaeus*

(Washington: Lowdermilk, 1901); Théodore Reinach and Aimé Puech, *Alcée/ Sapho* (Paris: Sociéte D'Edition "Les Belles Lettres," 1937); Wilfried Barner, *Neuere Alkaios-Papyri aus Oxyrhynchos* (Hildesheim: Georg Olms, 1967).

3. Eduard Fraenkel, *Horace* (Oxford: Clarendon Press, 1957), p. 154; also, *Tucker v. Alexandroff*, 183 U.S. 424, 438, cited in Don H. Kennedy, *Ship Names: Origin and Usage During 45 Centuries* (Newport News: Mariner's Museum and the University Press of Virginia, 1974), p. 9.

4. See Frank Kermode, *The Classic* (New York: Viking, 1975), especially on Virgil's *Aeneid* and the *translatio imperii,* the carrying of polity and power from Troy to Rome to Northern Europe and America.

5. An intriguing violation of the practice of male-only crews is Herodotus' account of Artemisia, the Greek-born commander of a Persian warship. The result was a shipwreck, deliberately ordered by Artemisia, and to the ultimate advantage of the Greek cause. See my "Public and Private."

6. John Locke, *Second Treatise of Government* (Indianapolis: Hackett Publishing, 1980): V, pp. 18–30.

7. Alexander Hamilton, James Madison, John Jay, *The Federalist Papers,* ed. Clinton Rossiter (New York: Mentor, 1961), Federalist 9, p. 73.

8. Henry Adams, *History of the United States in the Administration of James Madison,* vol. 4 (New York: Charles Scribner's Sons, 1890): VII.13, pp. 316–321.

9. Ibid., IX.10, p. 228.

10. Herman Melville, *Moby Dick* (Oxford: Oxford University Press, 1988), p. 71.

11. Tony Tanner, "Introduction," *Moby Dick,* p. x.

12. A matter of present concern; see Robert D. Putnam, *Bowling Alone: The Collapse and Revival of American Community* (New York: Simon & Schuster, 2000).

13. Tanner, xix.

14. Alfred Thayer Mahan, *The Influence of Sea Power Upon History* (Boston: Little, Brown, 1890).

15. See Paul Kennedy, *Strategy and Diplomacy 1870–1945* (London: George Allen & Unwin, 1983), pp. 43–85, and John Hattendorf, ed., *The Influence of History on Mahan* (Newport, Rhode Island: Naval War College Press, 1991).

16. Gaddis Smith, et al., *The Amistad Incident: Four Perspectives, The Connecticut Scholar,* No. 10, 1992. *Wooden Boat,* 155 (July/August 2000): 68–75.

Bibliography

Abel, Elizabeth, ed. *Writing and Sexual Difference*. Chicago: University of Chicago Press, 1982.

Ackerman, Bruce and Anne Alstott. *The Stakeholder Society*. New Haven: Yale University Press, 1999.

Adams, Henry. *History of the United States in the Administration of James Madison*. Volume 4. New York: Charles Scribner's Sons, 1890.

Adams, Timothy Dow. *Telling Lies in Modern American Autobiography*. Chapel Hill: University of North Carolina Press, 1990.

Alexander, Liz Anne. "The Best Regimes of Aristotle's *Politics*." *History of Political Thought* XXI, 2 (Summer 2000): 189–216.

Alkon, Paul K. "Visual Rhetoric in *The Autobiography of Alice B. Toklas*." *Critical Inquiry* 1, 4 (June 1975): 849–881.

Ambler, Wayne. "Aristotle on Nature and Politics: The Case of Slavery." *Political Theory* 15 (1987): 390–410.

Anderson, Warren D. *Ethos and Education in Greek Music: The Evidence of Poetry and Philosophy*. Cambridge: Harvard University Press, 1966.

Annas, Julia. "Plato's *Republic* and Feminism." *Philosophy* 51 (July 1976): 307–321.

Arendt, Hannah. *The Origins of Totalitarianism*. New York: Harcourt Brace Jovanovich, 1973.

Aristotle. *Nicomachean Ethics*. Translated by H. Rackham. Cambridge: Harvard University Press, 1982.

———. *Politics: Books I and II*. Translation and commentary by Trevor J. Saunders. New York: Clarendon Press, 1995.

———. *The Politics*. Translated by Carnes Lord. Chicago: University of Chicago Press, 1984.

Arkes, Hadley. "Machiavelli and America." In Machiavelli, *The Prince*. Translated by Angelo Codevilla. New Haven: Yale University Press, 1997.

Arneil, Barbara. *Politics and Feminism*. Oxford: Blackwell Publishers, 1999.

Ascoli, Albert Russell and Victoria Kahn, eds. *Machiavelli and the Discourse of Literature*. Ithaca: Cornell University Press, 1993.

Augustine. *Confessions*. Translated by W. Watts. Two volumes. Cambridge: Harvard University Press, 1989.

Ausland, Hayden W. "On Reading Plato Mimetically." *American Journal of Philology* 118 (Fall 1997): 371–416.

Austin, Norman. *Archery at the Dark of the Moon*. Berkeley: University of California Press, 1975.

———. *Helen of Troy and Her Shameless Phantom*. Ithaca: Cornell University Press, 1994.

Barber, Benjamin R. "Foundationalism and Democracy." In Seyla Benhabib, ed., *Democracy and Difference: Contesting the Boundaries of the Political*, pp. 348–359. Princeton: Princeton University Press, 1996.

———. "Misreading Democracy: Peter Euben and the *Gorgias*." In Josiah Ober and Charles Hedrick, eds., *Dēmokratia: A Conversation on Democracies, Ancient and Modern*, pp. 361–375. Princeton: Princeton University Press, 1996.

Barner, Wilfried. *Neuere Alkaios-Papyri aus Oxyrhynchos*. Hildesheim: Georg Olms, 1967.

Bar On, Bat-Ami, ed. *Modern Engendering: Critical Feminist Readings in Modern Western Philosophy*. Albany: State University of New York Press, 1994.

Bauerlein, Mark. *The Pragmatic Mind*. Durham: Duke University Press, 1997.

Bauval, Robert and Graham Hancock. *Keeper of Genesis: A Quest for the Hidden Legacy of Mankind*. London: Heinemann, 1996.

Beer, Francis A. and Robert Hariman, eds. *Post-Realism: The Rhetorical Turn in International Relations*. East Lansing: Michigan State University Press, 1996.

Behrendt, Stephen C., ed. *Approaches to Teaching Shelley's Frankenstein*. New York: The Modern Language Association of America, 1990.

Behuniak-Long, Susan. "The Significance of Lucrezia in Machiavelli's *La Mandragola.*" *Review of Politics* 51 (Spring 1989): 264–280.

Berger, Harry, Jr. "Levels of Discourse in Plato's Dialogues." In Anthony J. Cascardi, ed., *Literature and the Question of Philosophy*, pp. 75–100. Baltimore: Johns Hopkins University Press, 1987.

Berthoff, Warner. *The Ferment of Realism: American Literature, 1884–1919*. New York: The Free Press, 1965.

Beye, Charles Rowan. "Male and Female in the Homeric Poems." *Ramos* 3, 2 (1974): 87–101.

Blackmore, Steven, ed. *Burke and the French Revolution: Bicentennial Essays*. Athens, Georgia: University of Georgia Press, 1992.

Blair, Elena Duvergès. "Women: The Unrecognized Teachers of the Platonic Socrates." *Ancient Philosophy* 16 (1996): 333–350.

Bloom, Allan. *Love and Friendship*. New York: Simon & Schuster, 1993.

Bloom, Harold, ed. "Introduction." In *Modern Critical Views: Gertrude Stein*, pp. 1–6. New York: Chelsea House Publishers, 1986.

——, ed. "Introduction." In *Modern Critical Views: Mary Shelley*, pp. 1–10. New York: Chelsea House Publishers, 1985.

Bloom, Lynn Z. "Gertude is Alice is Everybody: Innovation and Point of View in Gertrude Stein's Autobiographies." *Twentieth Century Literature* 24 (1978): 81–93.

Bluestone, Natalie Harris. *Women and the Ideal Society: Plato's Republic and Modern Myths of Gender*. Amherst: University of Massachusetts Press, 1987.

Blumenberg, Hans. *Shipwreck with Spectator*. Cambridge: The MIT Press, 1997.

Boegehold, Alan L. and Adele C. Scafuro, eds. *Athenian Identity and Civic Ideology*. Baltimore: The Johns Hopkins University Press, 1994.

Booth, William J. "Politics and the Household: A Commentary on Aristotle's *Politics* Book One." *History of Political Thought* II, 2 (Summer 1981): 203–226.

Boulton, James T. *The Language of Politics in the Age of Wilkes and Burke*. Toronto: University of Toronto Press, 1963.

Bowie, A. M. "Homer, Herodotus and the 'Beginnings' of Thucydides' *History*." In H. D. Jocelyn, ed., *Tria Lustra: Essays and Notes presented to John Pinsent*, pp. 141–147. Liverpool Classical Papers, 3; 1993.

Braque, Georges, with Eugene and Maria Jolas, Henri Matisse, André Salmon, and Tristan Tzara. *Testimony Against Gertrude Stein*. Supplement to *Transition* (February, 1935).

Breslin, James E. "Gertrude Stein and the Problems of Autobiography." In

Michael J. Hoffman, ed., *Critical Essays on Gertrude Stein*, pp. 149–159. Boston: G. K. Hall and Co., 1986.

Brickhouse, Thomas C. and Nicholas D. Smith. *Plato's Socrates*. New York: Oxford University Press, 1994.

Bridgman, Richard. *Gertrude Stein in Pieces*. New York: Oxford University Press, 1970.

Bromwich, David. "The Sublime Before Aesthetics and Politics." *Raritan* 16 (Spring 1997): 30–51.

——. "Wollstonecraft as a Critic of Burke." *Political Theory* 23, 4 (November, 1995): 617–633.

Broome, J. H. *Rousseau: A Study of His Thought*. London: Edward Arnold Publishers, 1963.

Brown, Wendy. *Manhood and Politics: A Feminist Reading in Political Theory*. Totowa, New Jersey: Rowman and Littlefield, 1988.

Bruns, Gerald L. *Tragic Thoughts at the End of Philosophy: Language, Literature, and Ethical Theory*. Evanston: Northwestern University Press, 1999.

Burgelin, Pierre. "L'Éducation De Sophie." *Annales De La Société Jean-Jacques Rousseau* 35 (1959–1962): 113–130.

Burger, Ronna. *Plato's Phaedrus: A Defense of a Philosophical Art of Writing*. Tuscaloosa: University of Alabama Press, 1980.

Burke, Edmund. *The Correspondence of Edmund Burke*. Volume VI. Edited by Alfred Cobban and Robert A. Smith. Chicago: University of Chicago Press, 1967.

——. *Philosophical Enquiry into the Origin of Our Ideas of the Sublime and Beautiful*. Edited with introduction by Adam Phillips. New York: Oxford University Press, 1990.

——. *Reflections on the Revolution in France*. Edited by J. G. A. Pocock. Indianapolis: Hackett Publishing Company, 1987.

Butler, Samuel. *The Authoress of the Odyssey*. Chicago: University of Chicago Press, 1897 (reprint, 1967).

Caeser, James W. "Political Science, Political Culture, and the Role of the Intellectual." In Ken Masugi, ed., *Interpreting Tocqueville's Democracy in America*, pp. 287–325. Savage, Maryland: Rowman and Littlefield, 1991.

Cantor, Paul A. and Michael Valdez Moses. "Teaching *Frankenstein* from the Creature's Perspective." In Stephen C. Behrendt, ed., *Approaches to Teaching Shelley's Frankenstein*, pp. 127–132. New York: The Modern Language Association of America, 1990.

Caramello, Charles. *Henry James, Gertrude Stein, and the Biographical Act*. Chapel Hill: University of North Carolina Press, 1996.

Carne-Ross, D. S. and Kenneth Haynes, eds. *Horace in English*. New York: Penguin, 1996.

Cartledge, Paul. "The Silent Women of Thucydides: 2.45.2 Re-viewed." In Ralph Rosen and Joseph Farrell, eds., *Nomodeiktes: Greek Studies in Honor of Martin Ostwald*, pp. 125–132. Ann Arbor: University of Michigan Press, 1993.

——. "Spartan Institutions in Thucydides." Appendix C in the revised edition of the Richard Crawley translation, edited by Robert B. Strassler and introduced by Victor Davis Hanson, *The Landmark Thucydides: A Comprehensive Guide to The Peloponnesian War*. New York: Touchstone, 1998.

Castoriadis, Cornelius. "The Greek Polis and the Creation of Democracy." *Graduate Faculty Philosophy Journal* 9, 2 (Fall 1983): 79–115.

Cavarero, Adriana. *In Spite of Plato: A Feminist Rewriting of Ancient Philosophy*. Translated by Serena Anderlini-D'Onofrio and Áine O'Healy. Foreword by Rosi Braidotti. Cambridge: Polity Press, 1995, 1990.

Caws, Peter, ed. *The Causes of Quarrel: Essays on Peace, War, and Thomas Hobbes*. Boston: Beacon Press, 1989.

Chambers, Mortimer H. "Aristotle's Historical Method." In Stanley M. Burstein and Louis A. Okin, eds., *Panhellenica: Essays in Ancient History and Historiography in Honor of Truesdell S. Brown*, pp. 57–67. Lawrence, Kansas: Coronado Press, 1980.

Chessman, Harriet Scott. *The Public is Invited to Dance: Representation, the Body, and Dialogue in Gertrude Stein*. Stanford: Stanford University Press, 1989.

Christenson, Ron. "The Political Theory of Male Chauvinism: J. J. Rousseau's Paradigm." *The Midwest Quarterly* Volume XIII, Number 3 (April, 1972): 291–299.

Clark, Lorenne M. G. and Lynda Lange. *The Sexism of Social and Political Theory: Women and Reproduction from Plato to Nietzsche*. Toronto: University of Toronto Press, 1979.

Cobban, Alfred. *Rousseau and the Modern State*. Hamden, Connecticut: Archon Books, 1964.

Cogan, Marc. *The Human Thing: The Speeches and Principles of Thucydides' History*. Chicago: University of Chicago Press, 1981.

Cohen, Beth, ed. *The Distaff Side: Representing the Female in Homer's Odyssey*. New York: Oxford University Press, 1995.

Colmo, Ann Charney. "What Sophie Knew." In Pamela Grande Jensen, ed., *Finding a New Feminism*, pp. 67–91. Lanham, Maryland: Rowman & Littlefield, 1996.

Connor, W. Robert. *Thucydides*. Princeton: Princeton University Press, 1994.

——. "Tyrannis Polis." In John D'Arms and John W. Eadie, eds., *Ancient and Modern: Essays in Honor of Gerald F. Else*. Ann Arbor: University of Michigan Press, 1977.

Cook, Albert. *The Stance of Plato*. Lanham, Maryland: Littlefield Adams Books, 1996.

Coole, Diana. *Women in Political Theory: From Ancient Misogyny to Contemporary Feminism*. Hemel Hempstead: Harvester Wheatsheaf, 1993.

Couser, G. Thomas. *American Autobiography: The Prophetic Mode*. Amherst: University of Massachusetts, 1979.

——. "Of Time and Identity: Walt Whitman and Gertrude Stein as Autobiographers." *Texas Studies in Literature and Language* 17 (Winter 1976): 787–804.

Crane, Gregory. *The Blinded Eye: Thucydides and the New Written Word*. Lanham, Maryland: Rowman and Littlefield Publishers, 1996.

Cropsey, Joseph. "The Dramatic End of Plato's Socrates." *Interpretation* 14, 2 & 3 (1986): 155–175.

——. *Plato's World: Man's Place in the Cosmos*. Chicago: University of Chicago Press, 1995.

——. *Political Philosophy and the Issues of Politics*. Chicago: University of Chicago Press, 1980.

Dahrendorf, Ralf. *The Modern Social Conflict*. New York: Weidenfeld and Nicolson, 1988.

D'Amico, Jack. "Machiavelli and Memory." *Modern Language Quarterly* 50, 2 (June 1989): 99–124.

——. "The Virtù of Women: Machiavelli's *Mandragola* and *Clizia*." *Interpretation* 12, 2 & 3 (May and September 1984): 261–273.

Davis, Michael. *The Politics of Philosophy: A Commentary on Aristotle's Politics*. Lanham, Maryland: Rowman and Littlefield Publishers, 1996.

Davy, Kate. "Richard Foreman's Ontological-Hysteric Theatre: The Influence of Gertrude Stein." *Twentieth Century Literature* 24,1 (Spring 1978): 108–125.

DeJean, Joan. *Literary Fortifications: Rousseau, Laclos, Sade*. Princeton: Princeton University Press, 1984.

DeKoven, Marianne. "Gertrude Stein and the Modernist Canon." In Shirley Neuman and Ira B. Nadel, eds., *Gertrude Stein and the Making of Literature*, pp. 8–20. Boston: Northeastern University Press, 1988.

Derrida, Jacques. *Dissemination*. Translated with introduction and notes by Barbara Johnson. Chicago: University of Chicago Press, 1981.

———. *Of Grammatology*. Translated by Gayatri Spivak. Baltimore: Johns Hopkins University Press, 1976.

Dietz, Mary. "Trapping the Prince: Machiavelli and the Politics of Deception." *American Political Science Review* 80, 3 (September 1986): 777–798.

Dobbs, Darrell. "Aristotle's Anticommunism." *American Journal of Political Science* 29, 1 (February 1985): 29–46.

———. "Choosing Justice: Socrates' Model City and the Practice of Dialectic." *American Political Science Review* 88, 2 (June 1994): 263–277.

———. "Family Matters: Aristotle's Appreciation of Women and the Plural Structure of Society." *American Political Science Review* 90, 1 (March 1996): 74–89.

———. "Natural Right and the Problem of Aristotle's Defense of Slavery." *The Journal of Politics* 56, 1 (1994): 69–94.

———. "Reckless Rationalism and Heroic Reverence in Homer's *Odyssey*." *American Political Science Review* 81, 2 (June 1987): 491–508.

Doherty, Lillian Eileen. *Siren Songs: Gender, Audiences, and Narrators in the Odyssey*. Ann Arbor: The University of Michigan Press, 1995.

Donaldson, Ian. *The Rapes of Lucretia: A Myth and Its Transformations*. Oxford: Clarendon Press, 1982.

Dumont, Louis. *Essays on Individualism: Modern Ideology in Anthropological Perspective*. Chicago: University of Chicago Press, 1986.

Dydo, Ulla E. "Must Horses Drink." *Tulsa Studies in Women's Literature* 4, 2 (Fall 1985): 272–280.

———. "*Stanzas in Meditation:* The Other Autobiography." In Richard Kostelanetz, ed., *Gertrude Stein Advanced: An Anthology of Criticism*. Jefferson, North Carolina: McFarland and Company, 1990.

Easby-Smith, James S. *The Songs of Alcaeus*. Washington: Lowdermilk, 1901.

Eisenstein, Zillah R. *The Radical Future of Liberal Feminism*. Boston: Northeastern University Press, 1981, 1993.

Ellrich, Robert J. *Rousseau and His Reader: The Rhetorical Situation of the Major Works*. Chapel Hill: The University of North Carolina Press, 1969.

Elshtain, Jean Bethke. *Public Man, Private Woman: Women in Social and Political Thought*. Princeton: Princeton University Press, 1981.

Fata, Frank. "Machiavellian Strategies in *Mandragola*." *Machiavelli Studies* 2 (1988): 89–101.

Ferguson, Robert A. *The American Enlightenment, 1750–1820*. Cambridge: Harvard University Press, 1994.

Fermon, Nicole. *Domesticating Passions: Rousseau, Women, and Nation*. Hanover, New Hampshire: University Press of New England, 1997.

Ferrari, G. R. F. *Listening to the Cicadas: A Study of Plato's Phaedrus*. Cambridge: Cambridge University Press, 1987, 1990.

Flaumenhaft, Mera J. "The Comic Remedy: Machiavelli's *Mandragola*." *Interpretation* 7,2 (May 1978): 33–73.

Foley, Helene P. *Reflections of Women in Antiquity*. New York: Gordon and Breach Science Publishers, 1981.

——. "'Reverse Similes' and Sex Roles in the *Odyssey*." *Arethusa* 11, 1–2 (Spring and Fall 1978): 7–26.

Forde, Steven. *The Ambition to Rule: Alcibiades and the Politics of Imperialism in Thucydides*. Ithaca: Cornell University Press, 1989.

——. "Gender and Justice in Plato." *American Political Science Review* 92, 3 (September 1997): 657–670.

——. "Varieties of Realism: Thucydides and Machiavelli." *Journal of Politics* 54, 2 (May, 1992): 372–393.

Fortenbaugh, W. W. "On Plato's Feminism in *Republic* V." *Apeiron* 9, 2 (1975): 1–4.

Fraenkel, Eduard. *Horace*. Oxford: Clarendon Press, 1957.

Fuller, Lon. *The Morality of Law*. New Haven: Yale University Press, 1969.

Furniss, Tom. *Edmund Burke's Aesthetic Ideology: Language, Gender, and Political Economy in Revolution*. Cambridge: Cambridge University Press, 1993.

Fuss, Diana. *Essentially Speaking: Feminism, Nature and Difference*. New York: Routledge, 1989.

——. "The 'Risk' of Essence." In Sandra Kemp and Judith Squires, eds., *Feminisms*, pp. 250–258. Oxford: Oxford University Press, 1997.

Gardiner, Judith Kegan. "On Female Identity and Writing by Women." In Elizabeth Abel, ed., *Writing and Sexual Difference*, pp. 177–191. Chicago: University of Chicago Press, 1982.

Garver, Eugene. *Machiavelli and the History of Prudence*. Madison: University of Wisconsin Press, 1987.

Gatens, Moira. "'The Oppressed State of My Sex': Wollstonecraft on Reason, Feeling, and Equality." In Mary Lyndon Shanley and Carole Pateman, eds., *Feminist Interpretations and Political Theory*, pp. 112–128. University Park: Pennsylvania State University Press, 1991.

Gilbert, Sandra. M and Susan Gubar. "Mary Shelley's Monstrous Eve." In J. Paul Hunter, ed., *Mary Shelley: Frankenstein*, pp. 225–240. New York: Norton & Company, 1996.

Gill, Christopher and Mary Margaret McCabe, eds. *Form and Argument in Late Plato*. Oxford: Clarendon Press, 1996.

Gomme, A. W. *A Historical Commentary on Thucydides*. Volume 1: *Intro-*

duction and Commentary on Book I. Oxford: Clarendon Press, 1971, 1945.

Gourevitch, Victor. "Rousseau on Lying: A Provisional Reading of the Fourth Rêverie." *Berkshire Review* 15 (1980): 93–107.

Grant, Ruth W. *Hypocrisy and Integrity: Machiavelli, Rousseau, and the Ethics of Politics*. Chicago: University of Chicago Press, 1997.

Greene, Thomas M. "The End of Discourse in Machiavelli's *Prince*." *Yale French Studies* 67 (1984): 57–71.

Grene, David. *Greek Political Theory: The Image of Man in Thucydides and Plato*. Chicago: University of Chicago Press, 1965.

Griswold, Charles L., Jr. *Adam Smith and the Virtues of Enlightenment*. Cambridge: Cambridge University Press, 1999.

——. "*E Pluribus Unum?* On the Platonic 'Corpus.'" *Ancient Philosophy* 19 (1999): 361–397.

——, ed. *Platonic Writings, Platonic Readings*. New York: Routledge, 1988.

——. *Self-Knowledge in Plato's Phaedrus*. New Haven: Yale University Press, 1986.

Habermas, Jürgen. *The Philosophical Discourse of Modernity*. Translated by Frederick Lawrence. Cambridge: The MIT Press, 1987.

——. *The Structural Transformation of the Public Sphere: An Inquiry into a Category of Bourgeois Society*. Translated by Thomas Burger with Frederick Lawrence. Cambridge: The MIT Press, 1991.

Halperin, David M. "Plato and the Erotics of Narrativity." In James C. Klagge and Nicholas D. Smith, eds., *Methods of Interpreting Plato and His Dialogues*. *Oxford Studies in Ancient Philosophy*, pp. 93–129, supplementary volume. Oxford: Clarendon Press, 1992.

Hampshire, Stuart. *Innocence and Experience*. Cambridge: Harvard University Press, 1989.

Hancock, Graham and Robert Bauval. *Keeper of Genesis: A Quest for the Hidden Legacy of Mankind*. London: Heinemann, 1996.

Hancock, Ralph C. "The Uses and Hazards of Christianity in Tocqueville's Attempt to Save Democratic Souls." In Ken Masugi, ed., *Interpreting Tocqueville's Democracy in America*, pp. 348–393. Savage, Maryland: Rowman and Littlefield, 1991.

Hansen, Mogens Herman, ed. "Introduction." In *The Ancient Greek City-State*, pp. 7–29. *Historisk-filosofiske Meddelelser* 67 Commissioner: Munksgaard Copenhagen, 1993.

——, ed. *Polis and City-State: An Ancient Concept and Its Modern Equivalent*. *Historisk-filosofiske Meddelelser* 76 Commissioner: Munksgaard Copenhagen, 1998.

——, ed. *The Polis as an Urban Centre and as a Political Community*. *Historisk-filosofiske Meddelelser* 75 Commissioner: Munksgaard Copenhagen, 1997.

——, ed. *Was Athens a Democracy? Historisk-filosofiske Meddelelser* 59 Commissioner: Munksgaard Copenhagen, 1989.

Hansen, Mogens Herman and Kurt Raaflaub, eds. *More Studies in the Ancient Greek Polis*. Stuttgart: Steiner, 1996.

——. *Studies in the Ancient Greek Polis*. Stuttgart: Steiner, 1995.

Hariman, Robert. "Composing Modernity in Machiavelli's *Prince*." *Journal of the History of Ideas* 50 (January, March 1989): 3–29.

Hariman, Robert and Francis A. Beer, eds. *Post-Realism: The Rhetorical Turn in International Relations*. East Lansing: Michigan State University Press, 1996.

Harvey, David. "Women in Thucydides." *Arethusa* 18 (1985): 67–90.

Hattendorf, John. *The Influence of History on Mahan*. Newport, Rhode Island: Naval War College Press, 1991.

Haynes, Kenneth and D. S. Carne-Ross, eds. *Horace in English*. New York: Penguin, 1996.

Hedrick, Charles E., Jr. "The Zero Degree of Society: Aristotle and the Athenian Citizen." In J. Peter Euben, John R. Wallach, and Josiah Ober, eds., *Athenian Political Thought and the Reconstruction of American Democracy*, pp. 289–318. Ithaca: Cornell University Press, 1994.

Herodotus. *The History*. Translated by David Grene. Chicago: University of Chicago Press, 1987.

Hirschman, Albert O. *The Passions and the Interests: Political Arguments for Capitalism Before Its Triumph*. Princeton: Princeton University Press, 1977.

Hoffman, Michael J., ed. *Critical Essays on Gertrude Stein*. Boston: G. K. Hall and Co., 1986.

Homer. *The Iliad*. Translated by Robert Fagles and introduced by Bernard Knox. New York: Penguin, 1990.

——. *The Odyssey*. Translated by Robert Fagles with introduction and notes by Bernard Knox. New York: Penguin Books, 1996.

Horace. *The Odes and Epodes*. Translated by C. E. Bennett. Cambridge: Harvard University Press, 1968.

Hornblower, Simon. "The Religious Dimension to the Peloponnesian War, Or, What Thucydides Does Not Tell Us." *Harvard Studies in Classical Philology*, 94 (1992): 169–197.

Howland, Jacob. *The Paradox of Political Philosophy: Socrates' Philosophic Trial*. Lanham, Maryland: Rowman and Littlefield, 1998.

Hulliung, Mark. *Citizen Machiavelli*. Princeton: Princeton University Press, 1983.

Hunt, Lynn. "The Many Bodies of Marie Antoinette: Political Pornography and the Problem of the Feminine in the French Revolution." In Peter Jones, ed., *The French Revolution in Social and Political Perspective*, pp. 268–284. New York: St. Martin's Press, 1996.

Hunter, Virginia. *Past and Process in Herodotus and Thucydides*. Princeton: Princeton University Press, 1982.

Hyland, Drew A. *Finitude and Transcendence in the Platonic Dialogues*. Albany: State University of New York Press, 1995.

——. "Plato's Three Waves and the Question of Utopia." *Interpretation* 18, 1 (Fall 1990): 91–109.

Immerwahrr, Henry R. "Pathology of Power and the Speeches in Thucydides." In Philip A. Stadter, ed., *The Speeches in Thucydides*, pp. 16–31. Chapel Hill: University of North Carolina Press, 1973.

Irigaray, Luce. *Speculum of the Other Woman*. Translated by Gillian C. Gill. Ithaca: Cornell University Press, 1985, 1974.

Jacobs, William. "Plato on Female Emancipation and the Traditional Family." *Apeiron* 12, 1 (1978): 29–31.

Jensen, Pamela Grande, ed. *Finding a New Feminism*. Lanham, Maryland: Rowman and Littlefield, 1996.

Jimack, Peter. "La Genèse et la rédaction de *l'Emile* de Jean-Jacques Rousseau." *Studies on Voltaire and the 18th Century* 13 (1960): 15–418.

Johnson, Barbara. "My Monster/My Self." In Mary Shelley, *Frankenstein*, pp. 241–251. Edited by J. Paul Hunter. New York: Norton and Company, 1996.

Johnson, Samuel. *The Letters of Samuel Johnson*. Volume 1, collected and edited by R. W. Chapman. Oxford: Clarendon Press, 1952.

Jones, A. H. M. *Athenian Democracy*. Oxford: Basil Blackwell, 1969.

Jones, Ann Rosalind. "Writing the Body: Toward an Understanding of l'Écriture Féminine." In Elaine Showalter, ed., *The New Feminist Criticism: Essays on Women, Literature and Theory*, pp. 361–377. New York: Pantheon, 1985.

Kagan, Donald. *The Archidamian War*. Ithaca: Cornell University Press, 1974.

——. *The Fall of the Athenian Empire*. Ithaca: Cornell University Press, 1987.

——. *The Outbreak of the Peloponnesian War*. Ithaca: Cornell University Press, 1969.

——. *The Peace of Nicias and the Sicilian Expedition*. Ithaca: Cornell University Press, 1981.

———. *Pericles of Athens and the Birth of Democracy*. New York: The Free Press, 1991.

Kahn, Charles H. *Plato and the Socratic Dialogue: The Philosophical Use of a Literary Form*. Cambridge: Cambridge University Press, 1996.

Kahn, Victoria. *Machiavellian Rhetoric, from the Counter-Reformation to Milton*. Princeton: Princeton University Press, 1994.

Kahn, Victoria and Albert Russell Ascoli, eds. *Machiavelli and the Discourse of Literature*. Ithaca: Cornell University Press, 1993.

Kallet-Marx, Lisa. "Thucydides 2.45.2 and the Status of War Widows in Periclean Athens." In Ralph Rosen and Joseph Farrell, eds., *Nomodeiktes: Greek Studies in Honor of Martin Ostwald*, pp. 133–143. Ann Arbor: University of Michigan Press, 1993.

Katz, Leon. "Weininger and *The Making of Americans*." *Twentieth Century Literature* 24,1 (Spring 1978): 8–26.

Kavanagh, Thomas M. *Writing the Truth: Authority and Desire in Rousseau*. Berkeley: University of California Press, 1987.

Kelly, Christopher. "Rousseau and His Readers." *The Political Science Reviewer* XII (Fall, 1982): 315–336.

———. *Rousseau's Exemplary Life: The Confessions as Political Philosophy*. Ithaca: Cornell University Press, 1987.

———. " 'To Persuade without Convincing': The Language of Rousseau's Legislator." *American Journal of Political Science* 31, 2 (1987): 321–335.

Kennedy, Don H. *Ship Names: Origin and Usage During 45 Centuries*. Newport News: Mariner's Museum and the University Press of Virginia, 1974.

Kennedy, Paul. *Strategy and Diplomacy 1870–1945*. London: George Allen & Unwin, 1983.

Keohane, Nannerl O. " 'But for Her Sex. . .': The Domestication of Sophie," *University of Ottawa Quarterly* Vol. 49, 3–4 (July and October 1979): 390–400.

Kerber, Linda K. "Separate Spheres, Female Worlds, Woman's Place: The Rhetoric of Women's History." *The Journal of American History* 75,1 (June 1988): 9–39.

Kermode, Frank. *The Classic*. New York: Viking, 1975.

Keyt, David. "Three Basic Theorems in Aristotle's *Politics*." In David Keyt and Fred D. Miller, Jr., eds., *A Companion to Aristotle's Politics*, pp. 118–141. Cambridge: Basil Blackwell, 1991.

Kierkegaard, Søren. *The Concept of Irony, with Continual Reference to Socrates*. Translated by Howard V. Hong and Edna H. Hong. Princeton: Princeton University Press, 1989.

——. *Stages on Life's Way*. Translated by Walter Lowrie. London: Oxford University Press, 1940.

Klagge, James C. and Nicholas D. Smith, eds. *Methods of Interpreting Plato and His Dialogues*. *Oxford Studies in Ancient Philosophy*, supplementary volume. Oxford: Clarendon Press, 1992.

Klein, Jacob. *A Commentary on Plato's Meno*. Chapel Hill: University of North Carolina Press, 1965.

Knippenberg, Joseph. "Virtue, Honor and Reputation: Machiavelli's Appropriation of Christianity in the 'Rape' of Lucrezia." In *Poets, Princes and Private Citizens: Literary Alternatives to Postmodern Politics*, edited by Joseph M. Knippenberg and Peter Augustine Lawler, pp. 21–38. Lanham, Maryland: Rowman and Littlefield, 1996.

Knoepflamacher, U. C. and George Levine, eds. *The Endurance of Frankenstein: Essays on Mary Shelley's Novel*. Berkeley: University of California Press, 1979.

Kostelanetz, Richard, ed. *Gertrude Stein Advanced: An Anthology of Criticism*. Jefferson, North Carolina: McFarland and Company, 1990.

Kramnick, Isaac. *The Rage of Edmund Burke: Portrait of An Ambivalent Conservative*. New York: Basic Books, 1977.

Kullman, Wolfgang. "Man as a Political Animal in Aristotle." In David Keyt and Fred D. Miller, Jr., eds., *A Companion to Aristotle's Politics*, pp. 94–117. Cambridge: Basil Blackwell, 1991.

Lacey, W. K. *The Family in Classical Greece*. Ithaca: Cornell University Press, 1968.

Lange, Lynda and Lorenne M. G. Clark. *The Sexism of Social and Political Theory: Women and Reproduction from Plato to Nietzsche*. Toronto: University of Toronto Press, 1979.

Larmore, Charles. *The Morals of Modernity*. Cambridge: Cambridge University Press, 1996.

Lebow, Richard Ned and Barry S. Strauss, eds. *Hegemonic Rivalry: From Thucydides to the Nuclear Age*. Boulder: Westview Press, 1991.

Lefkowitz, Mary. *Not Out of Africa: How "Afrocentrism" Became an Excuse to Teach Myth as History*. New York: Basic Books, 1996.

Levine, George. "The Ambiguous Heritage of Frankenstein." In George Levine and U. C. Knoepflamacher, eds., *The Endurance of Frankenstein: Essays on Mary Shelley's Novel*, pp. 3–30. Berkeley: University of California Press, 1979.

Lindsay, Thomas K. "Was Aristotle Racist, Sexist, and Anti-Democratic? A Review Essay." *Review of Politics* 56,1 (Winter, 1994): 127–151.

Lipking, Lawrence. "*Frankenstein*, the True Story: or Rousseau Judges

Jean-Jacques." In J. Paul Hunter, ed., *Mary Shelley: Frankenstein*, pp. 313–331. New York: Norton and Company, 1996.

Lipset, Seymour Martin. *The First New Nation: The United States in Historical and Comparative Perspective*. New York: Doubleday, 1967.

Livy. *The Early History of Rome: Books I-V of The History of Rome from Its Foundation*. Translated by Aubrey De Sélincourt and introduced by R. M. Ogilvie. New York: Penguin Books, 1960, 1971.

Locke, John. *Second Treatise of Government*. Indianapolis: Hackett Publishing, 1980.

Loraux, Nicole. *The Children of Athena: Athenian Ideas about Citizenship and the Division Between the Sexes*. Translated by Caroline Levine, foreword by Froma I. Zeitlin. Princeton: Princeton University Press, 1993.

——. *The Experience of Tiresias: The Feminine and the Greek Man*. Translated by Paula Wissing. Princeton: Princeton University Press, 1995.

——. *The Invention of Athens: The Funeral Oration in the Classical City*. Translated by Alan Sheridan. Cambridge: Harvard University Press, 1986.

Lord, Carnes. "On Machiavelli's *Mandragola*." *Journal of Politics* 41 (August 1979): 806–827.

Loriaux, Michael and Sara Monoson. "The Illusion of Power and the Disruption of Moral Norms: Thucydides' Critique of Periclean Policy." *American Political Science Review*. 92, 2 (June 1998): 285–297.

McAuslan, Ian and Peter Walcot, eds. *Women in Antiquity*. New York: Oxford University Press 1996.

McCabe, Mary Margaret and Christopher Gill, eds. *Form and Argument in Late Plato*. Oxford: Clarendon Press, 1996.

Machiavelli, Niccolò. *Discourses on Livy*. Translated by Harvey C. Mansfield and Nathan Tarcov. Chicago: University of Chicago Press, 1996.

——. *Mandragola*. Translated with introduction and notes by Mera J. Flaumenhaft. Prospect Heights, Illinois: Waveland Press, 1981.

——. *The Prince*. Translated with an introduction by Harvey C. Mansfield, Jr. Chicago: University of Chicago Press, 1985.

Macleod, Colin. *Collected Essays*. Oxford: Clarendon Press, 1983.

Mahan, Alfred Thayer. *The Influence of Sea Power Upon History*. Boston: Little, Brown, 1890.

de Man, Paul. *Blindness and Insight: Essays in the Rhetoric of Contemporary Criticism*. Introduced by Wlad Godzich. Second edition. Minneapolis: University of Minnesota Press, 1983.

Manent, Pierre. *Tocqueville and the Nature of Democracy*. Foreword by

Harvey C. Mansfield. Translated by John Waggoner. Lanham, Maryland: Rowman and Littlefield Publishers, 1996.

Mansfield, Harvey C., Jr. *Machiavelli's New Modes and Orders: A Study of the Discourses on Livy*. Ithaca: Cornell University Press, 1979.

———. *Machiavelli's Virtue*. Chicago: University of Chicago Press, 1996.

Martinez, Ronald L. "The Pharmacy of Machiavelli: Roman Lucretia in *Mandragola*." *Renaissance Drama* New Series XIV (1983): 1–43.

Masugi, Ken, ed. *Interpreting Tocqueville's Democracy in America*. Savage, Maryland: Rowman and Littlefield, 1991.

Mathie, William. "God, Woman, and Morality: The Democratic Family in Tocqueville." *Review of Politics* 57,1 (Winter 1995): 7–30.

Mellor, Anne K. *Mary Shelley: Her Life, Her Fiction, Her Monsters*. New York: Routledge, 1988.

Melville, Herman. *Moby Dick*. Introduced by Tony Tanner. Oxford: Oxford University Press, 1988.

Melzer, Arthur M. *The Natural Goodness of Man: On the System of Rousseau's Thought*. Chicago: The University of Chicago Press, 1990.

Merrill, Cynthia. "Mirrored Image: Gertrude Stein and Autobiography." *Pacific Coast Philology* 20, 1–2 (November 1985): 11–17.

Meyer, Steven J. "Gertrude Stein Shipwrecked in Bohemia: Making Ends Meet in the *Autobiography* and After." *Southwest Review* 77, 1 (Winter 1992): 12–33.

———. "Stein and Emerson." *Raritan* 10,2 (1990): 87–119.

Miller, Fred D., Jr. *Nature, Justice and Rights in Aristotle's Politics*. Oxford: Clarendon Press, 1995.

Miller, Nancy K., ed. *The Poetics of Gender*. New York: Columbia University Press, 1986.

Mitchell, Joshua. *The Fragility of Freedom: Tocqueville on Religion, Democracy, and the American Future*. Chicago: University of Chicago Press, 1995.

Mitchell, W. J. T. *Iconology: Image, Text, Ideology*. Chicago: University of Chicago Press, 1987.

Moers, Ellen. "Female Gothic: The Monster's Mother." In J. Paul Hunter, ed., *Mary Shelley: Frankenstein*, pp. 214–224. New York: Norton and Company, 1996.

Molho, Anthony, Kurt Raaflaub and Julia Emlen, eds. *City-States in Classical Antiquity and Medieval Italy*. Ann Arbor: University of Michigan Press, 1991.

Monoson, Sara. "Citizen as *Erastes*: Erotic Imagery and the Idea of Reciprocity in the Periclean Funeral Oration." *Political Theory* 22, 2 (May 1994): 253–276.

Monoson, Sara and Michael Loriaux. "The Illusion of Power and the Disruption of Moral Norms: Thucydides' Critique of Periclean Policy." *American Political Science Review*. 92, 2 (June 1998): 285–297.

Morton, F. L. "Sexual Equality and the Family in Tocqueville's *Democracy in America*." *Canadian Journal of Political Science*, XVII: 2 (June 1984): 309–324.

Mosher, Michael A. "The Skeptic's Burke: *Reflections on the Revolution in France*, 1790–1990," *Political Theory* 19, 3 (August 1991): 391–418.

Murray, Oswyn. "*Polis* and *Politeia* in Aristotle." In Mogens Herman Hansen, ed., *The Ancient Greek City-State*, pp. 197–210. *Historisk-filosofiske Meddelelser* 67 Commissioner: Munksgaard Copenhagen, 1993.

Myers, Mitzi. "Politics from the Outside: Mary Wollstonecraft's *First Vindication*." In Ronald C. Rosbottom, ed., *Studies in Eighteenth-Century Culture*, pp. 113–132. Madison: University of Wisconsin Press, 1977.

Nadel, Ira B. and Shirley Neuman, eds. *Gertrude Stein and the Making of Literature*. Boston: Northeastern University Press, 1988.

Nederman, Cary J. "The Puzzle of the Political Animal: Nature and Artifice in Aristotle's Political Theory." *Review of Politics* 56,2 (Spring 1994): 283–304.

Nehamas, Alexander. *The Art of Living: Socratic Reflections from Plato to Foucault*. Berkeley: University of California Press, 1998.

Nelson, Hilde Lindemann. "Sophie Doesn't: Families and Counterstories of Self-Trust." *Hypatia* 11,1 (Winter 1996): 91–104.

Neuman, Shirley C. *Gertrude Stein: Autobiography and the Problem of Narration*. Victoria, British Columbia: English Literary Studies, University of Victoria, 1979.

Neuman, Shirley and Ira B. Nadel, eds. *Gertrude Stein and the Making of Literature*. Boston: Northeastern University Press, 1988.

Nichols, Mary P. *Citizens and Statesmen: A Study of Aristotle's Politics*. Savage, Maryland: Rowman and Littlefield, 1992.

Nielsen, Thomas Heine, ed. *Yet More Studies in the Ancient Greek Polis*. Stuttgart: Steiner, 1997.

Nietzsche, Friedrich. *Beyond Good and Evil*. Translated with commentary by Walter Kaufmann. New York: Random House, 1966.

———. *The Birth of Tragedy* and *The Case of Wagner*. Translated with commentary by Walter Kaufmann. New York: Random House, 1967.

———. *Untimely Meditations*. Translated by R. J. Hollingdale and introduced by J. P. Stern. New York: Cambridge University Press, 1983.

Norris, Christopher. *Derrida*. Cambridge: Harvard University Press, 1987.

Ober, Josiah. *The Athenian Revolution: Essays on Ancient Greek Democracy and Political Theory*. Princeton: Princeton University Press, 1996.

Okin, Susan Moller. *Justice, Gender, and the Family*. New York: Basic Books, 1989.

——. "Reason and Feeling in Thinking about Justice." In Cass Sunstein, ed., *Feminism and Political Theory*, pp. 15–36. Chicago: The University of Chicago Press, 1982.

——. "Rousseau's Natural Woman." *Journal of Politics* 41 (May 1979): 393–416.

——. *Women in Western Political Thought*. Princeton: Princeton University Press, 1979, 1992.

Olson, S. Douglas. "The Stories of Helen and Menelaus (*Odyssey* 4.240–89) and the Return of Odysseus." *American Journal of Philology* 110 (1989): 387–394.

Onians, John. *Bearers of Meaning: The Classical Orders in Antiquity, the Middle Ages, and the Renaissance*. Princeton: Princeton University Press, 1988.

Oost, Stewart Irvin. "Thucydides and the Irrational: Sundry Passages." *Classical Philology* LXX, 3 (July 1975): 186–196.

Orwin, Clifford. *The Humanity of Thucydides*. Princeton: Princeton University Press, 1994.

——. "Machiavelli's Unchristian Charity." *American Political Science Review* 72 (1978): 1217–1228.

——. "Rousseau's Socratism." *Journal of Politics* 60,1 (February 1998): 174–187.

Ozouf, Mona. *Women's Words: Essay on French Singularity*. Translated by Jane Marie Todd. Chicago: University of Chicago Press, 1997.

Parry, Adam M. *The Language of Achilles and Other Papers*. Oxford: Clarendon Press, 1989.

Pateman, Carole and Mary Lyndon Shanley, eds. *Feminist Interpretations and Political Theory*. University Park: Pennsylvania State University Press, 1991.

Patterson, Cynthia. "'Here the Lion Smiled': A Note on Thucydides 1.127–38." In Ralph Rosen and Joseph Farrell, eds., *Nomodeiktes: Greek Studies in Honor of Martin Ostwald*, pp. 145–152. Ann Arbor: University of Michigan Press, 1993.

Paulson, Ronald. *Representations of Revolution (1789–1820)*. New Haven: Yale University Press, 1983.

Pelikan, Jaroslav. *The Mystery of Continuity: Time and History, Memory and Eternity in the Thought of Saint Augustine*. Charlottesville: University Press of Virginia, 1986.

Pitken, Hanna Fenichel. *Fortune Is a Woman: Gender & Politics in the Thought of Niccolò Machiavelli*. Berkeley: University of California Press, 1984.

Plato. *Five Dialogues*. Translated by G. M. A. Grube. Indianapolis: Hackett Publishing Company, 1981.

——. *The Laws*. Translated with notes and essay by Thomas L. Pangle. New York: Basic Books, 1980.

——. *Phaedo*. Translated with introduction and commentary by R. Hackforth. Cambridge: Cambridge University Press, 1955.

——. *Phaedrus*. Translated with introduction and commentary by R. Hackforth. New York: Cambridge University Press, 1982.

——. *The Republic*. Translated with notes, essay and introduction by Allan Bloom. New York: Basic Books, 1968.

——. *The Republic*. Translated by G. M. A. Grube, revised by C. D. C. Reeve. Indianapolis: Hackett Publishing Company, 1992.

——. *Symposium*. Translated with introduction and notes by Alexander Nehamas and Paul Woodruff. Indianapolis: Hackett Publishing Company, 1989.

——. *Timaeus*. Translated by Benjamin Jowett, in Edith Hamilton and Huntington Cairns, eds., *The Collected Dialogues of Plato*. Princeton: Princeton University Press, 1961.

Plutarch. *Moralia*. Volume III. Translated by Frank Cole Babbitt. London: William Heinemann, 1931.

——. *Plutarch on Sparta*. Translated with introduction and notes by Richard J. A. Talbert. New York: Penguin Books, 1988.

——. *The Rise and Fall of Athens: Nine Greek Lives*. Translated with introduction by Ian Scott-Kilvert. New York: Penguin Books, 1960.

Pocock, J. G. A. *The Machiavellian Moment: Florentine Political Thought and the Atlantic Republican Tradition*. Princeton: Princeton University Press, 1975.

Poirier, Richard. *Poetry and Pragmatism*. Cambridge: Harvard University Press, 1992.

——. *The Renewal of Literature: Emersonian Reflections*. New York: Random House, 1987.

——. *Trying It Out in America: Literary and Other Performances*. New York: Farrar, Strauss and Giroux, 1999.

Polansky, Ronald. "The Dominance of Polis For Aristotle." *Dialogos* 33 (1979): 43–56.

Pomeroy, Sarah B. "Feminism in Book V of Plato's *Republic*." *Apeiron* 8 (1974): 33–35.

——. *Goddesses, Whores, Wives and Slaves*. New York: Schocken Books, 1975.

Poovey, Mary. *The Proper Lady and the Woman Writer*. Chicago: University of Chicago Press, 1984.

Porter, Dennis. *Rousseau's Legacy: Emergence and Eclipse of the Writer in France*. New York: Oxford University Press, 1995.

Posner, Richard A. *Law and Literature: A Misunderstood Relation*. Cambridge: Harvard University Press, 1988.

Press, Gerald. "The Dialogical Mode in Modern Plato Studies." In Richard Hart and Victorino Tejera, eds., *Plato's Dialogues: The Dialogical Approach*, pp. 1–28. Lewiston, New York: Edwin Mellen Press, 1997.

Puech, Aimé and Théodore Reinach. *Alcée/Sapho*. Paris: Société D'Edition "Les Belles Lettres," 1937.

Putnam, Robert D. *Bowling Alone: The Collapse and Revival of American Community*. New York: Simon & Schuster, 2000.

Raaflaub, Kurt A. "Homer to Solon: The Rise of the Polis. The Written Sources." In Mogens Herman Hansen, ed., *The Ancient Greek City-State*, pp. 41–49. *Historisk-filosofiske Meddelelser* 67 Commissioner: Munksgaard Copenhagen, 1993.

Raaflaub, Kurt A. and Mogens Herman Hansen, eds. *More Studies in the Ancient Greek Polis*. Stuttgart: Steiner, 1996.

——. *Studies in the Ancient Greek Polis*. Stuttgart: Steiner, 1995.

Rahe, Paul A. "Thucydides' Critique of Realpolitik." *Security Studies* 5, 2 (Winter 1995/1996): 105–141.

Randall, John Herman, Jr. *Plato: Dramatist of the Life of Reason*. New York: Columbia University Press, 1970.

Rawlings, Hunter R. Rawlings III. *The Structure of Thucydides' History*. Princeton: Princeton University Press, 1981.

Rebhorn, Wayne A. *Foxes and Lions: Machiavelli's Confidence Men*. Ithaca: Cornell University Press, 1987.

Redfield, James. "*Homo Domesticus*." In Jean-Pierre Vernant, ed., *The Greeks*, pp. 153–183. Chicago: University of Chicago Press, 1995.

——. *Nature and Culture in the Iliad: The Tragedy of Hector*. Chicago: The University of Chicago Press, 1975.

Reid, B. L. *Art by Subtraction: A Dissenting Opinion of Gertrude Stein*. Norman: University of Oklahoma Press, 1958.

Reid, Christopher. "Burke's Tragic Muse: Sarrah Siddons and the 'Feminization' of the *Reflections*." In Steven Blackmore, ed., *Burke and the French*

Revolution: Bicentennial Essays, pp. 1–27. Athens, Georgia: University of Georgia Press, 1992.

Reinach, Théodore and Aimé Puech. *Alcée/Sapho*. Paris: Société D'Edition "Les Belles Lettres," 1937.

Richardson, John. "Thucydides 1.23.6 and the Debate about the Peloponnesian War." In E. M. Craik, ed., *'Owl to Athens': Essays on Classical Subjects Presented to Sir Kenneth Dover*, pp. 155–161. Oxford: Clarendon Press, 1990.

Roberts, Jennifer Tolbert. "The Creation of a Legacy: A Manufactured Crisis in Eighteenth-Century Thought." In J. Peter Euben, John R. Wallach, and Josiah Ober, eds., *Athenian Political Thought and the Reconstruction of American Democracy*, pp. 81–102. Ithaca: Cornell University Press, 1994.

Rood, Tim. *Thucydides: Narrative and Explanation*. Oxford: Clarendon Press, 1998.

Rorty, Richard. *Contingency, Irony, and Solidarity*. Cambridge: Cambridge University Press, 1989.

——. *Essays on Heidegger and Others*. Cambridge: Cambridge University Press, 1991.

——. *Philosophy and the Mirror of Nature*. Princeton: Princeton University Press, 1979.

——. "The Priority of Democracy to Philosophy." In Merrill D. Peterson and Robert C. Vaughan, eds., *The Virginia Statute for Religious Freedom: Its Evolution and Consequences in American History*, pp. 257–288. New York: Cambridge University Press, 1988.

Rosen, Stanley. *The Ancients and the Moderns: Rethinking Modernity*. New Haven: Yale University Press, 1989.

Rousseau, Jean-Jacques. *The Basic Political Writings*. Translated by Donald A. Cress and introduced by Peter Gay. Indianapolis: Hackett Publishing Company, 1987.

——. *Emile, or On Education*. Introduced and translated with notes by Allan Bloom. New York: Basic Books, 1979.

——. *Emile and Sophie, or Solitary Beings*. Translated by Alice W. Harvey. In Pamela Grande Jensen, ed., *Finding a New Feminism: Rethinking the Woman Question for Liberal Democracy*, pp. 193–235. Lanham, Maryland: Rowman and Littlefield Publishers, 1996.

——. *Essay on the Origin of Languages*. Edited, translated, and annotated by Victor Gourevitch. New York: Harper and Row, 1986.

Runciman, W. G. "Doomed to Extinction: The Polis as an Evolutionary

Dead-End." In Oswyn Murray and Simon Price, eds., *The Greek City: From Homer to Alexander*, pp. 347–367. Oxford: Clarendon Press, 1990.

Rutherford, R. B. *The Art of Plato: Ten Essays in Platonic Interpretation.* Cambridge: Harvard University Press, 1995.

Ryan, Alan. *Property.* Minneapolis: University of Minnesota Press, 1987.

Salkever, Stephen G. *Finding the Mean: Theory and Practice in Aristotelian Political Philosophy.* Princeton: Princeton University Press, 1990.

Saunders, Judith P. "Gertrude Stein's *Paris France* and American Literary Tradition." In Harold Bloom, ed., *Modern Critical Views: Gertrude Stein*, pp. 121–129. New York: Chelsea House Publishers, 1986.

Saxonhouse, Arlene W. *Athenian Democracy: Modern Mythmakers and Ancient Theorists.* Notre Dame: University of Notre Dame Press, 1996.

——. "Classical Greek Conceptions of Public and Private." In S. I. Benn and Gerald Gauss, eds., *Conceptions of Public and Private in Social Life*, pp. 363–384. New York: St. Martin's Press, 1983.

——. "Family, Polity & Unity: Aristotle on Socrates' Community of Wives." *Polity* XV, 2 (Winter 1982): 202–219.

——. *Fear of Diversity: The Birth of Political Science in Ancient Greek Thought.* Chicago: University of Chicago Press, 1992.

——. "The Philosopher and the Female in the Political Thought of Plato." In Nancy Tuana, ed., *Feminist Interpretations of Plato*, pp. 67–85. University Park: Pennsylvania State University Press, 1994.

——. *Women in the History of Political Thought: Ancient Greece to Machiavelli.* New York: Praeger, 1985.

Sayre, Henry M. "The Artist's Model: American Art and the Question of Looking Like Gertrude Stein." In Shirley Neuman and Ira B. Nadel, eds., *Gertrude Stein and the Making of Literature*, pp. 21–41. Boston: Northeastern University Press, 1988.

Scafuro, Adele C. and Alan L. Boegehold, eds. *Athenian Identity and Civic Ideology.* Baltimore: The Johns Hopkins University Press, 1994.

Schaps, David. "The Women of Greece in Wartime." *Classical Philology* 77, 3 (July 1982): 193–213.

Schein, Seth L. "Female Representations and Interpreting the *Odyssey*." In Beth Cohen, ed., *The Distaff Side: Representing the Female in Homer's Odyssey*, pp. 17–27. New York: Oxford University Press, 1995.

——. *The Mortal Hero: An Introduction to Homer's Iliad.* Berkeley: University of California Press, 1984.

——, ed. *Reading the Odyssey: Selected Interpretive Essays.* Princeton: Princeton University Press, 1996.

Schmitz, Neil. "Doing the Fathers: Gertrude Stein on U. S. Grant in *Four in America*." *American Literature* 65, 4 (December 1993): 751–760.

——. *Of Huck and Alice: Humorous Writing in American Literature*. Minneapolis: University of Minnesota Press, 1983.

Schütrumpf, Eckart. "Aristotle on Sparta." In Anton Powell and Stephen Hodkinson, eds., *The Shadow of Sparta*, pp. 323–345. New York: Routledge, 1994.

——. *Die Analyse Der Polis Durch Aristoteles*. Amsterdam: R. R. Grüner, 1980.

Schwartz, Joel. *The Sexual Politics of Jean-Jacques Rousseau*. Chicago: University of Chicago Press, 1984.

Scully, Stephen. *Homer and the Sacred City*. Ithaca: Cornell University Press, 1990.

Seaford, Richard. *Reciprocity and Ritual*. New York: Oxford University Press, 1994.

Sedley, David. "The Dramatis Personae of Plato's *Phaedo*." In Timothy Smiley, ed., *Philosophical Dialogues: Plato, Hume, Wittgenstein*, pp. 3–26. Oxford: Oxford University Press, 1995.

Senior, Nancy. "*Les Solitaires* as a Test for Emile and Sophie." *The French Review* XLIX, 4 (March 1976): 528–535.

Shanley, Mary Lyndon and Carole Pateman, eds. *Feminist Interpretations and Political Theory*. University Park: Pennsylvania State University Press, 1991.

Shapiro, Ian. *Democratic Justice*. New Haven: Yale University Press, 1999.

Shelley, Mary. *Frankenstein*. Edited by J. Paul Hunter. New York: Norton and Company, 1996.

——. *Frankenstein*. Edited by D. L. Macdonald and Kathleen Scherf. Orchard Park, New York: Broadview Press, 1998.

Shklar, Judith N. *Men and Citizens: A Study of Rousseau's Social Theory*. New York: Cambridge University Press, 1969, 1987.

——. "Rousseau's Images of Authority." In Maurice Cranston and Richard S. Peters, eds., *Hobbes and Rousseau: A Collection of Critical Essays*, pp. 333–365. Garden City, New York: Doubleday & Company, 1972.

Showalter, Elaine, ed. *The New Feminist Criticism: Essays on Women, Literature and Theory*. New York: Pantheon, 1985.

Simon, Linda. *Gertrude Stein Remembered*. Lincoln: University of Nebraska Press, 1994.

Smith, Adam. *The Theory of Moral Sentiments*. Introduction by E. G. West. Indianapolis: Liberty Classics, 1976.

Smith, Bruce James. *Politics and Remembrance: Republican Themes in*

Machiavelli, Burke, and Tocqueville. Princeton: Princeton University Press, 1985.

Smith, Charles Forster. "Traces of Epic Usage in Thucydides." *Transactions and Proceedings of the American Philological Association* XXXI (1900): 69–81.

Smith, Nicholas D. and James C. Klagge, eds. *Methods of Interpreting Plato and His Dialogues. Oxford Studies in Ancient Philosophy*, supplementary volume. Oxford: Clarendon Press, 1992.

Smith, Nicholas D. and Thomas C. Brickhouse. *Plato's Socrates*. New York: Oxford University Press, 1994.

Smith, Rogers M. "Beyond Tocqueville, Myrdal, and Hartz: The Multiple Traditions in America." *American Political Science Review* 87, 3 (September 1993): 549–567.

——. *Civic Ideals: Conflicting Visions of Citizenship in United States History*. New Haven: Yale University Press, 1997.

Sommerstein, Alan H. "Introduction." In Alan H. Sommerstein, Stephen Halliwell, Jeffrey Henderson, and Bernhard Zimmermann, eds., *Tragedy, Comedy and the Polis*, pp. 11–19. Bari, Italy: Levante Editori, 1993.

Spiegelberg, Herbert, ed., with Bayard Quincy Morgan. *The Socratic Enigma: A Collection of Testimonies Through Twenty-Four Centuries*. Indianapolis: Bobbs-Merrill, 1964.

Stadter, Philip A. "The Form and Content of Thucydides' Pentecontaetia (1.89–117)." *Greek, Roman and Byzantine Studies* 34, 1 (Winter 1993): 35–72.

Stahl, Hans-Peter. *Thukydides: Die Stellung des Menschen im geschichtlichen Prozess*. Munich: C. H. Beck, 1966.

Stanford, W. B. *The Ulysses Theme: A Study in the Adaptability of a Traditional Hero*. Ann Arbor: University of Michigan Press, 1976.

Starobinski, Jean. *Jean-Jacques Rousseau: Transparency and Obstruction*. Translated by Arthur Goldhammer and introduced by Robert J. Morrissey. Chicago: University of Chicago Press, 1988.

Stein, Gertrude. *The Autobiography of Alice B. Toklas*. In Catharine R. Stimpson and Harriet Chessman, eds., *Gertrude Stein: Writings 1903–1932*, pp. 653–913. New York: The Library of America, 1998.

——. *Everybody's Autobiography*. New York: Random House, 1937.

——. *Four in America*. Introduction by Thornton Wilder. New Haven: Yale University Press, 1947.

——. *The Geographical History of America*. In Catharine R. Stimpson and Harriet Chessman, eds., *Gertrude Stein: Writings 1932–1946*, pp. 365–488. New York: The Library of America, 1998.

——. *Lectures in America*. Introduced by Wendy Steiner. Boston: Beacon Press, 1935, 1985.

——. *The Making of Americans*. New York: Something Else Press, 1925, 1966.

——. *Narration: Four Lectures*. Introduction by Thornton Wilder. Chicago: University of Chicago Press, 1935.

——. *Paris France*. New York: Charles Scribner's Sons, 1940.

——. *Picasso*. New York: Dover Publications Inc., 1938, 1984.

——. *A Primer for the Gradual Understanding of Gertrude Stein*. Edited by Robert Bartlett Haas. Los Angeles: Black Sparrow Press, 1971.

——. *Tender Buttons*. In Catharine R. Stimpson and Harriet Chessman, eds. *Gertrude Stein: Writings 1903–1932*, pp. 313–355. New York: The Library of America, 1998.

——. *Wars I Have Seen*. New York: Random House, 1945.

——. *What Are Masterpieces*. Foreword by Robert Bartlett Haas. New York: Pitman Publishing Corporation, 1940, 1970.

Stein, Leo. *Journey Into the Self*. Edited by Edmund Fuller and introduced by Van Wyck Brooks. New York: Crown Publishers, 1950.

Steiner, Deborah Tarn. *The Tyrant's Writ: Myths and Images of Writing in Ancient Greece*. Princeton: Princeton University Press, 1994.

Stewart, Allegra. *Gertrude Stein and the Present*. Cambridge: Harvard University Press, 1967.

Stimpson, Catharine R. "Gertrude Stein and the Transposition of Gender." In Nancy K. Miller, ed., *The Poetics of Gender*, pp. 1–18. New York: Columbia University Press, 1986.

——. "The Mind, the Body, and Gertrude Stein." *Critical Inquiry* 3, 3 (Spring 1977): 489–506.

Strauss, Barry S. and Richard Ned Lebow, eds. *Hegemonic Rivalry: From Thucydides to the Nuclear Age*. Boulder: Westview Press, 1991.

Strauss, Leo. *Natural Right and History*. Chicago: University of Chicago Press, 1953.

——. *The Political Philosophy of Hobbes: Its Basis and Its Genesis*. Chicago: University of Chicago Press, 1963.

——. *Thoughts on Machiavelli*. Glencoe, Illinois: The Free Press, 1958.

Streuver, Nancy S. *Theory as Practice: Ethical Inquiry in the Renaissance*. Chicago: University of Chicago Press, 1992.

Sullivan, Vickie B. *Machiavelli's Three Romes: Religion, Human Liberty, and Politics Reformed*. DeKalb, Illinois: Northern Illinois Press, 1996.

Sumberg, Theodore A. "*La Mandragola*: An Interpretation." *The Journal of Politics* 23 (1961): 320–340.

Sutherland, Donald. *Gertrude Stein: A Biography of Her Work*. New Haven: Yale University Press, 1951.

Swanson, Judith A. *The Public and the Private in Aristotle's Political Philosophy*. Ithaca: Cornell University Press, 1992.

Tate, Allen. *Memoirs and Opinions, 1926–1974*. Chicago: The Swallow Press, 1975.

Thompson, Norma. *Herodotus and the Origins of the Political Community: Arion's Leap*. New Haven: Yale University Press, 1996.

——. "Public or Private? An Artemisian Answer." *Arion* 7, 2 (Fall 1999): 49–63.

Thornton, Bruce S. *Eros: The Myth of Ancient Greek Sexuality*. Boulder: Westview Press, 1997.

Thucydides. *The Landmark Thucydides: A Comprehensive Guide to the Peloponnesian War*. Revised edition of the Richard Crawley translation, edited by Robert B. Strassler and introduced by Victor Davis Hanson. New York: Touchstone, 1998.

Tigerstedt, E. N. "Plato's Idea of Poetical Inspiration." *Commentationes Humanarum Litterarum* 44, 2 (1969): 5–76.

Tocqueville, Alexis de. *The Ancien Régime*. Translated by John Bonner and introduced by Norman Hampson. London: J. M. Dent & Sons, 1988.

——. *Democracy in America*. Translated by George Lawrence and edited by J. P. Mayer. New York: Harper Collins Publishers, 1969.

Tuana, Nancy, ed. *Feminist Interpretations of Plato*. University Park: Pennsylvania State University Press, 1994.

Vander Waerdt, Paul A., ed. *The Socratic Movement*. Ithaca: Cornell University Press, 1994.

Veeder, William. "Gender and Pedagogy: *The Question of Frankenstein*." In Stephen C. Behrendt, ed., *Approaches to Teaching Shelley's Frankenstein*. New York: The Modern Language Association of America, 1990.

——. *Mary Shelley and Frankenstein: The Fate of Androgyny*. Chicago: University of Chicago Press, 1986.

Vlastos, Gregory. "The Historical Socrates and Athenian Democracy." *Political Theory* 11, 4 (November 1983): 495–516.

——. *Socrates: Ironist and Moral Philosopher*. Ithaca: Cornell University Press, 1991.

Walcot, P. "The Funeral Speech, A Study of Values." *Greece and Rome* 20 (1973): 111–121.

Walcot, Peter, and Ian McAuslan, eds. *Women In Antiquity*. New York: Oxford University Press, 1996.

Walker, Andrew D. "*Enargeia* and the Spectator in Greek Historiography." *Transactions of the American Philological Association* 123 (1993): 353–377.

Walker, Jayne L. "History as Repetition: *The Making of Americans*." In Harold Bloom, ed., *Modern Critical Views*, pp. 177–199. New York: Chelsea House Publishers, 1986.

Weaver, Richard M. *The Ethics of Rhetoric*. Davis, California: Hermagoras Press, 1985.

Weiss, Penny. *Gendered Community: Rousseau, Sex, and Politics*. New York: New York University Press, 1993.

———. "Rousseau, Antifeminism, and Woman's Nature." *Political Theory* 15,1 (February 1987): 81–98.

Westlake, H. D. "Thucydides on Pausanias and Themistocles—A Written Source?" *Classical Quarterly* 27 (1977): 95–110.

Wexler, Victor G. "'Made for Man's Delight': Rousseau as Antifeminist." *American Historical Review* 81, 2 (April 1976): 266–291.

White, James Boyd. *When Words Lose Their Meaning: Constitutions and Reconstitutions of Language, Character, and Community*. Chicago: University of Chicago Press, 1984.

White, Stephen K. *Edmund Burke: Modernity, Politics, Aesthetics*. Thousand Oaks, California: Sage Publications, 1994.

Wiedemann, Thomas E. J. "Thucydides, Women, and the Limits of Rational Analysis." *Greece and Rome* XXX, 2 (October 1983): 163–170.

Wight, Martin. *Power Politics*. Edited by Hedley Bull and Carsten Holbraad. Harmondsworth, England: Penguin Books, 1986.

Willett, Cynthia. "Hegel, Antigone, and the Possibility of a Woman's Dialectic." In Bat-Ami Bar On, ed., *Modern Engendering: Critical Feminist Readings in Modern Western Philosophy*, pp. 167–181. Albany: State University of New York Press, 1994.

Winkler, John J. *The Constraints of Desire: The Anthropology of Sex and Gender in Ancient Greece*. New York: Routledge, 1990.

Winnett, Susan. "Coming Unstrung: Women, Men, Narrative, and Principles of Pleasure." In J. Paul Hunter, ed., *Mary Shelley: Frankenstein*, pp. 287–301. New York: Norton and Company, 1996.

Winthrop, Delba. "Tocqueville's American Women and 'The True Conception of Democratic Progress.'" *Political Theory* 14, 2 (May 1986): 239–261.

Wohl, Victoria Josselyn. "Standing by the Stathmos: Sexual Ideology in the *Odyssey*." *Arethusa* 26 (1993): 19–50.

Wolin, Sheldon S. "Transgression, Equality, and Voice." In Josiah Ober and

Charles Hedrick, eds., *Dêmokratia: A Conversation on Democracies, Ancient and Modern*, pp. 63–90. Princeton: Princeton University Press, 1996.

Wollstonecraft, Mary. *A Vindication of the Rights of Men* and *A Vindication of the Rights of Woman*. Edited by D. L. Macdonald and Kathleen Scherf. Orchard Park, New York: Broadview Press, 1997.

Yack, Bernard. *The Problems of a Political Animal: Community, Justice, and Conflict in Aristotelian Political Thought*. Berkeley: University of California Press, 1993.

Zeitlin, Froma. "Playing the Other: Theater, Theatricality, and the Feminine in Greek Drama." *Representations* 11 (1985): 63–94.

Zerilli, Linda M. G. *Signifying Woman: Culture and Chaos in Rousseau, Burke, and Mill*. Ithaca: Cornell University Press, 1994.

Žižek, Slavoj. *The Ticklish Subject: The Absent Centre of Political Ontology*. London: Verso, 1999.

Zuckert, Catherine H. "Aristotle on the Limits and Satisfactions of Political Life." *Interpretation* 2, 2 (1983): 185–206.

———. *Postmodern Platos*. Chicago: University of Chicago Press, 1996.

Index

Adams, Henry, 170
aristocracy, in contrast to democracy, 3, 124–27
Aristotle, 12, 36–51, 75, 169; balance, importance of, 165; compared to democrats, 48–50; definition of polis, 36–38, 45–46; gender, treatment of, 45, 47–51, 165; on the kallipolis, 61–70; marital rule, 48–49; master-slave relationship, 45–48; misogynism, 45; musical metaphor, 165; *Nicomachean Ethics*, 43, 114–15; *nous*, 50; on Plato and Socrates, 61–64; political community, 43–44; *Politics*, 37, 43, 45–46, 61–63, 165; referenced by Machiavelli, 84; religious tradition, 129; on statecraft, 44, 46–47; views on modera-

tion, 43; views on Sparta, 40–43
Athens, 168–69; compared to Sparta, 24–25, 38, 42, 44, 51; gender, treatment of, 162–63; as polis, 24–25, 32–36; Solon, 38–40
The Autobiography of Alice B. Toklas (Stein), 137, 140–43, 147, 151–57; literary style of, 143

balance, 5, 39, 50–51, 69, 161; Aristotle, 165; Burke, Edmund, 94; democracy, 61, 128, 166, 171; democratic thinking, 61; gender, 101–2; human nature, 164, 166; Melville, Herman, 170–71; Plato, 61; of polis, 36, 73; political community, 158; Rousseau, Jean-